GV 346 .L36 1987

Lapchick, Richard Edward.

On the mark

BRADNER LIBRARY
SCHOOLCRAFT COLLEGE
LIVONIA, MICHIGAN 48152

On the Mark

On the Mark

Putting the Student Back in Student–Athlete

Richard E. Lapchick
with Robert Malekoff

Center for the Study of Sport in Society,
Northeastern University

Lexington Books
D.C. Heath and Company
Lexington, Massachusetts/Toronto

GV
346
.L36
1987

Library of Congress Cataloging-in-Publication Data

Lapchick, Richard Edward.
  On the mark.

  Includes index.
    1. School sports—United States.   2. Athletes—
United States.   3. College sports—United States.
4. Students—Counseling of—United States.
I. Malekoff, Robert.   II. Title.
GV346.L36   1986   371.8′9   85-45944
ISBN 0-699-13824-X (alk. paper)
ISBN 0-699-12604-7 (pbk.: alk. paper)

Copyright © 1987 by D.C. Heath and Company

All rights reserved. No part of this publication may be reproduced
or transmitted in any form or by any means, electronic or
mechanical, including photocopy, recording, or any information
storage or retrieval system, without permission in writing from the
publisher.

Published simultaneously in Canada
Printed in the United States of America
Casebound International Standard Book Number: 0-669-13824-X
Paperbound International Standard Book Number: 0-669-12604-7
Library of Congress Catalog Card Number: 85-45944

The paper used in this publication meets the minimum
requirements of American National Standard for Information
Sciences—Permanence of Paper for Printed Library Materials, ANSI
Z39.48-1984. ∞™

ISBN 0-669-12604-7

87 88 89 90 8 7 6 5 4 3 2

For Joe Lapchick and Bob Douglas, who helped to inspire their own players and other coaches to stay on the mark, to play to win, but to play with dignity.

Contents

Foreword

Anita DeFrantz
Two-time Olympian and Medalwinner
Senior Vice-President of the 1984
   Los Angeles Olympic Organizing Committee
Member of International Olympic Committee

On the Mark is a remarkable book. The information in it has been critically needed for a long time. This is a unique book that gives essential guidance to the student who is also an athlete. *On the Mark* is dedicated to the young men and women who have developed their talent and love of sport to the extent that they aspire to athletic excellence, as well as becoming educated. Written to address the needs of these special individuals, this book charts a path through the labyrinth of rules and regulations. It provides true stories that will both shock and inspire. And, most important, it provides a clear picture of the hard realities of attempting to enter the world of sports as a profession.

NEWS ITEM: Talented sophomore woman ruled ineligible to play by NCAA Infraction Committee. Her ineligibility is a result of rule violations when she was recruited by her school. She will lose at least one year of college basketball.

NEWS ITEM: Talented junior man ruled ineligible to play for academic reasons. For no apparent reason, he dropped all of his spring semester courses. He may not be permitted to play in the following year.

Both of these items appeared on the same day in the sports section. Sadly, this was not an unusual day. Indeed, it is a rare period of time when some athlete is not ruled ineligible—when some young woman or man who has worked hard for many many years at the dream of being a college or professional athlete has those dreams dashed by a rule that makes them ineligible. Why this waste? Why do so many of our young people get caught in a trap that makes it impossible for them to fulfill their dreams?

How often do we see such stories?

NEWS ITEM: Top flight prep pick arrested in drug raid. This youngster was thought to be the next generation of running back—a potential Heisman Trophy winner.

NEWS ITEM: Olympic team hopeful banned for eighteen months from track and field competition. This current world record holder failed his doping test and is suspected of using steroids.

Why? Why do these athletes, some of our most talented and creative youngsters, find their way into the news for reasons that have nothing to do with successful competition?

NEWS ITEM: A five-foot nine sixteen-year-old attempts suicide, saying there was no future for him in basketball.

Why? Why do sports become so important to these young people that their personal futures are tossed aside in pursuit of sport? How can we permit this to happen?

Far too many youngsters are led down a primrose path to self-destruction and disaster every year. Too often, well-intended but tragically misinformed advice only cripples and scars our most talented youth. This is all the more heartbreaking because most of the tragedies that we read about in the sports news could have been avoided. If only the athlete's parents, coaches, counselors, or other people important to the student–athlete, had taken the time to understand the world of sports and its pitfalls before pushing the athlete down the road to disaster.

On the Mark is a very special book. Within these pages, you will not only find stories like the ones previously mentioned, but you will hear from the athletes themselves. These athletes share the inside story of their fall from grace, with the hope that the next generation will not be caught in the traps that destroyed their future. Never before have so many athletes come forward to share their experiences with up-and-coming athletes. They care about you, the reader. They care about the future of sport in America. They care about whether student–athletes can fulfill their educational needs.

Professional and top-level sport cannot be a lifetime profession, but it can be a lifelong pastime. A short sixteen-year-old can enjoy sports throughout his life. An athlete can hold a world record without using drugs. An athlete can demand and receive a quality education.

Congratulations to you, the reader, for finding this book. It will assist you, and it will help others through you. Congratulations also to the authors, Richard E. Lapchick and Robert Malekoff. Instead of just reading the headlines, they have, through this book, done something positive to prevent the continuation of these tragedies.

Please read these pages and take them to heart. It is well past time for such a publication. Perhaps if enough people read and understand this book, the headlines will be of success, not tragedy. The world of sports can truly be a lifetime of joy.

Acknowledgments

We would like to thank all the people who have been involved in this project. The list is too long to mention everyone, but many must be singled out!

This book would not have been possible without the dozens of athletes, administrators, and coaches who granted us interviews or who made their views available to us. The list is a long one and includes Kareem Abdul-Jabbar, Bruce Arians, Evelyn Ashford, Eva Auchincloss, Merilee Dean Baker, Jack Bicknell, Larry Bird, Bill Bradley, Lou Carnesecca, Al Coccoluto, Tony Elliott, Leslie Evans, Doug Flutie, Lisa Garrett, Dwight Gooden, Elvin Hayes, Nancy Hogshead, Stefan Humphries, Mike Jarvis, Magic Johnson, Sean Jones, Bob Knight, Steve Moore, Bobby Orr, Joe Paterno, Digger Phelps, Mary Lou Retton, Rumeal Robinson, Debbie Ryan, Kim Silloway, Dean Smith, Vivian Stringer, Mosi Tatupu and Gary Williams.

We would also like to thank Anita DeFrantz, one of the nation's most prominent women athletes and sports administrators, for writing the foreword to this book and Robert Bovenschulte of Lexington Books who has been a strong supporter of this project. Organizations that have given us invaluable material include the NCAA, the Women's Sports Foundation, and the College Board.

Last but certainly not least, we thank the staff, both official and unofficial, of the Center for the Study of Sport in Society for their support in this project. We must especially single out Tom "Satch"

Sanders, who has been our sounding board; Jacques Eusebe, who has helped with technical details; and Ernest Leon Parker, who helped collect material and offered invaluable advice. Jennifer Collis and Bill Dutczak were instrumental with the Help Section.

Introduction

Every year millions of our country's athletes play their hearts out, dreaming of a shot at big-time sports.

The home run. The winning touchdown. The last-second shot. The tie-breaking goal. The dream of sports success. Maybe everyone who ever played had that dream. But it is reality for very few people. Only 1 in 12,000 makes it to the pros.

If success comes for the others—the vast majority—it will come with hard work in the classroom, with the training, diplomas, and degrees that prepare young people to prove themselves in the real world of work.

All too many students are losing their chances at life's success by neglecting their schoolwork to pursue athletic dreams. They are betting their futures against almost impossible odds. Of the millions of high school athletes like you, only 1 in 50 will get a scholarship to play in college. And of the top players who receive scholarships in big-money sports like football and basketball, fewer than 30 percent will graduate from college after four years. Can you beat those odds? Better to bet on your books than bank on the game. It's a lot safer.

Furthermore, the characteristics that make you a good athlete—discipline, hard work, developing goals and team spirit—will make you a success after your sports days are over. You can bank on that.

From TV and newspaper stories, you may have heard about the outrageous abuses of our system of sports and education: recruiting violations, improper payments, and drug abuse. But the problem goes deeper than these scandals. When our schools and colleges fail to prepare young athletes for careers in the real world, some of our nation's potential is lost.

This is a problem for parents, coaches, educators—anyone who lets the short-term excitement of sports success blind them to their long-term responsibility for your future. But most of all, it can be a problem for you, the student–athlete. If you are not aware of the potential problems you can face by concentrating too much on sports, then troubles can begin.

However, if you *are* aware, then sports can be all the fun it's meant to be. This book was written to make you aware so you can benefit as much as possible from your own sports experience.

The book has been written by the director of the Center for the Study of Sport in Society at Northeastern University, with the assistance of its research director. It focuses on the needs of students and athletes from junior high school to high school. It is a guide for people who may never play in college or the pros, and also for people who beat the long odds. If you are recruited to play ball after high school, it can help you choose your college. This book will also help you stay within the rules so your college sports career is never threatened.

The Center for the Study of Sport in Society is dedicated to improving the sports system and to providing information for the student–athlete. The Center works closely with athletes your age, professional athletes, teams and leagues, and the news media. This book is a result of that work. We hope you find it is helpful. Well-known sports stars supporting the Center and quoted throughout *On the Mark* are:

Kareem Abdul-Jabbar
Evelyn Ashford
Larry Bird
Doug Flutie
Dwight Gooden
Nancy Hogshead
Magic Johnson
Bobby Orr
Mary Lou Retton

They want you to become the best person you can be. So do your parents, teachers, and coaches. We hope that *On the Mark* can help you do that.

Courtesy of the Los Angeles Lakers

"

We always hear the term student–athlete. Well, 'student' always comes first, and it should. Very few high school athletes go on to become college athletes, and even fewer become pros. The odds against it are tremendous. But far more high school students can become college students. And a college degree is the key that unlocks the door to your future, whatever you want it to be. Stay in school, but, more important, learn while you're in school.

Magic Johnson
Los Angeles Lakers

"

How to Use This Book

The following is a guide to each chapter.

1 • A Tale of Two Athletes

This chapter is for all student–athletes, parents, coaches, and school administrators. It discusses the careers of the Chicago Bears' Stefan Humphries and of Fred Buttler. Humphries graduated and made it big in sports. Buttler, a one-time pro prospect, focused on sports too much, ignored his studies, and ended up with very few employable skills.

By their examples, the chapter shows how things can go well with proper guidance and how things can go downhill. The chapter concludes with stories of pro athletes who are trying to help younger student–athletes learn how to succeed both on and off the playing field.

2 • The Educated Consumer

The educated consumer is you, the high school athlete. This chapter is really for anyone who hopes to attend college, whether or not you intend to play ball in college. It will help you research and consider colleges. It takes you through all the choices ahead of you. It answers questions like: How does the college admissions process work? How important is your grade-point average? How about college entrance exams? How do I fill out the application? Should I have an interview at the college? What should I do to prepare in my junior year? This chapter has a special section for athletes that tells you how to get the most out of a campus visit and what questions to ask the head coach. Finally, this chapter helps you consider important facts such as climate, location, the size of the college, housing and dining facilities, the academic program (including academic support services for athletes), and campus social life.

3 • Drugs and Alcohol

Because drugs and alcohol are such a widespread problem in high school, this chapter is definitely for everyone. But it is especially for all student–athletes and their parents. It looks at the extent of drug and alcohol abuse among high school students and at the effects of the abuse. There are also real-life examples of superstar athletes whose lives have nearly been destroyed by abuse. We concentrate on Micheal Ray Richardson, Tony Elliott, Bob Welch, and Steve Courson.

4 • Gambling

This chapter is especially important for the athletes going on to play in college, and their parents and coaches. We bring you close to the point-shaving scandals that have rocked the sports world since the 1950s. Because many of the athletes who became involved with gamblers started their gambling activities in high school, you should learn from the mistakes of superstars like John "Hot Rod" Williams and Art Schlichter.

5 • Recruiting

This chapter is for student–athletes who are being recruited to play in college. It is important for parents and coaches. This chapter will help you create a smart game plan for this exciting experience. Being recruited can be wonderful, but if you make mistakes, your college playing career could end before it even begins. As examples, we zero in on two athletes. First, Rumeal Robinson, the nation's top guard in 1985–86, who chose the University of Michigan after a well-planned search that included his coach, his family, and school counselors. The second is Sean Stopperich, who let illegal financial inducements move him to the wrong school. Finally, we listen to some highly respected college coaches: Penn State's Joe Paterno, Indiana's Bobby Knight, and Notre Dame's Digger Phelps. A section on boosters tells you how to avoid them and why.

6 • Rules of the Game

This chapter is for all student–athletes, parents, coaches, and school administrators. Starting in high school, you will face dozens of rules in your athletic career. Here, we cover these rules, starting with minimum high school academic standards. Most of the chapter is for athletes who want to play in college. Based on high school records, Proposition 16 sets academic standards that freshmen have to meet to be eligible for Division I college programs. The NCAA has more than forty regulations about recruitment, and many college athletes are now losing their eligibility for violating these rules. This chapter presents the rules in an easy-to-understand fashion, with commonsense ways to make sure you adhere to the NCAA's policies.

7 • Women as Student–Athletes

This chapter is devoted to the millions of middle and high school girls who are taking advantage of the opportunity to participate in athletics. It discusses the history of women's athletics since the inception of Title IX, and points to the dramatic rise in the number of women who are involved in organized sports. Commonly believed myths such as "women are not physically strong enough to play some sports," and "female athletes cannot maintain their femininity" are discussed and dispelled. Finally, we take a close look at the college career of Kim Silloway, who truly epitomizes the woman student–athlete.

Help Section

This section is a very important part of *On the Mark*. It is filled with information that will be useful to students, parents, coaches, and school administrators. The Help Section discusses how a college guide book can make your college search more comprehensive, the pluses and minuses of standardized test aids, and a step-by-step approach to applying for college financial aid. This section also furnishes you with names and addresses of organizations that can be of particular help in regard to combatting drug and alcohol or gambling abuse. A complete copy of the *NCAA Guide for the College-Bound Student Athlete* is included, as well as information regarding the services of such organizations as the Women's Sports Foundation and the Center for the Study of Sport in Society.

On the Mark

Courtesy of the Chicago Bears

"

I'm not saying that it was easy for me to balance football and academics, but if you are determined it can be done. I know how lucky I am to be playing pro ball, especially for a championship team. I also know that by having worked hard on my studies, my life won't stop once my football career is over.

Stefan Humphries
Chicago Bears

"

1 A Tale of Two Athletes

It seems as though people have always viewed athletes as "dumb jocks." Somehow, as an athlete you aren't expected to be as smart as other students. If you have a strong body, you're not supposed to have a well-developed brain, too. Non-athletes joke about your intelligence, and athletes even joke among themselves. A bad grade becomes funny to mask the pain. Sound familiar?

It's easy to see how the pattern begins for you. If you are a really good player, have you ever felt that one of your teachers helped boost your grade just a bit so you could keep playing? Or that a teacher was more tolerant of you when you handed in a late assignment? Or that a guidance counselor told you to take a lighter class load or an easier course during the season?

Of course, this doesn't happen to everyone. If you are determined, and if you demand the best of yourself both as an athlete and a student, then you won't become just another statistic. But *beware* of how easy it is to go in the other direction!

Too often the American educational system takes academic responsibility away from you if you are an athlete. Don't let this happen to you. Instead, be one of the growing number of athletes who are taking back that responsibility. Be a winner in the classroom—and in life! The message is clear: *Prepare your mind while you are preparing your body.*

What follows is a tale of two athletes. The first won big, the other lost big. Listen to their stories.

The Superbowl Champion

Super Bowl Championship, drummer in the video "Super Bowl Shuffle"—1986 was a heady year for second-year pro Stefan Humphries of the Chicago Bears. But this could be expected of someone who was featured in *Sports Illustrated* while he was still in high school. In his senior year at the University of Michigan, *Sports Illustrated* ran another story on Humphries, as a man who had lived up to all his promise. The story of this youthful giant is unique and inspiring.

" ———————————————————————————

All Stefan Humphries stands for is everything this game is supposed to be about. Football is always important to him, but never, never to the exclusion of academics. He wants nothing—including football—to interfere with his pursuit of education. He has broader interests than just football, and I like that.

Bo Schembechler
Football Coach, University of Michigan
in *Sports Illustrated*

——————————————————————————— **"**

Stefan's athletic skill was obvious to everyone from the moment he first stepped onto a college practice field. He became a starting offensive lineman at Michigan in his sophomore year. Stefan spent many of his Saturday afternoons in Michigan Stadium throwing key blocks for the nationally ranked Wolverine football team. But on one particular Saturday there were no running backs to lead up-field on the power sweep. Humphries was not knocking heads with a heavyweight defensive tackle from Ohio State or Purdue on this spring afternoon. Instead, on this June day he traded in his helmet for a cap, and his number 76 football jersey for a gown. Stefan Humphries shared the field with the majority of his classmates as he quietly celebrated his greatest victory at Michigan—earning his college degree.

That was no small accomplishment because, as you read earlier, 70 percent of his football brothers across America who entered college with him did not graduate. But Stefan had different priorities.

Like other college football players, he faced 40–60 hours a week of practice and films, and had his body punished by the rigors of the game. But unlike the 70 percent who don't finish their studies, Humphries got a degree—and did so with distinction.

During his four-year stay in Ann Arbor, Humphries chalked up achievements both on and off the football field that may not be matched for some time. Here's a sampling of his accomplishments:

1982 and 1983 All-Big Ten
1982 and 1983 Academic All-American
1983 first Team All-American
1983 Outland Award Finalist
1983 National Football Foundation and Hall of Fame Scholar

At the same time that he became an All-American player, Humphries also found time to truly excel in the classroom, and he became an Academic All-American. As an engineering major, he graduated with a 3.67 grade-point average and was named Outstanding Student in the engineering school. He earned nine A-pluses and fifteen As and received only one grade lower than B while balancing the rigors of football practice with his demanding academic schedule.

Things didn't come easily for Stefan Humphries at Michigan, and they certainly didn't come easily for him when he was growing up in Fort Lauderdale, Florida. At a very early age he learned that the quickest route to accomplishment was through hard work and perseverance.

As a child, Humphries grew up with a disease opthamologists call ptosis. This left him with "lazy" or "drooping"eyes. Three operations corrected 85 percent of the problem, but Stefan was still teased constantly by friends, who nicknamed him "Sleepy." Thornton Humphries, Stefan's father and a middle school principal, felt that the disease turned out to be a blessing in disguise. "I think Stefan's eye disorder was one of the real motivating factors in his life. It gave him a very strong incentive to achieve in all areas."

Thornton Humphries also discussed the direction and guidance that Stefan received at home. "Both my wife and I have always believed in the importance of setting goals for all of our children," explained the senior Humphries. "And once those goals were set, we made sure that Stefan and his sisters did everything possible to make sure they were meeting them. I really think that young people need some direction, and goal-setting can provide just that."

Stefan's father added that "there is no reason that a young person cannot excel on the athletic field *and* in the classroom. The problem is that many times as a top athlete, people like to do things for you. No one can do the job for you when it comes to education.

"The great things you do as an athlete are publicized on television and in the newspapers. Everyone knows who scored the big touchdown in the championship game, but students who excel in the classroom are many times not properly recognized. I was every bit as proud of Stefan's educational accomplishments as I was of his athletic success because I knew education held the real key to his future. When he headed off to college, he was prepared academically, athletically, and socially."

Stefan shares his father's opinion about the importance of balancing academics and athletics. "I was really lucky to have parents that worked in school systems and stressed the importance of a quality education," he said. "When I was younger I really didn't know why my schoolwork was so important. . . . I just worked at it because my parents told me to and because both of my sisters were excellent students. Now I know why my parents encouraged me to hit the books.

"When I went to Michigan I pursued a very demanding course of study. My coach, Bo Schembechler, was really supportive of my academic goals. He didn't want guys on the team to let football be their whole lives, and really encouraged everyone to work hard in the classroom and to enjoy college.

"When I was visiting colleges during my senior year in high school I was first looking for a quality academic program; a competitive football program second; and a comfortable environment which would give me an opportunity to grow as a person and to enjoy myself. I found all three at Michigan."

Humphries says his ultimate goal in life is to pursue a career in medicine. "I'm not saying that it was easy for me to balance football and academics, but if you are determined it can be done. I know how lucky I am to be playing pro ball, especially for a championship team. I also know that by having worked hard on my studies, my life won't stop once my football career is over."

The Tragic Athlete

Fred Buttler's fate was very different from Stefan Humphries'. Buttler is only one tragic example of a young man who didn't make it in the pros and is now paying the price for failing to receive a proper education.

Like Stefan Humphries' parents, Fred's mother wanted her son to earn a solid education. At Warren Lane Elementary School in Inglewood, California, Fred showed outstanding athletic potential. He was clearly the best athlete in his grade, and he even beat older children at virtually every sport he decided to try. After a while, he began to believe what everyone in school told him: that he would be a professional athlete when he grew up. This promise became all that mattered to everyone—except Fred's mother. As sports began to dominate his life more and more, Mrs. Buttler watched her son begin to suffer in the classroom.

" ——————————————————————————————

I think some of the coaches were probably happy I couldn't read because that meant I wouldn't waste time on schoolwork since that way I could concentrate on playing for them.

Fred Buttler
former football player at Cal-LA State
in *New Times Magazine*

—————————————————————————————— **"**

She noticed that he was not able to do his daily schoolwork assignments. Worried about her son, she asked that he be held back in the third grade so he could improve his weak reading skills. But this request was denied. Two years later, Mrs. Buttler questioned school officials when they promoted Fred to Monroe Junior High School after the sixth grade. She was told that Fred was progressing at a normal pace, and that she needn't be concerned.

Fred immediately became a football star at Monroe, but he still couldn't read. One day, to his great shock, he and four other athletes were told that they were "just too bright to be in the eighth grade." Therefore, they were being skipped into Morningside High School straight from the seventh grade. Mrs. Buttler complained to the Monroe administration that it wasn't fair to send a student who couldn't read to high school. But she was told that the move was being made "in Fred's best interest."

In his three years at Morningside, Fred accumulated a C+ average, even though he never opened a book. He never had to study because many teachers made special arrangements for the school's star football player. At times he handed in blank exams only to have them returned to him with all the correct answers. At other times he was given oral exams that he always seemed to pass—despite having no knowledge of the subject matter. Most of the time he didn't have to take exams. There was no point. He couldn't read them.

Buttler told *New Times Magazine* that his teachers always made him feel good and gave him confidence that he would make the pros. "No matter how much trouble I had understanding things in class, I always figured I would make a good living playing ball for the pros. . . . Football was just going to make me famous. And I knew I wasn't just dreaming because everyone told me I was good."

When he graduated from Morningside, Fred had the reading ability of a second-grader—about the same level he had nine years before when his mother asked for him to be held back in third grade. Despite the fact that he couldn't read the playbook, Fred received a football scholarship from El Camino Junior College. There, Buttler took mostly "activity classes," a term college people use for subjects like golf and tennis. Somehow he managed to stay eligible. As a cornerback, he helped lead El Camino to two outstanding seasons. Fred assumed that after two more years of college he would end up with a pro football contract.

Fred decided to attend Cal-LA State. His junior college advisor spent two days filling out Buttler's complicated admission and grant-in-aid forms. Fred was promised reading help at LA State, but never received it. He noted, "I think some of the coaches were probably happy I couldn't read because that meant I wouldn't waste time on schoolwork since that way I could concentrate on playing for them." The dream continued during his first one-and-a-half years at LA State.

At first he maintained a C+ average and played well. But when his four years of college eligibility ran out at the end of the fall semester, so did the great interest and the support from the faculty. Suddenly the former football star was a failing student and he flunked out of LA State within months.

In the end, Fred Buttler had no degree, no offers to play pro football, and no skills to use in other employment. And he still could not read.

Further tragedy entered Fred's life when he was involved in the accidental shooting death of his father. He tried to go to the cemetery to visit his father's grave but he was not even able to read the signs that would have directed him to the grave site.

The differences in the stories of Stefan Humphries and Fred Buttler are clear. If Stefan Humphries is cut from the Chicago Bears or suffers an injury that ends his football career, his life will not stop. From a very early age he understood the importance of a proper education, and he demanded the opportunity to pursue his education. By not putting "all his eggs in the athletic basket" he has made sure that several doors of opportunity will be open to him when his football career is just a memory.

When Fred Buttler lost his dream of becoming a professional football player, he had nowhere to turn. The doors that would open for Stefan Humphries were tightly locked for Fred. He assumed that football would be his ticket to the big-time and allowed himself to be academically exploited throughout his youth. If Buttler had demanded a quality education in return for his outstanding athletic contributions, his story might have had a happier ending.

Tom "Satch" Sanders, associate director of the Center for the Study of Sport in Society and former Boston Celtic great, sounds an ominous warning. "I remember when a high draft pick was cut from the Celtics one year, and he sat in front of his locker with his head down crying out 'what am I going to do now?' The young man did not have a college degree, and without basketball felt completely lost. I was to see this scene repeated many times during my career as a player and coach. Those of us who made it can count dozens of others who weren't prepared for the big fall. They are the tragedies. Buttler's story is not unique."

You might say that Stefan Humphries was lucky because of his good upbringing, and because he was always taught that there is more to life than playing ball. You might also argue that if Fred Buttler had been a stronger, more assertive person, he wouldn't have ended up in trouble. Clearly, Humphries was lucky to have supportive parents who played a major part in his success.

Not every young athlete will be as lucky as Stefan, and you may be in circumstances beyond your control. If you don't have support from your parents, then it becomes your responsibility to demand a quality education. This way, no matter what happens in your sports career, you can help insure for a brighter future for yourself.

If Only I Had Done It Right the First Time

Steve Moore, a starting offensive tackle for the AFC-champion New England Patriots, is working hard to build a solid foundation to fall back on when his playing days are over. Moore is one of the very few players who has been lucky enough to realize his pro dream.

Achieving the dream was costly for Moore, as it is for so many others. In 1980 Steve was one of twenty-six freshmen who accepted a football scholarship to Tennessee State University. Four years later, only three of the twenty-six had graduated. Steve Moore wasn't among them. He wasn't even close to graduation, because university officials and coaches told him to take activity classes so that his grades would be good enough to keep him eligible to play football.

In effect, the university officials perhaps assumed that Moore was yet another "dumb jock." So only the sports-related subjects of Steve's courses changed each year, and Steve never missed a game because of grades. But if going to college is supposed to produce an education, then somebody cheated Steve Moore. Steve was also cheating himself. This part of Steve's story is not unusual, nor is Tennessee State's role. It's typical of what happens at many universities.

Courtesy of the University of Notre Dame Office of Sports Information

"

What good is a basketball player to our program if he doesn't have the basic skills necessary at the college level? And what value is a young person to a potential employer if that person doesn't have the basic abilities and knowledge to do a particular job well?

Digger Phelps
Notre Dame University basketball coach

"

Looking back, Steve Moore now understands what happened: "The school got what they wanted out of us. They knew that most of us wanted to be pros. We were only there to play sports. We practiced and watched films until 10 P.M. every night. There was no way to go back to the dorm to study then. We won almost all of our games while I was there, but not many of us graduated.

"I couldn't, wouldn't get up for those eight o'clock classes. I'm not a dumb jock. I was there to play football, then to make it in the NFL. I did, but the great majority of the others didn't. They didn't get much of an education either. It was the end of the road for them."

Steve Moore certainly isn't a dumb jock. He stopped believing the people who told him what courses to take. Instead, he enrolled in a degree-completion program at Northeastern University in Boston. Now he dreams of the day when he will become a college graduate. "Now that I've made the pros, I want to reach another goal—getting a degree at Northeastern. I promised my mother and myself that I would get this degree."

Mosi Tatupu, Moore's New England Patriot teammate at running back, echoes Steve's thoughts on the importance of getting a well-rounded education. "I had all the choices, all the same opportunities as everyone else to study. But I was missing too many classes because it's tough to play major college football and attend class. Tough, but not impossible. Pat Haden was my teammate. Not only did he become a pro quarterback, but he also got a Rhodes Scholarship. He was totally committed. I wasn't, most of us weren't. He got himself something to fall back on after football."

Sean Jones, a defensive lineman for the Los Angeles Raiders, also returned to Northeastern to complete his degree—which he did in 1985. His message for young student–athletes is important. Jones reflected that "football is not my entire life. I have confidence that I can be at least as successful in other fields. Success lulls you to sleep and makes you complacent. I haven't accomplished a lot of what I want to do with my life." Sean's brother's experiences influenced him. After several years in the NFL and the USFL, the defensive back fell on his knee, and the accident ended his pro career. But Sean noted his brother had "a college degree from the University of Massachusetts, and insured his body. He was smart enough to plan ahead." Are you planning ahead?

Giving Something Back: The New Breed of Athletes

All kinds of athletes, former athletes, and coaches are beginning to speak out about the importance of balancing athletics and education. They are highly aware of the great odds against students who dream of a professional sports career. They also understand the need to prepare for life after sport. *They are talking to you!*

Larry Bird and Ervin "Magic" Johnson are generally considered to be two of the very best all-around basketball players in the National Basketball Association. Both of these superstars have made it big in the world of professional sports, but warn you to back up any athletic dreams you have with a meaningful education.

"We always hear the term student–athlete," Johnson commented. "Well, 'student' always comes first, and it should. Very few high school athletes go on to become college athletes, and even fewer become pros. The odds against it are tremendous. But far more high school students can become college students. And a college degree is the key that unlocks the door to your future, whatever you want it to be. Stay in school but, more important, learn while you're in school."

Bird adds, "I've worked hard and received many awards from playing basketball, both at Indiana State and with the Celtics. But to me my most important award was receiving my diploma from Indiana State. Working hard at my education and receiving my diploma made me feel as if I had just scored 100 points in a game. Work hard at your sport, but get your degree."

Olympic gold medal swimmer Nancy Hogshead had no professional league or big contract to look forward to at the conclusion of her amateur career. She warns that "top athletes won't try to compete in their sports without the proper equipment. The brightest of these superstars see their athletic careers end by 30—mine ended at 22. Your equipment for the remaining 45 years of your life is your education. Don't be ill equipped."

Elvin Hayes enjoyed a spectacular sixteen-year career in the National Basketball Association. He retired in 1984 as the league's third all-time leading scorer and rebounder, and he is a sure bet to be voted into the Basketball Hall of Fame. Despite all of his amazing athletic accomplishments, Hayes felt that he had missed something in life. He returned to the University of Houston to finish his degree. "I feel this is the most important thing I've done in my whole life. I wanted young people to know that it was important to Elvin Hayes to become a total person. Obtaining my degree has brought balance to my life."

Julius Erving, the magnificent Dr. J., has returned to the University of Massachusetts to finish his degree—even though he was earning nearly $2 million a year. He said that part of the reason for going back was to give a message to America's young athletes that finishing their education *is* important.

Pro football players like Steve Moore, Mosi Tatupu, and Brian Holloway of the Patriots devote much of their off-season time to spreading the same message, talking to students in schools around the country.

Digger Phelps, Notre Dame's basketball coach, has long spoken out about the importance of education for the nation's young athletes. "What good is a basketball player to our program if he doesn't have the basic skills necessary at the college level?" asks Phelps. "And what value is a young person to a potential employer if that person doesn't have the basic abilities and knowledge to do a particular job well?"

Senator Bill Bradley of New Jersey knows all about balancing athletics and education. Bradley was a three-time All-American basketball player at Princeton University and a starting forward for the New York Knickerbockers. While with the Knicks, Bradley was a key member of two world championship teams. He was also an honor student at Princeton, and went on to earn a Rhodes Scholarship.

Bradley commented that "Time devoted to games, practice, and travel may frequently interfere with your studies. Practice as hard as you can to be the best you can be, but understand that overwhelming numbers of student athletes in college, not to mention high school, will never become or even have the opportunity to be-

Courtesy of Princeton University Office of Sports Information

"

Time devoted to games, practice, and travel may frequently interfere with your studies. Practice as hard as you can to be the best you can be, but understand that overwhelming numbers of student–athletes in college, not to mention high school, will never become or even have the opportunity to become a pro. Of those that do, relatively few will play long enough to earn a living for themselves and security for their families.

Senator Bill Bradley
Former three-time All-American at Princeton University
and forward for the New York Knicks

"

come a pro. Of those who do, relatively few will play long enough to earn a living for themselves and security for their families."

Kareem Abdul-Jabbar, perhaps the longest-lasting and most dominant player in the history of any sport, warned that "I hope that young people realize that developing athletic skills is only doing one-half of the job. Just remember, a mind is a terrible thing to waste."

So dream those dreams. You *are* a special person. Not everyone has made it as far as you have in sports. Just remember that only a select few will go on to excel in college—and only the very top athletes will have the opportunity to be pros. The qualities that make you a good athlete will serve you well in other areas. Use them to become that whole person that your heroes tell you to be. Your education is your insurance policy against these dreams not coming true, or suddenly ending. Regardless of your ability as an athlete, you must be prepared to play the most important game—the game of life. In the end, it will be the most important game to win.

Courtesy of the New Jersey Generals

"

I'll always be remembered for "The Pass" at Boston College. But getting a good education at Boston College was also very important to me. Don't drop my pass; get a good education.

Doug Flutie
Chicago Bears

"

Courtesy of Boston College Office of Sports Information

"

Pretend for a minute that you don't play a sport. Would you still be interested in that school? I've seen kids pick a school for some crazy reasons . . . because the stadium has a dome; because they want to play on astroturf; because they like the football team's uniforms. If you are not interested in a college for any reasons other than athletics, I would recommend that you not consider that school.

Jack Bicknell
Boston College football coach

"

2 *The Educated Consumer*

If you are going to attend college, choosing the right one is without question one of the most difficult and important decisions that you will ever be asked to make. The college which you eventually attend will have a tremendous effect on you, both during your years there and later in life. If you happen to be an athlete, the complex decision will be further complicated by sports-related considerations—especially the entire athletic recruiting process.

Perhaps the most important point to remember while researching and considering schools is the fact that there are many excellent colleges and universities throughout the country. Your task is to choose the right one for you. There is no "best" school. However, there may be a particular school that is best for your personal needs and goals.

To make the best possible selection, you must consider all of the factors that might help make your college years as enjoyable and worthwhile as possible. You can't learn too much about a school. Obviously, the more information that you collect, the better your chances are of making an educated, successful decision.

High School Preparation

Regardless of how great an athlete you are, the odds against your making a living in professional sports are staggering. As you know from the first chapter, only 1 in every 12,000 high school athletes will be fortunate enough to make it to the top of the mountain and become a pro. The world is full of former high school All-County, All-State, and even All-American athletes who—despite their exceptional abilities—were not talented or lucky enough to make it in the National Football League, National Basketball League, National Hockey League, Major League Baseball, or one of the other professional sports. For every Dr. J, there are thousands of high school athletes whose closest connection with professional sports will be as spectators.

If you can play in college, you should continue to dedicate yourself to your sport. You will have already beaten almost 50 to 1 odds against a high school athlete playing in college. That's quite an accomplishment in itself. However, beating 50 to 1 odds isn't the same as topping 12,000 to 1 odds.

Sports can be a very worthwhile part of your total college experience. However, as you begin to think about choosing a college, try to balance your athletic dreams with the importance of a positive academic and social experience.

College Admissions

Admission standards at colleges and universities throughout the country vary greatly. Qualifications that make you an excellent candidate in the eyes of college A, may leave you judged a longshot at college B. When they rate an applicant, college admissions officers take several key factors into account. The following sections tell you what these factors are.

Grade-Point Average

Generally speaking, your grade-point average (GPA) is the most important academic factor that admissions officers will consider. Your GPA shows what you have accomplished in the classroom over your four years in high school, not what your test scores were on one morning. If you are a poor test taker, a high GPA will help admissions officers overlook a low test score.

As you begin high school, you should be aware that your work in

Courtesy of Bob Woolf Associates, Inc.

"

Top athletes won't try to compete in their sports without the proper equipment. The brightest of these superstars see their athletic careers end by thirty—mine ended at twenty-two. Your equipment for the remaining forty-five years of your life is your education. Don't be ill equipped.

Nancy Hogshead
Olympic gold-medal swimmer

"

the ninth and tenth grades will be added into your final GPA. As a high school junior, if you look back and realize that you haven't done your best in the classroom, don't panic. College admissions officers are usually impressed with signs of great improvement. A strong academic showing in the junior and first half of the senior years can often overshadow a weaker freshman and sophomore performance. The higher your final GPA or your rank in class, the more college options will be available to you.

“

Many times high school guidance counselors encourage students to take courses that do not fulfill core requirements. Every student should set up his schedule in such a way that when it comes time to apply to colleges, he has as many avenues open to him as possible. The skills you gain in core courses are important even if you choose not to go to college.

Dean Smith
North Carolina basketball coach

”

If you are a high school athlete interested in college sports, you should be sure that you are entered in the core curriculum courses, as discussed in chapters 5 and 6. Dean Smith, North Carolina's basketball coach, talks about recruited athletes who fell short in core course requirements. "Many times high school guidance counselors encourage students to take courses that do not fulfill core requirements. Every student should set up his schedule in such a way that when it comes time to apply to colleges, he has as many avenues open to him as possible. The skills you gain in core courses are important even if you choose not to go to college."

College Entrance Examinations

The most commonly used college entrance tests are the Scholastic Aptitude Test (SAT) and the American College Test (ACT). Admissions officers use the results of these tests along with GPA information to determine the overall academic potential of an applicant. High test scores can partly make up for a low GPA, but may be taken as signs of underachievement. The higher your test scores, the better your chances of admission, but don't be fooled into thinking that high test scores alone will ensure admission to most colleges.

Low test scores can make you ineligible to play in your freshman year in Division I schools. You now need a 700 combined score on the SAT or 15 on the ACT in order to qualify to play. For the next three years there will be some flexibility in this scale, as indicated in chapters 5 and 6.

There is much debate about whether you can improve your test score by studying or by enrolling in SAT/ACT preparation courses. Although these courses will not guarantee a high test score, they probably can't hurt your chances of performing well. For information on SAT/ACT preparation services, see the Help Section at the end of the book.

You are allowed to take the SAT and ACT tests as many times as you want. Usually, a college will consider only your highest score. Be sure to contact the admissions offices at all the schools you are considering and see if this is the case. Some schools will take an average of all test scores.

If you are playing a sport, you should be sure to check the SAT and ACT testing dates as far as a year in advance. Many times the test will be offered at the same time as an athletic contest. Usually schools will come to some agreement about rescheduling the sports event, but you should be aware of all testing opportunities well in advance so you can make arrangements to clear your schedule.

The Application

Depending upon the college, how well you fill out your application may have a lot of influence on your chance for admission. Be sure to type or print clearly when filling out the application. Remember that your application could be one of the last of many forms that the admissions officer reads in a day, and if it is sloppy he or she may not bother to try to read it carefully. In addition, a careless application may cause the admissions officer to draw negative conclusions about your work habits.

The essay part of the application should be completed only after you've written some practice essays on scratch paper. Ask your guidance counselor or English teacher to look at these practice essays, and ask for advice on how they might be improved. Don't brag, but don't be afraid to sell yourself.

The more positive things that the admissions officers can learn about you, the better your chances will be to gain entrance. Colleges are looking for students with unique backgrounds or characteristics, so include all types of qualifications, such as musical talents, interest in the arts, leadership experience, and so on. *This is not the time to be modest.* Include specific reasons why you feel the school you are applying to can best meet your needs and goals. Admissions officers are not only interested in what you have to offer to make the university better, they also want to know how well you will fit in at their school.

Be sure that the teachers who write recommendations for you know you well, and will take the time to do a good job of supporting your application. You should explain to these teachers why you are interested in the particular school they are writing to, so that they can do a more complete job on your recommendation.

The Interview

Today, most colleges don't require interviews, but it makes sense for you to schedule one if you are planning a campus visit. The interview not only gives you another chance to show your strengths, but it also lets you ask questions and get a different point of view on the school you are considering. Most admissions officers agree that an applicant's chances are rarely hurt by interviewing.

Research before the Senior Year

Don't wait until your senior year to begin looking into college choices. As an athlete, you don't wait until the day before the first practice to get in shape. Instead, you start your training program well before the season begins, to give yourself enough time to get in top condition. The same reasoning can be applied to researching colleges. If you start early, you're more likely to have enough time to gather all the meaningful information you need to help you to make an intelligent final choice.

If you are a recruited athlete, you may begin receiving correspondence from college coaches in your junior year. It is important to learn as much as you can about each college and its sports program. Finding out as much as you can about the athletic programs at the schools you are considering will be another important part of your search if you hope to play a sport in college.

Junior Year Screening

Sometime during your junior year, set up a meeting with your guidance counselor, your coach, and your parents. At this meeting you can discuss in very general terms the types of schools you think you might be interested in. If you are being recruited, you should bring along some of the literature you have already received from college coaches. The point of this meeting is for you to begin to set an idea of exactly what you are looking for academically, athletically, and socially in a school.

Ask your guidance counselor to suggest a few schools where you might fit in particularly well. Encourage your coach to give you his honest opinion of your potential to compete athletically at different levels. You don't want this meeting to end before both you and your parents have a realistic picture of the types of schools that you can be successful at both academically and athletically.

By the end of your junior year, you should narrow down your choices to approximately ten schools. Remember, even if you are a highly recruited athlete, you can only visit a handful of campuses. The sooner you narrow your choices down, the sooner you will be able to learn more about the schools you are really interested in attending.

The Narrowing-Down Process

During the later part of your junior year and in the summer before your final year of high school, learn as much as you possibly can about the ten or so schools you are considering. The information you get should help you narrow down your choices even further. Ideally, by the beginning of your senior year you will have chosen three or four schools to concentrate on. Sometimes, however, it is difficult to reject schools that you once had a strong interest in.

Trying to visit ten schools during your senior year can be time-con-suming, and—most of all—costly. At the start of your senior year, set a maximum of six schools to consider. If you receive new infor-mation on a school you have eliminated, you can always reconsider your decision.

If you are being heavily recruited, there is a chance that you will place too much weight on athletic information during this narrow-ing-down period. Always remember to balance your athletic goals with your academic and social needs.

Jack Bicknell, Boston College football coach, advises: "Pretend for a minute that you don't play a sport. Would you still be interested in that school? I've seen kids pick a school for some crazy reasons . . . because the stadium has a dome; because they want to play on astroturf; because they like the football team's uniforms. If you are not interested in a college for any reasons other than athletics, I would recommend that you not consider that school."

Senior Year: Taking a Hard Look

The Campus Visit

Probably the most important and revealing part of deciding on a college is the campus visit. By reading catalogs and talking to guid-ance counselors you can learn a great deal about a school, but a visit is the best way to get a "true feel" for what a college is really like. Here are some suggestions for how to get the most out of your visit to a college:

- Plan your visit so that you will be on campus when classes are in session. Remember that you want to get a sense of what it's like to be a typical student at the college. It's hard to get a true feel if most of the students are in Florida on spring break while you are visiting.
- Start your visit on a Friday, or end it on a Monday. This way you can experience campus life on a weekday and on a weekend. Plan-ning to attend classes on a Monday might be your best bet, be-cause many schools have a limited class schedule on Fridays. Be sure you get a chance to sit in on a few classes—perhaps one lec-

Courtesy of St. John's University Office of Sports Information

" ————————————————————————————————

If you're not encouraged to mingle with the players during your
visit, something is very wrong. These are the guys that you'll be
spending a great deal of time with should you decide to attend
that university. You should really try to get to know what they're
like on and off the court. They are also the people who can answer some of your most important questions—don't be afraid to
pick their brains.

Lou Carnesecca
St. John's University basketball coach

———————————————————————————————— "

ture and one small discussion section or lab. Ask yourself if the subject matter seems reasonably understandable.

• Take a guided tour of the campus if there is a university tour service. You will be surprised by how much you can learn on these tours, and it will give you an opportunity to see almost all of the school, not just the athletic facilities. Normally these tours are led by students, so don't be afraid to ask questions about life at that particular school. A different viewpoint may be very enlightening.

• If there is campus housing, make sure that you will be housed in the dormitory room of one of the players on the team. Also, be sure to eat at least some of your meals on campus. Being put up in a fancy hotel may do wonders for your ego, but you won't learn much about what it's like to be a college student at the school.

Lou Carnesecca, St. John's basketball coach, warned that, "If you're not encouraged to mingle with the players during your visit, something is very wrong. These are the guys that you'll be spending a great deal of time with, should you decide to attend that university. You should really try to get to know what they're like on and off the court. They are also the people who can answer some of your most important questions—don't be afraid to pick their brains."

• If possible, try to schedule your visit so you can see the team play and/or practice. You will learn a great deal about a team and its coach by observing them in action. Does the team have the type of attitude you're looking for? Are all the things you've heard about "the coach" true? Are you good enough to compete with these guys, or will you be in over your head? These are all questions you should be asking yourself while observing the team.

• Examine the academic facilities as well as the athletic facilities. Does the school seem to spend more money for new stadiums and arenas than it does for modern laboratory and classroom facilities?

• Request appointments with academic staff. If possible, meet with a professor who teaches a course in your main area of interest. Also, be sure to ask about academic support services for athletes, and speak with the person who heads that program.

At the end of your visit, you'll probably want to meet privately with the head coach. Up to this point, most of your contact has probably been with an assistant coach. He is certainly an important member of the staff and a valuable source of information. However, it is in your best interest to get to know the head coach as well as you possibly can.

"The assistant coaches are very important, but it's the head coach who will be making the final decisions that will affect you most," said Gary Williams. "You definitely want to spend some time with him during your visit."

Some of the questions you should discuss with the head coach are:

1. How do you feel I will fit in with your team and its style of play?
2. What position would you be likely to have me play?
3. Do you think I will have a good chance to start as a freshman? As a sophomore?
4. If I am not a starting player by the time I am a junior, will my athletic scholarship be taken away?

   North Carolina's coach Dean Smith explained his philosophy on athletic scholarships: "I have never taken away a scholarship for any reason as long as I have been head coach. One young man said he wanted to concentrate on his studies and no longer play basketball. He said he wanted to give up his scholarship and he could afford it. I said, 'no way: you have to keep it because we brought you to our school to graduate.' I think once you recruit and give an initial grant to a young man, you are really making a commitment to see that he earns a degree."
5. If I am injured and can no longer play, will the school still fund my education?
6. Are you recruiting any other high school seniors who play my position?
7. Will I have to live in an athletic dormitory?
8. Will the school pay for the courses I need to graduate, even after my four years of eligibility run out?
9. Will the school pay for summer courses that are necessary for my degree program?
10. Will I be able to miss practice if I have to attend a late class or lab session?
11. Does the school give free tutoring and counseling to athletes?
12. Are the tutors professionals, or work-study students?
13. Will I have an opportunity to make up classes I miss because of road games?

14. Will out-of-season practices interfere with my class schedule?
15. What is the graduation rate of athletes you have coached?
16. What is the employment rate for those athletes who graduate? In what professions?

When your campus visit is over, take some time to relax and try to evaluate what you saw and learned about the school. You might even want to make a balance sheet of the strong pluses and minuses. Try not to get too excited immediately after the visit. Remember, the chances are that they were really putting on a good show for you.

Jack Bicknell cautioned that "as a recruit, you receive constant attention. It is important to remember that once you start school in the fall, all the glory comes to a screeching halt. In most cases you'll find yourself at the bottom of the heap, trying to scratch and claw your way back up the hill. It can be a very tough experience for a young person."

Important Considerations

When you have done all your research, narrowed down the list, and visited the schools you are most interested in, you should consider these factors before making your final decision:

- **Climate.** If you are from southern California and are considering a school in Ohio or Pennsylvania, you should be sure that the cold winters and that white stuff they call snow won't bother you. Likewise, attending a school in an area where it is usually 85 degrees and sunny might do wonders for your tan—but not much for your grade-point average.
- **Location (distance from home).** Only you can decide whether it is important for you to attend a school close to your home town. "Do I want my parents and high school friends to be able to see me play often? Then maybe the favorite local college only thirty-five miles up the road is the place for me. Or perhaps the idea of living in another part of the country is exciting." Both choices obviously have their advantages. However, location probably shouldn't be a

Courtesy of the University of North Carolina Office of Sports Information

"

I have never taken away a scholarship for any reason as long as I have been head coach. One young man said he wanted to concentrate on his studies and no longer play basketball. He said he wanted to give up his scholarship and he could afford it. I said, 'No way—you have to keep it because we brought you to our school to graduate.' I think once you recruit and give an initial grant to a young man, you are really making a commitment to see that he earns a degree.

Dean Smith
University of North Carolina basketball coach

"

very important part of your decision unless your family's personal situation is a factor.

• **Size of school.** "Do I want to attend a small school, where I get a chance to really know people and build close friendships? Or do I want to get my education at a larger university, where I seem to see something new everyday?" Neither choice is right or wrong—it depends upon your personal preference.

• **Housing and dining facilities.** "As an athlete, will I be housed apart from the rest of the students, and will I eat separately? Does that appeal to me?" At Penn State, which has one of the top football programs in the nation, there is no football dorm. "I think a kid ought to come to college and be a nobody for awhile," explains Joe Paterno. "If he lives in a regular dorm, it will help a young man make a normal and healthy transition from high school to college."

• **Academic program.** "Does the school have the *exact* major I am interested in studying?"

"

If you want to major in accounting, don't be satisfied if the coach tells you, 'Oh yeah, we have a great business school.' Find out if you can major in accounting, and if not, what courses does the business school offer that are relevant to your academic interests. You should also find out if players are in degree completion programs, or just majoring in staying eligible.

Gary Williams
Ohio State basketball coach

"

• **An academic support system for athletes.** "What type of support programs does the university have to meet my special academic needs as an athlete? Is the tutoring program run by professionals or by work-study students? Is the job of the academic adviser to keep me eligible, or to help me learn?"

• **Athletic program.** "Can I play at this level? Would I be better off at a smaller school where I can start for four years, or do I want to compete at the highest possible level?"

- **Social life.** "Was I comfortable on the campus during my visit? Do I like a slower pace and a more laid-back atmosphere? Or would I prefer a school known for its great parties?"

The Decision

Obviously, the hardest part of the entire recruiting process is making that final decision. Even though you may be offered a place at more than one of the colleges you'd like to attend, you can only choose one school. As you try to make a final decision, write out a list that compares the good and bad points of each school. Talk to people you trust and get their opinions, but don't let them decide for you. Your own needs and goals are the most important factors.

If you base your decision on most of the guidelines suggested in this chapter, then your chances of making a good choice should be excellent. Once you make the decision, don't look back!

Courtesy of the Los Angeles Dodgers, Inc.

" ——————————————————

Sport is good to you. Education is good for you. Drugs and alcohol can kill you.

Pedro Guerrero
Los Angeles Dodgers

——————————————————— "

3 Drugs and Alcohol

The most frightening sports-related event of 1986 was undoubtedly the sudden, shocking death of Len Bias. In a three-day period, the 22-year-old Bias became the top draft choice of the world champion Boston Celtics, signed a million-dollar shoe contract, and died from a cocaine-related heart attack. The sports world mourned this superstar, this role model turned example.

But Bias's death was not the only sports drug story of 1986. As you read this chapter, you'll have to wonder what lure cocaine has that would make an athlete like Len Bias risk everything for that flash of instant pleasure, what power it possesses to have induced Don Rogers, the 1984 NFL Rookie-of-the-Year, to ingest enough cocaine to kill himself eight days after the Bias tragedy? If you read the sports page, you've probably read about the following stories:

- Seven New England Patriots were said to be "seriously" involved with drugs. This story was printed a day after the Patriots played in the Super Bowl.
- Micheal Ray Richardson was banned by the NBA after testing positive for cocaine for the third time.
- John Lucas was dropped by the Houston Rockets after he tested positive for the third time.
- Baseball Commissioner Peter Ueberroth announced sanctions against twenty-one former drug users in Major League Baseball.
- Fifty-seven of the top collegiate prospects for the NFL draft tested positive for drugs.

• NFL Commissioner Pete Rozelle and NFL Players Association Director Gene Upshaw battled over the issue of mandatory drug testing for NFL players.

For years, people close to pro sports have known that there is a serious drug problem. High incomes, boredom, and easy access to drugs have sucked all too many of our sports heroes into self-destruction.

The horror of Len Bias's death brought home that drugs were not limited to pro athletes. Doctors' testimony that a single exposure to cocaine could kill someone as physically fit as Bias might have woken up young athletes as no other incident could have. It appeared clear that other college basketball players were using coke. Yet only a short time before the death of Bias, sports fans seemed shocked when such a high percentage of college football stars tested positively at an NFL tryout camp. The pros blame the colleges; the colleges blame the pros and the high schools. But where you place the blame is not really important. What is important is that almost everyone connected with organized athletics agrees that there is a major drug abuse problem in sports at all levels.

But the real shocker is that millions of *high school* athletes are abusing drugs and alcohol. If you are one of them, you could be placing your entire future in serious danger. You are playing Russian roulette with your body and your life.

Before cocaine killed Len Bias and Don Rogers, you might have thought that, as an athlete, your superior physical strength would make you immune to the dangers of chemical abuse. But the deaths of Bias and Rogers are not the only drug stories that should have convinced you otherwise. Consider some of the people who might now be your athletic heroes—or some who might have been had their careers not been ended by drugs.

Sugar Man

Micheal Ray Richardson was the NBA's Comeback Player of the Year in the 1984–85 season. Usually the award is made to someone who has recovered from a serious injury. In Micheal Ray's case, however, it was because he had seemingly overcome his addiction to cocaine and was again becoming a force in the world of professional basketball. He was even featured with other players in a film about the dangers of cocaine abuse that was produced by the NBA Players Association.

Richardson was once again playing great ball in the 1985–86 season when things began to fall apart. This tragedy was caused by the overwhelming power of his addiction to cocaine.

In 1978, after playing four years of basketball at the University of Montana, Richardson was a first-round draft pick of the New York Knickerbockers. He quickly established himself as one of the top point guards in basketball by leading the NBA in assists and steals in only his second season. During his time with the Knicks he began to use cocaine.

Just before the start of the 1982–83 season, Richardson was traded to the Golden State Warriors. He was very upset by the trade, and he began to use cocaine more often. He told *The New York Times*, "I lost interest in playing. I didn't know what coke would do for me, but at least it got me away from reality."

In February 1983, Richardson was traded to the New Jersey Nets. He continued to use cocaine regularly, and his game suffered. One minute he would make the type of spectacular play that had become his trademark, and the next he would throw the ball away.

“

People assure you that its OK to try it . . . that the team won't find out. The first thing you know, you're back in it. I know I damn well reached my bottom. I was slowly but surely killing myself.

Micheal Ray Richardson
former New Jersey Nets All-Star guard, and the first active player banned by the NBA for drug use
in *Sports Illustrated*

”

He began to hang out with individuals who might be called the "wrong people." These "friends" encouraged his drug use and made it easy for him to get cocaine. "I wouldn't call them friends, though that's what I thought they were at the time," Richardson said later.

During the summer of 1983, Richardson spent time in two drug rehabilitation centers. In the early fall of the same year, he called a press conference and announced that he had recovered from his addiction.

He had not. It just wasn't that easy. Doctors will tell you that once you are an addict, you are always an addict. The best you can do is stay sober, day to day, month to month, year to year.

During the 1983 season, Richardson hit what seemed like rock bottom. His problems with cocaine abuse returned, and he refused to enter a rehabilitation center. The Nets, feeling they had no other choice, placed him on waivers. Because no other team in the NBA would claim him, Richardson entered a New York drug and alcohol rehabilitation center. When he left the center two weeks later, he continued with counseling for his addiction and was regularly tested for drug use.

Things began to look up. Richardson enjoyed a tremendous 1984–85 season, and he finally appeared to be making progress in his battle against drugs. In spring 1985, he was named the NBA Comeback Player of the Year. As Richardon's game picked up, the Nets began to make noises in the Eastern Conference of the NBA. They were gearing up for a serious run at the conference powerhouses, the Boston Celtics and the Philadelphia 76ers. With a record of 19-13, the Nets were breathing down the necks of the second-place Sixers. Was this finally going to be their year? Little did they know that more heartbreak lay ahead.

After a team Christmas party one Friday night, Richardson disappeared and was not seen for two days. On Saturday he missed morning practice, and then he failed to appear at the game with the Washington Bullets that night. On New Year's Eve, Richardson admitted that he had once again started using cocaine. He flew to California to enter yet another drug rehabilitation program. After spending a little over two weeks in California, Richardson returned to New Jersey and was reactivated by the Nets. His teammates knew that this would be Richardson's last chance to set himself straight as far as the Nets and the NBA were concerned.

As an all-star professional athlete, Richardson had faced many challenges on the court, and more often than not he had successfully met those challenges head on. Now Micheal Ray was involved in a battle with drug abuse that he *had* to win. There was much more than an NBA championship at stake—his life was at stake.

Richardson was again defeated by his addiction. He tested positive for cocaine use for the third time. In the eyes of the NBA, this was strike three. The NBA, in an agreement with the league's player's association, banned Micheal Ray from the league for at least two years. After the two years, he could reapply for admission, but there was no guarantee that he would ever again be allowed to play in the league. He had failed in his last chance.

As word of the suspension spread, members of the Net family expressed their dismay.

Otis Birdsong, Richardson's backcourt running mate, told the *Boston Globe* that it was "a great tragedy." "I had really gotten close to him. He said he was going to stay clean this time . . . that he wasn't going to blow it. That's why I'm shocked. That stuff is powerful. It's killing people."

And Tony Elliott sounded an ominous warning. "Now he's [Richardson] going to have to learn how to walk the earth like a normal person," said Elliott. "He's going to learn how tough it is to make a living when there's no $400,000-a-year job waiting for him.

"Most importantly, Micheal Ray is going to have to learn that there is no 'one last one for the road' when it comes to drug and alcohol abuse."

Perhaps more than any other current or former pro athlete, Tony Elliott should know what dragged Richardson down and what he might have to do to make his life whole—even if he never plays again.

With a Gun Pointed at My Head

From the time he was born up to the moment he faced the barrel of that .357 magnum, Tony Elliott's life was full of violence and fear. No one could have predicted that he would have survived. Tony simply calls it "a miracle."

Tony Elliott, who was almost destroyed by drugs, is now the starting nose tackle for the New Orleans Saints. Many other athletes who foolishly turned to drugs have seen their careers tragically end, but something about Tony's character begged the NFL powers to give him second and third chances. A few short years ago, a drug dealer's gun threatened his life, but now Elliott preaches to the nation's young students and student–athletes about the nightmare of his addiction to cocaine.

Anthony Robert Elliott was born in Bridgeport, Connecticut, in 1959. He was raised in a world of crime, drugs, and, finally, murder. At the age of four, Tony heard his mother screaming in the kitchen. He went in, and witnessed his father plunging a kitchen knife into his mother. When Tony looked down, he saw and then passed out in a pool of his mother's blood.

❝

> The dealer had a .357 magnum pointed at my head. Finally I realized that cocaine was my life, that I had been bought and sold by this drug. I was either going to die or give it up. I have been sober for nearly three years.
>
> *Tony Elliott*
> New Orleans Saints, recovering addict
> in the *New York Times*

❞

When Tony's father was sentenced to fifteen years for the murder of his mother, Tony and his two brothers were taken in by their Uncle Wilbert.

In junior high school, Tony began to experiment with alcohol. At first he would "hang out" with the guys and drink cheap wine. "It got to the point where I was drinking quite a bit of wine and beer, and it wasn't doing the job . . . getting me high," explained Elliott. "I figured I'd try a little hard liquor. I rationalized that a few shots of whiskey couldn't be any more harmful than a whole bottle of wine. Little did I know that I would continue to rationalize this way until it almost killed me."

Wilbert had become his father in Tony's mind by the time he was fourteen years old. Tony's world was slightly more secure. But shortly after Tony's real father was released from prison, he marched into Wilbert's house and killed him. Tony's life was once again ripped apart.

At age fifteen, Tony found himself without a family, and he was placed in a boy's home in Bridgeport, Connecticut. At the boy's home Tony first experimented with marijuana and cocaine. Using the home as his base of operations, Tony began to sell drugs.

At Warren Harding High School, the football coach, John Lewis, took Tony under his wing. Tony grew in size and talent, and quickly became one of the top players in Connecticut. He was selected for high school All-American teams in his junior and senior years.

Tony was heavily recruited by many big-time college football powers. He eventually chose to attend a Big Ten school that offered him an apartment and a car to sign a letter-of-intent. A local dentist became his "sugar daddy." All the rules of the game were being broken. The school knew it, and Tony knew it. Once again he rationalized by telling himself, "everybody does it."

At college, Tony smoked large amounts of marijuana every day. As was previously the case with alcohol, he found that marijuana was no longer satisfying his drug needs. Again, he began to rationalize. This time he convinced himself that a little cocaine couldn't possibly be any worse than all of that marijuana. Once again he was wrong.

At the start of his college football career, Tony was assigned to the role of a reserve for the first time in his athletic career. He became very insecure about his status on the team. After all, everything he ever had in life had come through sports. Fearing that he would lose everything, he dropped out of classes to concentrate on football. Still not starting he became deeply depressed. He felt unable to cope without the attention on the field, and he was about to flunk out of school. So Tony left college completely and joined the U.S. Marines in 1976. Unfortunately, he was not able to drop his cocaine habit as easily as he had dropped his college career.

After finishing his stint with the Marines, Elliott was accepted at junior college in Kansas. Again, a coach took care of all of his needs—including an apartment and a car. The people who Tony thought were helping him were, in fact, using him. Like many young athletes, he had no way of knowing that this type of special treatment can't go on forever.

After a year in junior college, Tony enrolled at North Texas State University in Denton, Texas. While at North Texas State he smoked marijuana regularly and began to experiment more and more with cocaine. Football continued to dominate his life. For two full seasons, State was rewarded by Tony's outstanding playing. He left North Texas State with tremendous confidence in his ability to play football, but with no degree, a drug habit, and a great deal of insecurity off the field.

However, when Coach Bum Phillips and the New Orleans Saints selected him in the fifth round of the NFL draft, Tony *knew* that he was headed for the pot of gold at the end of the rainbow. He had beaten the almost-impossible odds against making the pros, he had beaten back the horrors of his youth and family life, and he had achieved his greatest dream in life—playing in the National Football League.

Tony took his $30,000 signing bonus and went on a three-week cocaine binge. At the end of that time, he had blown the entire $30,000 with his friends.

In Tony's eyes, football had given him everything he had: money, cars, apartments, clothes, women, and success. It was his whole identity. He would do anything to protect this identity now that he was one of the "big guys." Although he excelled in training camp, it was clear that the rookie was not going to be a starter. Insecurity overwhelmed him, but this time he turned to cocaine to ease his tremendous fears. Cocaine gave Tony a false sense of escape from all his terrifying fears and insecurities. Tony said, "the cocaine also gave me friendship, I thought, and that would encourage me and build up my ego. Little did I know that I was only destroying myself."

Tony's rookie season was the year after the George Rodgers drug scandal. Rodgers, a winner of the Heisman Trophy Award and a star Saints running back, had admitted to being heavily involved with cocaine. The Saints coaching staff and front office were particularly worried about drug abuse spreading through the team.

As his addiction grew worse, Tony voluntarily sought help for his problem at the Timberline Drug Rehabilitation Center in Texas. During his short two-week stay at Timberline, all Tony could think about was getting back on the football field. He falsely believed that as long as he could play ball, the rest of his life would fall comfortably into place.

In the off-season after his rookie year, Tony managed to stay drug-free for six weeks. But then he found himself turning to cocaine again. He figured that it wouldn't hurt to have a little "fun" in the off-season. After all, he was a big man . . . a professional athlete . . . nothing could really hurt him.

Coach Phillips suspected that Tony was continuing to abuse drugs, and so he had Tony admitted to Hazelton Institute for Drug Rehabilitation in Minnesota. While at Hazelton, Tony felt he learned a great deal about drug addiction, but he still could not accept the fact that *he* was dependent on drugs. He still believed that *he* had no problem.

Tony's counselor at Hazelton told him that he was only going through the motions of kicking his habit. Until he surrendered to the fact that he was an addict, Tony could never really be cured. Tony knew that he couldn't get back into the NFL unless the doctors at Hazelton gave him the OK, so going through the motions became part of his routine. That routine was soon to collapse.

During his entire career, the people around him (including coaches, athletic administrators, teammates, and friends) helped him get everything he had. Like hundreds of others, all Tony had to do was produce on the field, and everyone would want to be his buddy. These "caring people" helped him avoid responsibility and care. In Tony's case, that made it easy for him to turn to drugs to escape all his inner fears. Within a year, he had lost everything.

Broke and desperate for drugs, Tony began selling all his possessions—his cars, furniture, appliances, his condominium, and even his wife's wedding ring. With nothing left, he turned to crime to supply his habit. At one point, Tony took a gun and went to rob his drug dealer. But when the dealer opened the door, he pointed his own .357 magnum at Tony's head. Tony suddenly knew that he was facing the same type of violent death that took the lives of his mother and uncle.

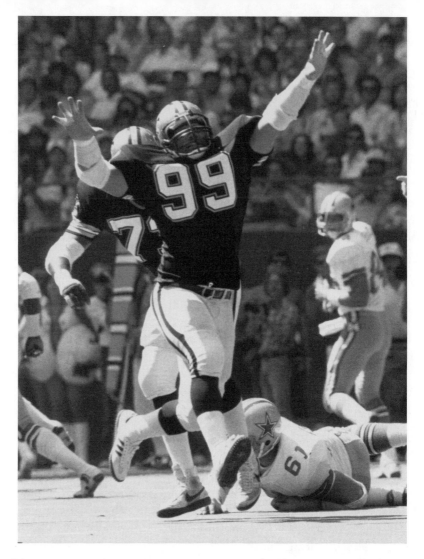

"

I have had a life filled with drugs and alcohol; I have experienced misery and misfortune. I allowed my coaches and advisers to take away all responsibilities from me. They did everything for me. All I had to do was play the game. They were wrong and I was wrong. But I was the one who almost died.

Tony Elliott
New Orleans Saints

"

He voluntarily admitted himself to DePaul Hospital Drug and Alcohol Rehabilitation Center in New Orleans. He was eventually released by the Saints. Finally he had hit rock bottom. With his career lifeline cut off, he was finally shocked back into reality. Tony had to decide whether football or his own life was most important to him.

He made a commitment to sobriety, and remained in DePaul for eighty-five days. From there he chose to move into a halfway house for recovering addicts and alcoholics. The most important step Tony had taken was to admit to himself that he was, in fact, addicted to cocaine.

"Denial is the drug abuser's worst enemy," he proclaimed. "I spent years convincing myself that I didn't really have a problem . . . that I was in control. I was wrong. The cocaine was in control."

According to Tony, what made his recovery more possible was his decision to visit junior high and high schools and urge youngsters to avoid the same perilous path he had taken. Bringing his message to others helped him keep his vow to stay drug-free. This message, coming from someone who lived through the horrors of drug addiction, is particularly forceful. He also speaks regularly at drug centers, prisons, and alcohol and drug rehabilitation institutions.

"Everytime I speak to a group about how I almost ruined my life, it serves as a reminder for me to not go down that road again," said Elliott. "My drug addiction was a living hell."

Looking back, he now says, "I have had a life filled with drugs and alcohol; I have experienced misery and misfortune. I allowed my coaches and advisers to take away all responsibilities from me. They did everything for me. All I had to do was play the game. They were wrong and I was wrong. But I was the one who almost died."

"Now, knowing the true, heartfelt feelings of sobriety, I am trying to help others. If through my efforts in my personal life or by speaking to groups, I save a few lives, then my life is worthwhile and there is truly a miracle in the works."

Commissioner Rozelle decided to readmit Tony to the NFL and he started every game in the 1985 season for the Saints.

Tony Elliott *is* a miracle, and his life, its lessons, and his courage are a gift to all of us.

One for the Road

Mention the name Bob Welch to an avid baseball fan, and chances are that his mind will turn back to the fall of 1978. In October of that year Welch, a rookie righthander for the National League Champion Los Angeles Dodgers took part in one of the most memorable confrontations in World Series history.

In the second game of the series at Dodger Stadium, Welch was summoned from the Dodgers bullpen in the bottom of the ninth inning to stop a New York Yankee comeback bid. With two outs and the go-ahead runs in scoring position, Reggie Jackson strode to the plate—the same Reggie Jackson who had been nicknamed "Mr. October" because of his past World Series exploits. Jackson had already driven in all three Yankee runs that night. Rookie unknown vs. veteran star. Fastball pitcher vs. fastball hitter. With the count at three balls and two strikes, Welch began to rear back and throw fastballs. Jackson stayed alive in the batter's box by barely fouling each pitch. Finally Welch threw a rising fastball past the swinging bat of Jackson. The Dodgers were winners and Welch's name would live in World Series history.

In the spring of 1980, Welch was involved in another confrontation, one that made facing Reggie Jackson in the World Series seem easy: Welch stood before his Dodger teammates and said, "I am an alcoholic. I always will be an alcoholic, but I'm trying to combat my illness. I now know how to stop drinking one day at a time, and that's what I'm going to do."

Welch told the painful story of his battle with alcoholism to George Vescey in their book *Five O'Clock Comes Early—A Young Man's Battle with Alcoholism.*

"It was inevitable that I would drink growing up," said Welch. "It was always there, wherever I went—family occasions, in the neighborhood, at school. Some people don't like it, but everybody tried it, and I liked it.

Welch continued to drink heavily in college. As part of an all-star team that toured Japan, he almost caused an incident at his Tokyo hotel after getting smashed. He later realized that he "was already suffering alcoholic blackouts."

Welch was drafted by the Dodgers and traveled to Vero Beach,

Florida, for his first Major League spring training camp in March 1978. There he met Don Newcombe, who was a former Dodger and the best pitcher in baseball in 1956. His career had been shortened by alcohol. Newcombe tried to warn young players in the Dodgers about the dangers of alcohol abuse. "I am an alcoholic. I have a weakness with alcohol, and I let it drag me down."

"

Drinking made everything easier. It was a wonder drug. I would get a buzz on and stop being afraid of girls. When I was starting in high school I was afraid to talk to them . . . But with a couple of beers in me, it was all right. In the tenth grade, eleventh grade, after a few beers, I'd feel part of the crowd.

Bob Welch
Los Angeles Dodgers pitcher, recovering alcoholic

"

Newcombe's words of warning had little effect on Welch. He was now a Major League pitcher, and he thought nothing could stop him. He continued to drink heavily. If he wasn't pitching, he would sneak into the Dodger weight-training room during games and have a few beers. Before a game with the San Francisco Giants, Welch was so drunk that he began cursing at members of the Giants and his own teammates alike. He had to be half-carried off the field by Rick Sutcliffe, then a member of the Dodger pitching staff.

In spite of his problems with alcohol, Welch continued to develop into one of the top young pitchers in baseball. There was no question that Bob Welch had enough talent to be a top pitcher for years to come. The question was, would he defeat alcohol, or would alcohol defeat him?

In 1980, with the help of Dodger General Manager Al Campanis, Welch finally began to realize that he had a problem. He agreed to attend an alcohol addiction treatment center known as The Meadows in Wickenburg, Arizona.

Welch spent over a month at The Meadows. After an extremely painful and difficult time, he finally came to grips with his drinking problem. The staff at The Meadows showed him that alcoholism is a disease. At last, Welch understood that he was trying to escape from things he couldn't handle by drinking.

"Kids shouldn't associate all good times with drugs and alcohol," said Welch. "I hope some kids will listen to me, because they can see what happened to me, how I almost blew my chance to play baseball because the drinking caught up with me."

The Truth about "Fun" Drugs and Alcohol

Micheal Ray Richardson, Tony Elliott, and Bob Welch all thought that they could abuse drugs and alcohol and still be star athletes. But they were fooling themselves and playing Russian roulette with their lives. Marijuana, cocaine, and alcohol have serious effects on your health and on your game. Every student–athlete should be aware of these effects and should understand why it's so important to avoid drugs.

Marijuana Use and Athletic Performance

- Marijuana use can cause drowsiness and can make you less alert.
- Marijuana use can decrease your hand-eye coordination.
- Marijuana use can increase your heart rate and blood pressure.
- Marijuana use can cause memory loss.
- Marijuana use can affect your vision.
- Marijuana use can slow down your reaction time.

Because marijuana can remain in your system for up to a month, it can negatively affect your athletic performance for that whole period of time. The joint you smoke a couple of nights before the big game will limit your effectiveness. Regular use of marijuana may not only destroy your athletic career—it can also threaten your ability to function in virtually all areas of life. If you use marijuana often, there is a real danger that you will be tempted to "graduate" to other drugs, such as cocaine—as Tony Elliott found out the hard way. This pattern has become all too familiar. Many young people have ruined their lives because of their desire to get high.

Cocaine Abuse and Athletic Performance

- Cocaine use can cause violent shifts in mood, from euphoria to depression.
- Cocaine use can lead to dizziness and vomiting.
- Cocaine use can make you short of breath.
- Cocaine use can cause rapid increases and decreases in blood pressure.
- Cocaine use can affect your depth perception.
- Cocaine use can slow down your reaction time.

In addition to the above-mentioned negative effects of cocaine, remember that *cocaine can cause death!* Used in high doses, it can cause fatal heart attacks. It can kill you slowly—or instantly. Stay away from cocaine. Your life may be at stake.

Alcohol Abuse and Athletic Performance

- Alcohol use can negatively affect your physical conditioning program.
- Alcohol use can result in muscle weakness.
- Alcohol use can slow down your reaction time.
- Alcohol use can affect your depth perception.
- Alcohol use can cause dizziness and vomiting.
- Alcohol use can make you less alert.
- Alcohol use can cause liver damage.

Simply put, there's no way alcohol can improve your athletic ability. It can not only make your athletic performance worse, but when alcohol is used regularly, it is a great danger to your physical and mental health. Alcoholism is one of the most common sicknesses in our society today. Don't let a few brews or a couple of shots start you on the road to self-destruction. Stay away from alcohol.

Performance-Enhancing Drugs: The Other Illusion

So far we have talked about drugs that young people get involved with for fun. They think alcohol or cocaine will relax them and help them have a good time. Through the eyes of athletes who told their stories for the benefit of others, we have learned about the life-threatening dangers of alcohol and drug abuse. But these are not the only dangerous drugs in the world of sports.

Today, many young athletes are using drugs that they hope will improve their athletic performance. The most common types of these drugs are amphetamines—or "speed"—and anabolic steroids, which build up your body weight. Such drugs are being illegally sold in some high schools, in the streets, at gyms, and on many college campuses. The evidence we are about to present to you clearly shows that these performance-enhancing drugs can be extremely dangerous to your overall health.

But first, let Steve Courson tell you what steroids did and didn't do for him. Courson is a starting offensive lineman for the Tampa Bay Buccaneers. He told *Sports Illustrated* about his involvement with steroids.

Courson began taking steroids the summer before his sophomore year in college. He felt they would help him become a stronger, better football player. By using the drugs, his body weight increased from 225 to 260 pounds in a month and a half. As a pro, Courson continued to use steroids. He took them for eight to twelve weeks in the off-seasons from 1982 to 1984.

"

The best thing I ever did was get off the drugs. I've found that I can compete in the NFL without them. Getting off them was hard; I was an addict, a steroid junkie. I thought about going back on. I still do. But . . . there are just too many medical risks. We'd all be better off if steroids weren't around—everyone would be better off.

Steve Courson
Tampa Bay Buccaneers

"

Although he vaguely knew about the risks, Courson believed that the benefits outweighed them. He thought he was less likely to be badly injured if he was stronger, and stronger meant using steroids. For Courson, his job was on the line—and that was the greatest risk of all.

But years later Courson changed his mind, and became steroid-free.

Courson claimed that getting off steroids had changed his life. Even though he was lighter and not as strong, he picked up speed and flexibility. His heart rate came way down, and the mood swings he had when he was a user were gone. The answers to the questions below will help you to understand why Courson gave up steroids.

Questions Often Asked about Performance-Enhancing Drugs

- Do amphetamines ("pep pills," "speed," "uppers") prevent an athlete from tiring and make him more aggressive?
  Although an athlete may feel more aggressive under the influence of amphetamines, studies show that the actual level of performance suffers. The athlete thinks that he or she is not tired, and so becomes a prime target for heat exhaustion. Amphetamines also cause a general rise in body temperature.
- Do amphetamines prevent an athlete from suffering injuries?
  Amphetamines tend to mask pain and increase the risk of serious injury to the athlete.
- Do amphetamines improve overall athletic ability?
  Numerous studies show that amphetamine use has negative effects on athletic performance. Timing and judgement skills are severely affected, even though the athlete wrongly believes that his or her performance is better than it actually is.
- Will anabolic steroids make an athlete stronger?
  Use of anabolic steroids may increase body weight,

mainly because they cause the body to retain water.
Some evidence suggests that anabolic steroid use
increases an individual's strength. However, experts
agree that the best way for a young athlete to increase
strength is through a comprehensive weight-training
program and through following high-quality nutritional
program.

• What are the negative effects of anabolic steroids for the
young athlete?
Anabolic steroid use can stunt your growth, cause liver
and heart disease, and can lead to stomach disorders. In
men, steroids can cause hair loss. There is also evidence
that steroids can make you sterile.

• Can the young female athlete suffer any additional
negative effects from anabolic steroid use?
Women athletes who take anabolic steroids to improve
performance can expect masculine side-effects, such as a
deeper voices, an enlarged clitoris, and increased facial
hair. These effects can be permanent.

• What are the long-term effects of anabolic steroid use?
The long-term side-effects of anabolic steroid use are
unknown, and will probably not be discovered for some
time. However, researchers are very concerned about the
possible long-term dangers of steroid use.

• Are there any drugs that can be effectively used to treat
injuries and speed an athlete's return to action?
Certain medications can reduce pain and swelling, and
can be helpful in *complementing* a treatment process.
However, recovery from an injury always takes time.
Although medications can mask the pain of an injury,
masking that pain can result in more serious damage if
the athlete goes back to the field too soon. Young athletes
should completely recover from an injury before
returning to competition.

As you can see, choosing to use drugs, whether for fun or to improve
your performance, can hurt you physically and emotionally. Drugs

and alcohol bring instant pleasure—that's why so many people use them. But the next time you are tempted to experience that pleasure, think about Len Bias. Think about Don Rogers.

"

I want those kids who come along years after this whole mess is forgotten to read every word . . . to see how it ruined lives and crippled careers. I want them to look at the pictures on the faces of these kids who are being put in jail and then, if they still turn crooked, they will deserve everything that happens to them.

Joe Lapchick
Former coach of St. John's University and the New York Knicks

"

4 Gambling

"I'll bet you five dollars that State beats Tech on Saturday night." A bet like this sounds as innocent as it is common. More than half of America's adults gamble—to the tune of over $70 billion a year! Betting sheets are just as available to high school athletes as they are to businessmen. Common? Innocent? Involvement in gambling can end your athletic career and ruin your life.

Whether we like it or not, gambling is a big part of the American sports scene. If it is not dealt with intelligently, gambling threatens everyone in organized athletics.

You are probably asking, "How does gambling affect me?" It's not likely to affect you very much during your high school years. But betting five dollars on a college game or on the Super Bowl can be where it all begins. People can become addicted to gambling, just like drugs. And there are Gamblers Anonymous organizations that—like Alcoholics Anonymous—help those who are addicted. If you come into contact with someone who is a serious gambler, you must be able to recognize this and act in your own best interests. *Don't get involved!*

In 1951, Joe Lapchick, the basketball coach of the New York Knicks, was busy putting together a scrapbook. This was not an ordinary scrapbook filled with articles about his team's many triumphs. This collection of newspaper and magazine clippings was about the point-shaving scandal of 1951 that shocked the world of college basketball. In all, seven schools were involved in the scandal, including championship teams from City College in New York and the University of Kentucky. A thorough investigation revealed that thirty-two players took part in the fixing of eighty-six games.

In a point-shaving scheme, players hold down their team's score so that its margin of victory is smaller, or its margin of defeat is greater, than the betting line set by the professional gamblers known as bookmakers.

Lapchick vowed that "I will show this [scrapbook] to every team I ever coach. I want those kids who come along years after this whole mess is forgotten to read every word in here, to see how it ruined lives and crippled careers. I want them to look at the pictures on the faces of these kids who are being put in jail and then, if they still turn crooked, then they will deserve everything that happens to them. At least I will know I have done my best."

In 1951, Lapchick's Knicks had just made it to the NBA finals. But their chance for the championship was ruined because their "big man" was missing from the team. Lapchick had been the nation's first great "big man" for the original Celtics, when they won more world championships than any other team in basketball's history. So he knew that Sherman White, star center at Long Island University, was the person that the Knicks needed. Best of all, White belonged to the Knicks through the NBA draft. But before he could make his move to the big-time, Sherman White became one of "those kids" involved in the scandal. *He never played a minute in the NBA.* The Knicks went to the finals again for the next two years, but they lost without White. They hadn't lost as much as White himself.

The case of Sherman White was sadly recalled when Tulane's John "Hot Rod" Williams and other teammates were accused of point-shaving in 1985. A sure first-round NBA draft choice with several million dollars in his future, Williams was said to have gambled for a few thousand dollars. He lost big.

On the first weekend of April in 1985, the eyes of the college basketball world were watching intently as four of the top teams in the nation prepared to compete for the NCAA Championship in Lexington, Kentucky. The Final Four—college basketball's show-case. Sadly, at the same time that Villanova and Georgetown were about to play one of the best games in the history of college hoops, the attention of basketball fans nationwide was shifted to New Orleans, Louisiana. There, eight Tulane University students—including five members of the Green Wave basketball team—were being charged with conspiring to fix basketball games.

"

Gamblers will try to get close to athletes in many different ways . . . girls, boosters, friends. It used to be just organized crime, but the Tulane scandal was largely precipitated by the athlete's classmates . . . and of course there is a real relationship between gambling and drugs.

Thomas French
FBI Supervisory Special Agent

"

The scandal cut so deep that Tulane dropped basketball. The following is an alleged version of the Tulane tragedy as reported by *Sports Illustrated.*

It all started when a Tulane undergraduate started to give Clyde Eads something for nothing.

Eads, a starting forward on the Tulane squad, was befriended by Gary Kranz, a Tulane undergraduate from New Rochelle, New York. According to investigators, Eads began supplying Kranz with Tulane basketball gear in exchange for cocaine. As time went on, Tulane team members began to visit Kranz's apartment, where they were given cocaine.

On the day of the Tulane–Southern Mississippi game, Kranz and two friends decided that Kranz should approach Eads and speak with him about fixing that evening's game. Eads talked the matter over with four of his teammates, and they decided to shave points.

Tulane was favored to defeat Southern Mississippi that night by at least ten points. Kranz and his friends wagered $7,000 that Tulane would not win by ten or more points. They paid Eads and his four teammates a total of $3,500 to make sure that Tulane did not win by this margin.

Tulane won the game 64–63. After the game, at a party at Kranz's apartment, one player remarked, "Hey, we won the game and still got all the money."

The players next accepted $13,500 (Williams was said to have received approximately $4,500) to "throw" the Memphis State game. At halftime, Tulane led the game by six points, but allowed State to come back early in the second half and eventually to win 60–49.

The authorities got wind of rumors of a point-shaving scandal. They investigated, and now eight more young men have been scarred for life.

Instead of spending the 1985–86 basketball season starring in the NBA, John "Hot Rod" Williams was tied up in a court of law. Although he was eventually acquitted of all charges brought against him, many people still believe that Williams may have unnecessarily risked his career—and more importantly his reputation—for a short-term financial fix.

Three other major college basketball point-shaving scandals were uncovered in between the time that Joe Lapchick sat down to put together his scrapbook and the Tulane humiliation. These scandals have also ruined lives and crippled careers.

Rick Kuhn obviously didn't read Lapchick's scrapbook, or if he did, he chose to ignore its warnings. In 1982 most of Kuhn's classmates from Boston College were beginning their careers in business or industry, or were heading off to continue their education at graduate school. Kuhn was about to receive another kind of education: he was sent to Lewisburg State Prison in Pennsylvania. He had been sentenced to ten years in prison for conspiring to point-shave in six BC games during the 1978–79 season. Rick Kuhn's story is a living nightmare. It is a sad example of the threat that involvement in gambling can be to anyone. You don't have to be a star athlete to be approached by gamblers. They will simply use anyone who can help them get more money. Kuhn learned this lesson the hard way.

Sports Illustrated told of how Kuhn's nightmare started innocently enough as most scandals of this nature do. Rick was a top reserve and an occasional starter on the BC basketball team. He played from 1976 to 1979, and although he was not a high scorer, he earned a lot of playing time because of his outstanding rebounding ability. In 1979, he became friendly with Tony Perla. Rocca, Tony Perla's younger brother, had been a high school classmate and close friend of Kuhn. Rick thought that the older brother was also becoming his friend when Tony began to help Rick financially. Tony Perla "lent" him the money to repair his car, and bought him a color television set.

Perla was actually trying to win Rick's friendship and confidence so that he could be persuaded to help fix Boston College basketball games. Sound familiar? It should, because this is very much how Clyde Eads was "cultivated" for his role in the Tulane scandal. Beware of someone you don't know well offering to give you something for nothing. Or, as former Marquette basketball coach Al McGuire warns, "for every pat on the back, there's a kick in the butt."

Perla arranged for Kuhn to meet Henry Hill, a convicted gambler with a long association with organized crime. During the meeting, Kuhn agreed to take part in point-shaving BC games. In return, Kuhn would receive $2,500 per game, and Hill would place bets on the games for him.

During the next few months, Kuhn took part in the point-shaving of at least six BC games. Henry Hill claims to have won between $75,000 and $100,000 by betting on these games. According to Hill, Kuhn probably made about $10,000 between illegal payoffs and bets.

The scheme began to fall apart when Hill became a government informer and sought immunity from his own conviction by telling the authorities of Kuhn's involvement in the point-shaving scandal.

For Ernie Cobb, things began to unravel the minute he became even slightly involved with the scandal. Cobb was found totally innocent of the charges that said he was part of the point-shaving schemes. But his case is an example of how your reputation can be badly damaged by being remotely connected to a scandal of this kind.

Cobb was the co-captain of the 1978–79 Boston College team, and he was without question its most talented player. As a junior, he averaged 21.9 points per game and received some All-American recognition. As a senior, he continued to average over 20 points per game. Almost everyone thought that he probably had a future as a professional basketball player in the NBA.

Cobb was approached by Perla before the Stonehill game and was asked how he thought BC would do. Cobb offered his opinion that it would be "no contest."

Cobb discussed the incident on ABC's *Sportsbeat.* "We did blow them away, and after the game he handed me $1,000 dollars. At the time I didn't think anything of it, but I sure would now. People don't give you anything for nothing. I didn't realize there was a string of people . . . criminals involved.

"I really believe I would be playing in the NBA today if this didn't happen," said Cobb. "I even had difficulty getting a tryout in the Continental Basketball Association. They were afraid my name was going to tarnish their league. The most important thing you have to offer is your reputation; once you put that on the line you're in trouble."

Gary Williams, basketball coach at Ohio State University, spoke out strongly about the danger of gambling involvement for young athletes. "You hope that high school athletes who might be good enough to play in college realize the harm of gambling involvement . . . not to their playing ability . . . but to their lives," said Williams. "When you get involved in point-shaving or illegal gambling and that becomes public knowledge, you carry that stigma with you for the rest of your life. If you apply for a job it will count heavily against you, even if it's something you did 10 or 20 years ago. I'm sure that the young men who were involved in scandals of this nature would give back any money that they got ten times if it would clear their names.

"If someone wants to give you something for nothing, they usually will want something from you down the road," added Williams. "A gambler's way of getting close to you is by doing you 'favors' or giving you some money. If you accept these gifts, it becomes easy for the gambler to ask for something in return. A couple of thousand dollars or a new stereo might seem like a lot when you are in high school or college, but it's not worth wrecking your life over.

"They even convince young athletes that there is nothing wrong with point-shaving. 'After all,' they will claim, 'I'm not asking you to lose, just make it close.'

"You have to know who the people you can trust are," said Williams. "Your parents, your coach, your guidance counselor . . . these are people that you know are looking out for your best interests. A guy you meet on the street or who approaches you after a game wanting to 'hang-out' with you might not be someone you should become involved with."

Courtesy of Ohio State University

"

You hope that high school athletes who might be good enough to play in college realize the harm of gambling involvement . . . not just to their playing ability . . . but to their lives. When you get involved in point-shaving or illegal gambling and that becomes public knowledge, you carry that stigma with you for the rest of your life.

Gary Williams
Ohio State University basketball coach

"

Coaches such as Williams have started awareness programs at their schools. These coaches have invited agents from the Federal Bureau of Investigation (FBI) to help educate their players on the dangers of gambling involvement.

So far we have talked about how athletes involved with gambling by intentionally playing below their ability to affect the final score of a game. You have seen how gamblers try to gain the confidence of an athlete and then use him for favors at a later time.

One of the so-called favors that gamblers often do for their athlete friends is to allow them to bet large sums of money on athletic contests—even if the athletes are losing and building a big debt. These gamblers know that athletes earn a lot of money, and that they usually have friends who will happily provide them with loans in order to be "in" with a big-time jock. In general, gamblers are more than willing to become involved with anyone who wants to bet—the higher the roller, the better.

Sports Illustrated told the story of how an addiction to gambling almost ruined the life of one of America's brightest young sports stars. As a senior in high school, Art Schlichter had it all ahead of him. Because he was quite possibly the country's top prep quarterback prospect, Schlichter was hotly pursued by college football powers from coast to coast. The question was not whether he would be an All-American college player, it was only how soon. Certainly he would someday be a top pro. Football fans, friends, scouts, college recruiters—it seemed that everyone wanted a piece of Art Schlichter.

As a way of escaping the pressures of his fame, he got into the habit of visiting a harness horse racetrack close to his rural Ohio home. While still in high school, he started betting on races. Because he normally didn't wager very much money, the activity seemed quite harmless. Schlichter enjoyed his days at the track. This pastime gave him some time away from the world of football and helped him relax.

In his sophomore year at Ohio State, he began living up to the potential he had shown in high school. He lead the Buckeyes to an 11–1 season. (The lone defeat was a heartbreaking 17–16 loss to the University of Southern California in the Rose Bowl.) Schlichter performed brilliantly all season long. People were calling him a Heisman Trophy candidate and a young man who could bring the national championship to Ohio State.

During his junior and senior seasons, however, Schlichter met with more frustration than success on the football field. The team never quite lived up to the great expectations. Because of a variety of injuries and personal problems, Schlichter felt very frustrated—both athletically and generally. People had extremely high hopes for Art Schlichter, and the pressure began to mount when some of these expectations were not fully met.

One of the ways that Schlichter found to relieve this pressure was to step up his gambling. He continued to visit the racetrack, but now the two-dollar bets, which had seemed so harmless, turned into twenty-dollar bets, which were anything but harmless. He also began to wager heavily on college basketball games. It all seemed so easy. He only had to pick up the phone to place a bet.

He found himself $2,000 in debt. You might think a debt that big would scare a person away from gambling forever. Unfortunately, it doesn't always work that way—and it certainly didn't for Schlichter. He borrowed money to pay off this debt, but the gambling bug had taken a very solid hold of him. He began to bet more aggressively than ever, and found himself $12,000 in the hole by the end of his senior year.

In 1982, Schlichter was drafted on the first round by the Baltimore Colts, which at the time was floundering and had no experienced quarterback. He was praised as the player who would follow in the footsteps of past Baltimore great field generals such as Johnny Unitas and Bert Jones. Surely the Colts would soon be a contender, with the rifle-armed Schlichter running the offense! Little did these loyal Baltimore fans realize that Schlichter was facing an opponent much more dangerous and certainly tougher to beat than the top teams in the NFL. He was quickly becoming addicted to gambling. It would take a great deal more than outstanding athletic ability to win this battle.

When Schlichter reported to training camp, he was out of shape physically and very confused mentally. Not only did he fail to win the starting quarterback job, but when the Colts broke camp, he found himself a third stringer. For the first time in his life he was not the star, and this was a tough pill to swallow. To deal with this disappointment, he again turned to his old friend, gambling. After all, he had plenty of money after just signing a contract that totaled over $500,000.

He began to bet thousands of dollars on college football, college basketball, and on the horses. The gambling sickness was dominating his life.

" ————————————————————

> It grabs you. You lose some money, then you start chasing. And you keep going and going and going. Your own mind is lying to you, telling you that your next bet is going to be better, that it's going to be the big winner. But it's not. It never is."

Art Schlichter
pro football quarterback
in *Sports Illustrated*

———————————————————— **"**

As Schlichter's gambling sickness got worse, he began to borrow money from anyone who would help him. His debts continued to grow, and he lost more control of his addiction with each passing day. Finally a friend helped Schlichter begin to turn away from gambling. He forced Schlichter to see that he had a serious gambling problem, and urged him to get help rather than "one more loan."

After suffering through a season-long suspension from the NFL because of gambling, Schlichter rejoined the Colts—only to be placed on waivers. To combat his addiction, he attended a therapy program, and now Schlichter believes that his problems with gambling are a thing of the past. Today he is looking forward to another opportunity to prove himself as a professional quarterback.

As you can see, involvement with gambling in any way, shape, or form is likely to lead you into trouble. Don't even touch betting in small, seemingly innocent ways. Most law enforcement officials who are trying to fight illegal gambling and point-shaving reluctantly admit that there will probably always be another "Tulane," and more lives will be ruined down the road. Make sure yours is not one of them!

"

Be yourself and have your own mind. Don't be pressured into doing things that you don't want to do.

Mary Lou Retton
Olympic gold-medal gymnast

"

Courtesy of Temple University Office of Sports Information

"

You know, it's very difficult for an eighteen-year-old to look ahead
and imagine what his life will be four or five years down the road.
Sometimes it's really easy to say yes to something that is being
offered to you right now, without bothering to consider the long-
range consequences. The main thing to remember is that if you
keep clean . . . you keep your integrity.

Bruce Arians
Temple University football coach

"

5 Recruiting

Unless you are one of the most exceptional high school athletes, one sad fact is that you will never be recruited. Ninety-eight percent of the people you are playing with and against will not receive a college athletic scholarship.

If you aren't approached by college coaches, don't let it get you down. If you have been more than just a player, if you have paid attention to the books, then you will be ready for life after sports. You will have already won the big game: *congratulations!*

If you haven't been pursued by college coaches and if you took a major in athletic eligibility, then you will need help to get the education you missed the first time around. There *is* help. Be sure to find it.

Nobody Wants Me

If you aren't recruited, but you still think you're good enough to play, you do have other choices.

Most college coaches begin to contact the student–athletes that they are interested in sometime in the athletes' junior year. If you aren't contacted, you shouldn't automatically assume that you're not a good enough athlete to compete at *some* level in college.

First, even though recruiting networks in all sports are very far-reaching, every year sports fans read about the "walk-on" that nobody ever heard of in high school who becomes a starting college player.

You should also keep in mind that while evaluating ability in sports like track and swimming is fairly clear-cut because of the times turned in by participants, evaluation in other sports can vary greatly—depending on the evaluator. For instance, a basketball coach at school A may be looking for players who are great ball handlers and favors an excellent controlled style. The coach at school B may place a high priority on natural athletic talent, and think speed and jumping ability are the keys to a successful team. Depending on your particular strengths, one of these coaches might see you as a fine prospect, while the other would not even bother to contact you because you don't fit in to *his* style.

If you have not been contacted by the end of your junior year, make an appointment to see your high school coach. He should be able to tell you if you can play at the Division I, II, or III level. Don't be afraid to also ask the opinions of club or summer league coaches.

If your college prospects are on the borderline, you must decide whether you want to be a big fish in a small pond, or a small fish in a big pond. Suppose your high school coach tells you to try a Division II or III school where he feels strongly that you could be a starter as a freshman. He thinks you might have a chance to play at the Division I level, but in all probability would end up struggling for a spot on the bench. The ball is now in your court. Only you can decide whether you would rather have the opportunity to play regularly at one level, or take a long shot at trying to make the grade against the top players. You should remember that Division II and III athletics are very competitive. You certainly don't have to play in Division I to have an enjoyable and worthwhile college sports experience.

Your next step is to contact the coaches at the schools you are interested in attending. You may feel that it's silly to contact a coach, because "if he wanted me, he would be recruiting me." Or you may feel that you are bothering the coach, or wasting his time. But it doesn't always work that way. Experienced coaches in all sports are more than willing to receive letters from high school athletes who are interested in their school. Most coaches will try to find out as much as they can about your athletic potential. They realize that they are not aware of *all* the good prospects at the high school level.

For an example of a "letter of interest" and a resumé that you can send to coaches at schools you might want to attend, look in the Help Section at the end of this book.

After reviewing all the information you send him and seeing a tape of you in competition, if the coach is interested in recruiting you, he will do everything he can to find out more about you.

The Coach Wants You

If you are approached, you have made it into the ranks of the finest two percent of America's athletes, who will earn a college scholarship and be recruited. *Congratulations!*

However, *be prepared* to deal intelligently with the recruiting process. Being a recruited athlete can be an enjoyable and worthwhile learning experience—if you handle it properly. You can make the recruiting system work for you, and end up at a school that is best for your academic, athletic, and social needs.

Being treated as such a special person by coaches is a real boost to your ego. However, if you let your ego become too inflated by people who may not be looking out for your best interests, you stand an excellent chance of being exploited by the system.

The following cases show what happened to two recent student–athletes. The first is an athlete who had an intelligent game plan for his sports career. The second athlete was under extraordinary family financial pressure. His game plan became confused and finally hit a dead end.

The High Road: How to Make Recruiting Reward Your Mind, Not Your Ego

``

He is a great player and a great kid. That's what makes him so attractive. There are a lot of great players, but he's also a fine individual who sincerely wants a degree

Bill Frieder
University of Michigan basketball coach

He has the potential to be the finest point guard in the country.

Mike Jarvis
Boston University basketball coach

"

The subject of this glowing praise is Rumeal Robinson, a senior at Rindge and Latin High School in Cambridge, Massachusetts. In 1985–86, he was one of the most highly sought-after basketball recruits in the entire nation. As often happens with potential superstars, he began hearing from college coaches as early as his sophomore year in high school. Once the flood started, he was overwhelmed with as many as forty letters a week.

"I couldn't possibly imagine what it would be like," said Robinson. "It's fun to a point, but after a while you can really get tired of it."

Robinson is the first to admit that the entire experience could have been a real nightmare if it hadn't been for "the committee." The committee was put together by Rumeal's high school coach, Al Coccoluto. It consisted of Robinson, Coccoluto, Rumeal's mother Helen Ford, his stepfather Lewis Ford, his guidance counselor Gordon Axtman, and a family friend Paul Chase. This group first met at the end of Rumeal's junior year. They discussed strategies for the best ways to deal with the recruiting process and keep it under control.

This was not the first time that Coccoluto was exposed to the whirlwind of big-time recruiting. He had been an assistant to Mike Jarvis, the former Rindge and Latin coach who is now head coach at Boston University. In that role, Coccoluto had first-hand involvement in the recruitment of Patrick Ewing, who graduated from Rindge and Latin in 1981.

"Mike knew that Patrick would be the top recruit in the country, and felt strongly that unless he set up some guidelines for recruiters, that the whole situation could get way out of hand," said Coccoluto. "Almost all of what we're trying to do with Rumeal comes from Mike's ideas that were put into use on Patrick's behalf.

"Our initial goal was to sift through the hundreds of letters that Rumeal received, and eliminate schools that Rumeal was not interested in, or did not meet his specific needs and/or goals. We first considered the overall academic programs of each school, and then took a look at the basketball programs."

When the committee finally finished its first review, seventeen universities were identified for Rumeal to further investigate and consider attending.

Coccoluto added, "there is no way that Rumeal could have thoroughly researched or visited each school, so our next step was to try to narrow the list of schools down to a maximum of five—which is the limit of expense-paid visits a recruit is permitted according to NCAA rules.

"We sent out letters to the coaches at all 17 schools and stressed that all written and telephone communication would have to go through me. I would be responsible for any messages and/or written correspondence to Rumeal.

"I really felt that it was important for Rumeal to be able to enjoy his senior year—as well as be able to concentrate on his schoolwork and college boards preparation. It really worked out well, mainly because a college coach does not want to risk the possibility of losing a blue-chip prospect like Rumeal, so they follow the guidelines. It also tends to eliminate the silly types of competition, like which coach will call the most or write the most letters."

The committee also constructed a questionnaire and mailed a copy to the coach at each school. It included questions about academic programs, tutorial services, graduation rates of basketball players, and so on. This unique approach was much more comprehensive than the information-collecting methods used by most other star high school players in the country. Rumeal noted that "we wanted to learn as much as we possibly could about each school without actually visiting. I think the questionnaire was a really great idea."

After receiving replies from most of the seventeen schools, the committee met again in September to narrow down the list to five or six schools. Although each member of the committee had a great deal of input, the final decision was in Rumeal's hands.

Coach Coccoluto explained the role of the committee. "Our job was to guide Rumeal, not to make decisions for him."

"It was really tough to narrow the choices down to five," said Robinson. "Every school had a lot to offer. Luckily, I had some great guidance from Mr. Coccoluto, Mr. Axtman, and my parents."

The five schools that Rumeal chose to consider were Boston University, Boston College, Michigan, Syracuse, and Villanova.

In early September, the coach from each of the five schools was invited to meet Rumeal and the entire committee to make a presentation and to answer questions about his school. These meetings took place at the high school, and were held before Rumeal made any campus visits.

As he met face to face with each coach, Rumeal realized that a difficult decision was ahead. "I was really impressed with each coach, and was very flattered that they were so interested in me," said Robinson. "Coach [Rollie] Massimino talked about the family atmosphere at Villanova. Coach [Gary] Williams talked about the advantages of playing in Boston and near home. Coach [Bill] Frieder seemed to really care about his players at Michigan. Coach [Mike] Jarvis stressed academics and what Boston University could do for me in the classroom. Coach [Jim] Boeheim was really sincere, and gave me a lot of information about Syracuse. All five coaches seemed really great, and for the first time I realized how tough it was going to be to have to say no to four of them."

In early October, Rumeal began to make his visits to the five schools. Each stay was scheduled to begin on a Friday and end on a Sunday. On a typical weekend, Rumeal sat in on classes and met with academic guidance personnel on Friday. Saturday afternoon usually included taking in a football game, and on Saturday night he might attend a movie or concert and then go to some sort of social gathering. On Sunday Rumeal would meet the head coach for a final talk, which usually centered around why his school would be the best choice.

Robinson reflected that "I enjoyed all the visits, but I was glad when they were over. It was nice to get back into my normal routine—especially to be able to play basketball on the weekend. I couldn't play during my visits. It didn't hurt to have the tremendous pressure begin to lift. No matter how great the coaches were, the pressure was tremendous."

When the visits were over, Rumeal met with Coach Coccoluto to begin the difficult process of narrowing his choices down to one school. Everyone seemed to have an opinion. Rumeal recalled, "it was funny how many people were talking to me and telling me where to go. I didn't realize so many people were so interested in me. A lot of people were trying to push one school or another, but Coach Coccoluto encouraged me to take my time and make my own decision."

Coach Coccoluto emphasized that "it was important that Rumeal had some time to think things out for himself, so I set up a guideline that there would be no contact from the college coaches after Rumeal's final school visit. At that point in time he wasn't going to learn anything new about the schools, and if he had any questions he could contact the coach on his own."

A clearer picture of exactly the type of school he was looking for began to form as Rumeal moved toward a final decision. "Sure, playing pro basketball is a dream of mine, but for right now it's in the back of my head." Robinson added, "my education comes first. If I get hurt or don't have enough ability to become a pro, I want to be sure that I have a quality education to fall back on. No one can take that away from me.

"I'd like to go to a school where I can really learn, and a place where I will be comfortable. As far as basketball is concerned, I'm looking for a team with a family atmosphere."

After many days of soul-searching, Rumeal came to a decision. He would attend the University of Mighigan. "I just felt very comfortable at Michigan," said Robinson. "The fact that it is one of the top academic schools in the country was what I based my decision on."

Courtesy of Les Kimbrough

"

Sure, playing pro basketball is a dream of mine, but for right now it's in the back of my head. My education comes first. If I get hurt or don't have enough ability to become a pro, I want to be sure that I have a quality education to fall back on. No one can take that away from me.

Rumeal Robinson
Rindge and Latin High School, Cambridge, Massachusetts

"

Coach Coccoluto was very happy about Rumeal's choice. "It was a great decision. I really think the idea of living in another part of the country was appealing to him, and he was obviously impressed with the people at Michigan."

"The really great thing about this whole process was that it would have been impossible for Rumeal to make a bad choice. The coaches and academic personnel at all five schools are such high quality people, that I'm sure Rumeal would have had a great experience regardless of his decision. I think this entire experience was a good one for Rumeal, and I give a lot of credit to each coach for being so honest and above board."

The Low Road: How to Allow Recruiting to Jeopardize Your Athletic Career

Sean Stopperich's recruiting story is quite different from Rumeal Robinson's. The *Dallas Morning News* told of Sean's experience, an excellent example of how a seemingly no-lose situation can turn into a nightmare.

Stopperich hails from Canonsburg, Pennsylvania, a small blue-collar town twenty miles south of Pittsburgh. From the start of Sean's high school football career, it was clear that he was a very special athlete. At six-foot four and 275 pounds, Sean had the physical strength that college football recruiters dream about. In 1984, he was selected to the Parade All-American football team and was named one of the top twenty-five football recruits in the nation by *USA Today*.

Unfortunately, while Sean's athletic career was on the rise, problems began in the Stopperich household. Sean's father Carl, a steel worker, lost his job during Sean's junior year in high school. Without his income, the family went into a financial tailspin.

Throughout the fall, recruiters from all over the country made a point of stopping in this small steel town to try to convince Sean that their school would be best for him. Sean had no committee and no well-thought-out plan for approaching his decision.

In late January, 1984, Sean decided he would attend the University of Pittsburgh. He had chosen Pitt over Southern Methodist University in Dallas, Texas, because he wanted to play football close to home. It was icing on the cake that Sean's idol, Bill Fralic, had played there. Fralic was then an offensive lineman for the Atlanta Falcons.

Sean's parents and friends were thrilled with his decision, as were many of his hometown's residents. The day after he made his choice public, the morning newspaper's headline proudly proclaimed "Stopperich Staying Home." Everyone seemed happy, most of all Sean Stopperich, who had an extremely bright future ahead. The only thing left was to enjoy the rest of his senior year before heading off to college. And then, of course, in four years it would be off to the National Football League.

Everything changed on February fifth, and the dream began to turn into a nightmare.

According to the NCAA, that was the day that a "representative of Southern Methodist's athletics interest" (a booster) visited Sean and other members of his family at a hotel near his home. The booster "gave at least $5,000 in cash to the family" and promised "assistance in finding employment for Mr. Stopperich in Dallas, Texas." The NCAA also found that the family was promised a rent-free apartment near the job and cash payment of $300 a month for Sean as long as he was enrolled at SMU.

Four days later Sean signed a national letter-of-intent with Southern Methodist. He later admitted that his parents' financial difficulties were the big reason why the illegal inducements from SMU were so tempting.

Tom Hisiro, Sean's high school coach, was shocked by the sudden switch. "After the football season [Sean's senior year] I accepted an administrative position in another school district," explained Hisiro. "However, all the college recruiters continued to go through me as if I were still in Canonsburg. The only school that didn't was SMU. I can't tell you the name of one coach at SMU that recruited Sean. As his high school coach, I find that hard to understand."

The Stopperich family moved to a small town just outside of Dallas in the summer of 1984. Sean's father had a job restoring damaged buildings, and the entire family took a liking to the Dallas area. The entire family except Sean.

"I was just never happy at SMU. I'm not sure why, but I was just never happy," said Stopperich.

Sean decided to withdraw from school in September of his freshman year, and he and his family moved back to the Pittsburgh area.

After being wined and dined by coaches from major college football programs throughout the country, Sean found himself with no school and no scholarship. He enrolled at Pitt for the second semester of the 1984–85 school year, but he couldn't get a football scholarship because of a knee injury that had begun to hamper his mobility. He decided to leave Pitt.

The dream that turned into a horror story for Sean Stopperich may yet have a happy ending. Bruce Arians, the Temple University football coach, has decided to give Sean a second chance.

Arians was contacted by coach Hisiro, who mentioned that Sean was interested in transferring to Temple. "I met with Sean and he seemed like a really nice kid," explained Arians. "He wanted a chance to start all over . . . and I am a big believer in giving people—especially young people—a second chance. When Sean decided to transfer to Temple, I told him not to look back . . . he started out with a clean slate in my book.

"You know, it's very difficult for an 18-year old to look ahead and imagine what his life will be four or five years down the road," warned Arians. "Sometimes it's really easy to say yes to something that is being offered to you right now, without bothering to consider the long range consequences. The main thing to remember is that if you keep clean . . . you keep your integrity."

Will You Choose the High Road?

Rumeal decided that what was most important for him—what would please him most—was to prepare not only for sports but also for life after sports. The opportunity for a great education plus a quality sports program became the basis for his selection of Michigan.

Confused by his sense of responsibility to his family, Sean was understandably attracted by the illegal inducements. Like many athletes, Sean succumbed to the temptation. With the NCAA ad-

Courtesy of Indiana University Office of Sports Information

"

Do you want to sell yourself like a piece of meat, or do you want to go to a college for legitimate reasons? You have a great opportunity here . . . do you want to blow it by selling yourself to the highest bidder? Only you can make that decision.

Bobby Knight
Indiana University basketball coach

"

mitting that a good college athlete in basketball or football can average $20,000 per year, and with stories of $100,000 pay-offs, it isn't surprising that the Sean Stopperichs of the world can get crushed in the recruiting process. Now in his third school, Sean has hopefully made the choice that will lead to a brighter future in and out of football.

Listen to the Coaches

As a high school athlete trying to choose which school to attend, the impressions that college coaches leave you with may have a great bearing on your final decision. Both the recruit and the recruiter have certain moral responsibilities that should be obeyed.

College coaches are under tremendous pressure to produce successful teams. Think about this as coaches approach you: of the 110 Division I basketball programs, 49 had at least three head coaches between 1970 and 1980! Coaches are often fired because they don't win enough to please university administrators and athletic boosters. Also, coaches resign because the pressure to win becomes too great. Obviously, to win consistently, a coach must attract talented and committed student–athletes to his school year after year.

Regardless of the pressures facing today's college coach, he is 100 percent wrong if he in any way attempts to involve a recruit in any violation of NCAA recruiting rules. It is important for you to understand that if he gets caught, both the coach *and the player* will be heavily penalized by the NCAA.

"It's a cop-out when coaches, alumns, and others say that they don't understand the NCAA rules," said University of Michigan basketball coach Bill Frieder. "I'm the first to admit that there are many rules that are confusing and need interpretation. There are also rules you could make an honest mistake on that are very incidental. However, everyone associated with the game knows that giving players cash payments, arranging for cars, stereos, wardrobes, and transportation is wrong."

Many coaches who have short contracts and little job security feel forced to show quick results, using any means available.

Penn State's Joe Paterno explained how the problem spreads. He pointed out that "sometimes a coach who has always been clean, sees another coach cheating and winning and becomes frustrated. The temptation to do whatever it takes to win can be very powerful, particularly for young coaches trying to make a name for themselves."

Most college coaches are careful to meet the NCAA recruiting standards. However, you are risking your future—both as a player and as a person—if you get involved with one of the few coaches who knowingly breaks the recruiting rules for their own advantage. You have to watch out for these individuals, and avoid involvement with them. If you are approached by a recruiter and offered an inducement that you are afraid might be illegal, immediately seek out assistance from your parents, your high school coach, and your guidance counselor.

Indiana's Bobby Knight was very forceful when asked how he might convince a high school recruit not to accept an illegal offer from a recruiter. "I would ask him: 'Do you want to sell yourself like a piece of meat, or do you want to go to a college for legitimate reasons? You have a great opportunity here . . . do you want to blow it by selling yourself to the highest bidder? Only you can make that decision.'"

As a recruit, it is also important that you understand the difficulty of the coach's job, and act accordingly.

"Recruited athletes can really be spoiled by the attention they receive," said Ohio State's Gary Williams. "I certainly realize that the recruiting process can become a little tiresome at times, but it's a once in a lifetime thing. I really believe it can be a positive experience if handled the right way.

"I think I speak for most of my colleagues when I say that a kid who acts like he's doing you a favor by talking to you is a real turn-off. Even though as a recruit you may be holding most of the cards, it is still important to treat people with respect. Be courteous, be on time, things like that mean a lot to a coach."

"I'm not interested in recruiting someone that I'll have to baby-sit," said Boston University's Mike Jarvis. "I'm a coach and a teacher, not a babysitter. I try to treat all my players with respect, and I expect the same in return."

Courtesy of Boston University Office of Sports Information

"

I'm not interested in recruiting someone that I'll have to babysit. I'm a coach and a teacher, not a babysitter. I try to treat all my players with respect, and I expect the same in return. I'm looking for young men who want an education.

Mike Jarvis
Boston University basketball coach

"

Beware the Booster—He Can Do You No Good

If you are talented and fortunate enough to be a recruited athlete, you will probably come into contact with people who have a strong emotional and sometimes financial attachment to the athletic fortunes of a particular school. They are known as athletic "boosters," and they can cause you a great deal of trouble.

College athletic boosters usually fall into one of two distinctly different categories.

Let's call one John Upright. John takes enormous pride in seeing his old college or the local university do well in all programs—from athletics to zoology. He donates money to university sports teams. John feels that athletics is an important part of the educational process and that it does a lot to create a good school spirit. When State U wins a big game he is happy. When State U loses a big game he says, "we'll get 'em next time." John wouldn't pretend to know what it takes to prepare a team, any more than he would want a coach telling him how to run his own business. Sports is a pleasant pastime for him.

The other type of booster is Bob Uptight. Bob also takes a great deal of pride in seeing his old college or the local university do well in all programs. But Bob's buddies at the office don't want to hear about the school's academic achievements. Therefore, Bob puts most of his energy into the athletic teams. He donates money to the football or basketball team so he can get prime seating locations, and so he will be invited to the select booster club parties. If he donates enough money, he feels that he should be able to get the coach's ear whenever he calls. When State U wins a big game Bob is overjoyed and he is sure to tell anyone who will listen that he played a big part in the victory. When State U loses a big game, he calls for the coach's job. Bob is a frustrated ex-jock, who knows very little about coaching—but thinks he could be the second coming of Don Shula. He will make sure to meet all the top recruits during their campus visits to State U, and he will make it clear that he is not above taking part in a financial deal to ensure that a top player will attend "his school." Stay away from the Bobs of the world.

Unfortunately, over the past ten years, more and more "university representatives" like Bob have arrived on the college athletic scene.

Since 1980, the NCAA has handed out seventy penalties for illegal recruiting practices, and forty-five of these have involved boosters. It's now fairly common to pick up the sports page and read about athletes being given large sums of money, automobiles, free airplane tickets, and so on.

It is not unusual for a top college athlete to shake the hand of a booster after a big win, only to find a few hundred-dollar bills left in his palm. The NCAA has begun to severely penalize college athletic programs that allow boosters to tempt recruits and reward enrolled athletes with illegal "gifts." As a recruited athlete, you too can pay the price—even for unknowingly breaking the rules.

If you come into contact with an athletic booster and accept any illegal inducements to attend the school he represents, you will seriously threaten your own future. You don't need to get involved with athletic boosters during the recruiting process. It is illegal for a school's representative to offer you a gift or even a small amount of money. You may be throwing out your opportunity to compete at the college level if you accept such an inducement.

By following the guidelines in the chapter on "The Educated Consumer," you should be well on the way up the high road. The coach will respect you more if you choose this path. If he doesn't, then you probably don't want to be playing for him.

The relationships between a recruited athlete and college coaches can be warm, rewarding, and special. Your only responsibilities are to be honest and sincere, and to try to choose the best school for your needs. You can create a no-lose situation for yourself. And, you can go a long way towards making sure you have a terrific college experience and a successful future.

Courtesy of Malek Abdul Mansour

"

I hope that young people realize that developing athletic skills is only doing one-half of the job. Just remember, a mind is a terrible thing to waste.

Kareem Abdul-Jabbar
Los Angeles Lakers

"

6 Rules of the Game

As a young athlete in today's complicated sports world, various rules and regulations can have a major effect on your athletic experience. It's very important for you to become familiar with these rules. If you have a thorough knowledge of the local, regional, and national regulations that govern our various sports programs, you will be able to use these regulations to protect your own best interests. Without a working knowledge of these rules, your athletic and educational options can be greatly limited.

High School Academic Standards

Bryan Smith from Burbank, California, painfully learned about the importance of knowing the rules on high school athletic eligibility. Smith's story was reported in the *Sacramento Bee*. Smith, a six-foot three point guard, was judged a sure bet to earn a college basketball scholarship.

But in his junior year at Burbank, Smith flunked a chemistry course. As a result, his grade-point average slipped below the 2.0 (C) level. Many school districts around the country are adopting the 2.0 minimum grade-point average for students to be eligible for extra-curricular activities—including all athletics. Burbank had this rule, so Smith found himself ineligible to play for the rest of the season. "I took things for granted," said Smith. "Once basketball season comes, there are a lot of distractions . . . girls, leisure time. My schoolwork wasn't a top priority."

Now in his senior year, Smith learned his lesson and improved his grades so he was able to showcase his basketball talents to college coaches during his senior year. But he learned an even greater lesson.

"
_____

> In the long run this will help me. I had to mature a lot. I don't take everything for granted anymore. I had to start thinking about what I would do after high school if I don't get a scholarship, or what I would do if I don't graduate. There are a million good basketball players in this country. Basketball doesn't need me. But I do need an education.
>
> *Bryan Smith*
> Star high school basketball player ruled ineligible because of grades

_____ **"**

Many states throughout the country are bringing in tougher minimum academic standards. A student in Colorado must carry five full-time classes, and cannot be failing more than one, either at the time of participation and or during the previous grading period. In order to take part in inter-scholastic athletics at most California high schools, a student must maintain a 2.0 (C) grade-point average and must be making normal progress towards graduation. Each state's minimum academic standards for athletic participation are listed in the Help Section at the back of the book.

The "no pass—no play" rule in Texas has been the most highly publicized and the most controversial. The rule says students who flunk one class during a six-week grading period can't take part in clubs and sports in the next six-week period. Many people believe that this is the strictest high school eligibility rule.

Texas Governor Mark White has been an outspoken supporter of the rule. The governor told the *Dallas Morning News*, "with the implementation of the 'pass, play' rule, we are saying to our students. "First you work, then you play." This rule is not an effort to penalize students. It is an effort to offer an incentive to ensure that

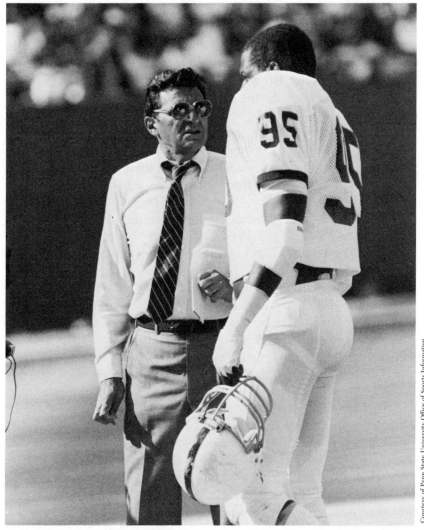

Courtesy of Penn State University Office of Sports Information

"

I am concerned with the subjects that are vital to a young person's future academic success. Minimum academic standards give a high school student a chance to be a legitimate student–athlete at some college or university.

Joe Paterno
Penn State University football coach

"

students make studying their Number One priority. . . . If an athlete isn't putting in 100 percent on the playing field and doing his best, what happens? He gets benched. And he stays on the bench until he shows the desire and discipline to work harder and improve."

College coaches such as Notre Dame's Digger Phelps and Penn State's Joe Paterno have come out in favor of minimum academic standards for high school students. When discussing the 2.0 minimum standard set up by the Los Angeles school system, Phelps noted, "over 5,000 students immediately became ineligible to participate in extra-curricular activities—including inter-scholastic athletics—and a lot of people were really upset. A year later more than half of those students improved their grades enough to be able to participate."

"I am concerned with the subjects that are vital to a young person's future academic success," said Paterno. "Minimum academic standards give a high school student–athlete a chance to be a legitimate student–athlete at some college or university."

The important issue here is not whether minimum academic standards for high school athletic participation are a good idea. The fact is that your school, school district, or state may have a minimum standard for eligibility that you haven't heard about. If so, you may be headed for trouble in the form of athletic ineligibility.

Speak to your coach, guidance counselor, or athletic director about whether or not your school has such a rule. Find out exactly what grades you have to earn to be able to represent your school on the athletic field. Bryan Smith can assure you that this is not a rule you want to learn about after it's too late.

Bryan and countless others who temporarily lost their eligibility will all tell you the same thing: some form of standards will be coming to your school, so *be prepared to stay eligible by studying now.*

NCAA Proposition #16 (formerly Proposition #48)

If you hope to play National Collegiate Athletic Association (NCAA) Division I athletics, then it's essential for you to be aware of NCAA

Proposition 16, which went into effect in August 1986. This rule states that all incoming freshman at Division I schools must fulfill the following high school requirements in order to be eligible to compete in intercollegiate competitions as freshmen:

- A 2.0 (C) grade-point average (GPA).
- A 700 combined score on the SAT examination or 15 on the ACT examination.
- Prospective athletes must pass a core curriculum of eleven high school courses. Students must complete three years of English, two years of math, two years of social science, and two years of natural or physical science. You will need a 2.0 (C) in these courses.

There will be a two-year transition period when incoming freshmen who fall slightly below one of the requirements will not be declared ineligible:

- In 1986–87, college freshmen with high school GPAs of 2.2 or higher in the core subjects can qualify with SAT scores as low as 660 or ACT scores of 13. Freshmen with GPAs of 1.8 will need to score 740 on the SAT or 17 on the ACT.
- In 1987–88, college freshmen with high school GPAs of 2.1 or higher in the core subjects can qualify with SAT scores as low as 680 or ACT scores of 14. Freshmen with GPAs of 1.9 will need to score 720 on the SAT or 16 on the ACT.

Some important points to remember about Proposition 16 are:

- This rule does not apply to Division II and III colleges.
- This rule establishes a minimum standard of eligibility only for college freshmen. A student can still be admitted to a Division I-A college or university without meeting the requirements of Proposition 16. A student can also receive financial aid on athletic grounds, without meeting the Proposition 16 requirements.
- The principal of your high school is responsible for deciding whether or not a course qualifies as a core course.

It is critical for you to understand that an athlete can be eligible to participate throughout high school, graduate from high school, and still not meet the requirements of Proposition 16.

Think about this: if Proposition 16 had been in effect in 1985–86, then more than half of the freshmen scholarship basketball and football players at many schools would have been ineligible.

The only way to make sure you don't become one of the Proposition 16 casualty statistics is to take your academic responsibilities seriously. If you want to play, you'll have to study.

If you hope to take part in intercollegiate athletics, you should check with your guidance counselor on a regular basis to make sure that you are meeting the minimum grade-point average and core curriculum requirements of Proposition 16. As soon as you can, you should also begin preparing for the SAT or ACT examinations. Check the Help Section at the back of the book for test preparation materials. And, again, consult your guidance counselor for his or her advice on getting ready for these tests.

College Recruiting: "Sign Our National Letter-of-Intent"

If you are being contacted by college coaches who want you to attend their schools, it is vitally important for you to get to know the NCAA recruiting rules. Forty of the major NCAA rules specifically refer to the recruiting of student–athletes. Failure to comply with one or more of these rules can seriously threaten your chances to compete at the college level or to earn an athletic scholarship.

As you begin to receive correspondence from coaches, you should sit down with your parents and/or your high school coach to carefully review these rules. Suggestions are contained in the chapter on "The Educated Consumer." If you are ever confused or unsure about an NCAA recruiting rule, immediately seek the advice of your coach, athletic director, or the administrator at your school who coordinates college athletic recruiting. The NCAA has staff members who will be more than happy to answer any questions you might have about these rules. Don't be afraid to call them—too much is at stake if you don't fully understand the rules. Their address and phone number are in the Help Section.

NCAA Rules on Recruiting

The entire set of NCAA rules on recruiting is listed in the Help Section at the back of the book. However, we have tried to go over them here in an easy-to-read fashion, with some examples of what can go wrong if you break the rules, or allow them to be broken on your behalf. Remember, it is *your* responsibility to know these rules.

What Can I Do?

It *is permissible* for a university to engage in the following activities if they are recruiting you as a prospective student–athlete:

Recruiting at your home or high school

1. You can be a guest of a genuine university alumni organization at luncheons, teas, or dinners. This applies to athletes and non-athletes in your own geographic area.

   Be aware: not all alumni or booster groups are legitimate. In fact, most athletes who got into trouble with the NCAA did so by accepting favors from boosters. Walter Byers, the executive director of the NCAA, flatly states that many good (not superstar) college athletes have received illegal offers of up to $20,000 a year from boosters. It's got to be tempting to take such money.

   But if you are tempted, consider the case of the 1985 Texas Christian University football team. In exchange for money, six TCU players traded the last years of their college eligibility, their future chances to make the pros, and most important, their dignity. They also set the TCU program back dramatically. In the long run, short-term payoffs will do you much more harm than good.

2. A representative of the university's athletic staff who wants to recruit you can make a total of three in-person contacts with you,

your relatives, or your legal guardian at any location off the college campus. However, they cannot spend any money to entertain any of you.

3. You can have three additional in-person, off-campus contacts at your high school, but only with the approval of an official of your school.

4. Regardless of the length or type of conversation that goes on, the following kinds of visits count toward the limits on in-person contacts:

   • Any meeting between you and an official that is prearranged;
   • or that takes place at your high school;
   • or that takes place at the site of an organized competition;
   • or that takes place at a practice you are involved in.

Depending on how good an athlete you are, these contacts can be very flattering—even ridiculously flattering. This constant attention can often leave you totally unprepared to adjust to the idea of just being one of the crowd when you get to college. All college freshmen face this problem—whether they are sports stars or not.

Chris Washburn, star center at North Carolina State University, has recently announced his intention to forego his final two years of college eligibility in order to play professional basketball. Washburn almost threw away his dream of an NBA career during his freshman year at State. As the top basketball recruit in the country in 1983–84, Washburn was coveted by college hoop coaches across the nation. Believe it or not, Washburn was contacted by North Carolina State more than *two hundred* times, either in person or by mail (primarily the latter).

Although these contacts were all quite legal under the guidelines set forth by the NCAA, this constant attention from State as well as countless other schools, may have hurt Chris Washburn more than helped him. When Chris arrived at N.C. State that fall he was *the* big man on campus. After all, he was going to take State to the Final Four for the next four years—or so many Wolfpack fans claimed. It didn't quite work out that way. During the fall of his freshman year, Chris was accused of stealing stereo equipment from another student's room. He had yet to learn that his superstar athletic status did not excuse him from the responsibilities, rules, and regulations that everyone must face. Because of this incident, Chris was not allowed to play during his freshman year, and could have seriously jeopardized his basketball career.

5. In-person, off-campus contacts can take place only during the following periods in the different sports:

Football:

- Between December 1 (or the date you complete your final high school contest) and March 1.
- No member of a Division I college's coaching staff can contact you during the annual convention of the American Football Coaches Association.

Men's basketball:

- Between September 1 and October 10, and between March 1 (or the date you complete your final high school game) and May 15.
- No contacts can be made by a member of a Division I or II coaching staff during the period beginning with the Thursday before the NCAA Division I Men's Basketball Championship game and ending at noon on the Tuesday after the game.

Women's basketball:

- The same dates as for men, but the exception applies during the period beginning with the Wednesday before the NCAA Division I Women's Basketball Championship game and ending at noon on the Monday after the game.

Women's gymnastics and volleyball:

- You can't be contacted by a member of a Division I college's coaching staff during a period beginning with the Wednesday before the Division I championships finals in each of those sports. For gymnastics, the period ends at noon on the Sunday after the championships. For volleyball, the period ends on noon the day after the championship game.

If you think these visitation restrictions sound trivial, consider the fate of six-foot-eleven Tito Horford. Tito was the nation's most heavily recruited high school basketball player in 1984–85. Like Chris Washburn, Horford was contacted by colleges from New York to

California. Eventually, he signed a letter-of-intent to attend the University of Houston, and was looking forward to helping the Cougars to an NCAA championship. But before Horford even had a chance to participate in one practice at Houston, it was revealed that a UH assistant coach had broken NCAA recruiting regulations. He had visited Tito during a period of time that coaches were not allowed to have in-person contact with high school recruits. Because of a rule that he probably wasn't even aware of, Horford was declared ineligible to participate in his freshman year. Stunned, Tito left Houston and began an ill-fated search for another place to play.

Taken with the Chris Washburn case mentioned in point 4, this meant that, for two years in a row, the nation's number one recruit did not play in his freshman year—directly or indirectly because of the recruiting process. You can make a strong argument that these two superb athletes got what they deserved, and it may be true. However, you can't help wondering if these stories wouldn't have been different if Washburn and Horford had been fortunate enough to get proper guidance during their whirlwind recruiting experiences. If the superstars can be exploited, obviously, less-talented players can also be prime victims.

6. An athletic supporter (for example, a booster) who represents a Division I or Division II college is not permitted to make in-person, off-campus recruiting contacts.

Visits to the university campus

7. You can receive one expense-paid visit to the campus. Some of the conditions are:
   - You can't make any expense-paid visits until after the beginning of classes in your senior year in high school.
   - Your expense-paid college visit can last no more than forty-eight hours.
   - Only actual round-trip transportation between your current home or high school and the campus may be paid.
   - If you fly, you must fly in economy class.
   - If you drive, or are driven by family or friends, the university can reimburse you for the actual and necessary transportation costs of traveling to the campus.

- The university can pay the actual reasonable cost of your room and board while you are traveling between your home and the campus on your one official expense-paid visit.
- If they accompany you on your one paid campus visit, your parents (or legal guardians) or spouse can be entertained and housed on the campus one time only. This must be done within a thirty mile radius of the campus. Such entertainment and housing should be on the level of normal student life.

8. You may not accept expense-paid visits to more than a total of five Division I and Division II member colleges.

9. The university can ask you to take a medical examination by the university's regular team physician when you visit the campus. This is done to determine whether you have any physical problems that might interfere with your ability to compete athletically.

In addition to the normal medical examination, more schools are including a urinalysis to test for drug use. A positive test will probably mean that you won't be offered an athletic scholarship. Think about it: smoking a joint four or five weeks before your visit could mean that you don't get a scholarship to the school of your choice. Marijuana stays in your system for that long. But read the stories of people like Tony Elliott and Micheal Ray Richardson in the chapter on drug and alcohol abuse, and then decide for yourself whether or not experimenting with drugs is worth the risk.

10. A staff member of the athletic department or an athletic representative can describe the university's grant-in-aid to you. Although that person can recommend you for such aid, you must understand that only the university financial aid officer can actually award the aid.

Get it in writing! Without a written statement from the financial aid office setting out the amount, the length of time, and the conditions and terms, a verbal promise of aid is unofficial and not binding on the university. If you suffer a bad injury during your senior year in high school after receiving a *verbal* scholarship offer, that offer is not binding. On the other hand, if you are offered a scholarship at a school that you definitely want to attend, you should sign the scholarship only after you have a written assurance that the financial grant will not be cut off if an injury leaves you unable to play.

11. You can receive another expense-paid visit (in addition to the one paid for by the athletic department) provided that the visit has nothing whatsoever to do with athletic recruitment. For example, a band trip, a senior day, or a fraternity or sorority weekend would be acceptable. However, be sure that the athletic department is not involved in any way in the arrangements for the visit.

Make sure such a visit is legitimate. If the university band leader invites you to visit the campus despite the fact that you have never picked up an instrument, say thanks anyway. If not, you could be playing with your eligibility.

12. You can visit the campus as many times as you like *at your own expense*. The only thing the university can provide on such visits is a maximum of three complimentary tickets to a campus sports event for you and anyone who may come with you on the visit. No meals can be provided unless you are visiting a Division II or III college, and then they must be served in on-campus student dining facilities. *Any* other expenditure besides this will cause the visit to be considered an expense-paid visit.

Understand what this means. Technically, if a Division I school buys you a sandwich—even if you paid for everything else—then this counts as an expense-paid visit. If you already had your expense-paid visit, then you could be ruled ineligible to play for the price of a ham on rye. Be careful. What you may view as a harmless "bending" of the rules, may be taken by the NCAA as a very clear violation.

After you sign the National Letter-of-Intent

13. Once you have signed a national letter-of-intent with a Division I or II college, there are no limits on the off-campus contacts that you, your relatives, or your legal guardian can have with representatives of that university.

What Can't I Do? Keep Your Eyes Wide Open

In June 1985, a group of college presidents known as the President's Commission tried to put a stop to the illegal activities and scandals that have been so harmful to intercollegiate athletics. The commission moved the NCAA to impose harsh penalties not only on universities that break NCAA rules, but also on high school athletes who accept illegal inducements from a school. Even though the following rules refer to what the university can or cannot do during the recruiting process, it is clearly in your best interests to thoroughly understand these guidelines. Don't risk unknowingly breaking the rules and losing your chance to participate in college.

It is *not permissible* for a university to engage in the following activities if they are recruiting you as a prospective student–athlete:

1. You can lose your eligibility unless the specific elements of your aid package are allowed by the NCAA, the university, and its athletic conference if it is a member of one. Any acceptance of an improper inducement could make you ineligible. Improper inducements include the following:

   • Cash, unless it's given in an approved category, such as in the place of campus room and board when there are no campus dorms.
   • The promise to employ you after college graduation.
   • Special discounts or payment arrangements on loans.
   • Employment of your relatives.
   • Providing loans to your relatives or friends.
   • Involvement in arranging professional and personal services, purchases, or charges.
   • Regular or occasional use of an automobile.
   • Transportation to or from a summer job or to any site other than the university's campus on an official visit.
   • Signing or co-signing a note for a loan.
   • The loan or gift of money or other objects (for example, clothes, cars, jewelry, electronic equipment).
   • Guarantees of bond in case of legal difficulties.
   • Purchasing items or sevices from you or your family at inflated prices.

Courtesy of Bob Woolf Associates, Inc.

"

I've worked hard and received many awards from playing basketball, both at Indiana State and with the Celtics. But to me my
most important award was receiving my diploma from Indiana
State. Working hard at my education and receiving my diploma
made me feel as if I had just scored 100 points in a game. Work
hard at your sport, but get your degree.

Larry Bird
Boston Celtics

"

- Transportation for you to enroll.
- Any financial aid other than that administered by the university's regular scholarship awards authority.
- Financial aid for a period beyond one year for a postgraduate education.

2. It is illegal for a university or its representative to offer, provide, or arrange financial assistance to pay all or part of the costs of your educational or other expenses for any period before your regular enrollment or after your regular enrollment if you apply for a postgraduate degree.

If you are offered any valuable item during the recruiting process, then be aware that the recruiter is acting illegally. If you decide to accept an illegal gift, then *you* are acting illegally.

3. It is a violation of NCAA policies for a university or its representative to:

- Pay any costs of an athletic talent scout for studying or recruiting you. Your coach and your parents should be the *only* ones involved in this.
- Pay back your high school coach for the costs of transporting you to visit the campus.
- Entertain your high school coach at any location except on the college campus, or in the community where the college is located. The university cannot pay for the coach's food and refreshments, room expenses, or the cost of transportation to and from the campus. Permissible entertainment for your coach is limited to two tickets to an athletic contest.

The NCAA rules even apply to people like your high school coach, who you feel are helping you find the right school. Although most high school coaches are certainly honorable people, if they make a mistake by not knowing a rule that applies to them, then you could pay the price for that mistake later. Be sure to go over all the NCAA recruiting rules with your high school coach before your senior year.

4. The university cannot provide you, your friends, or relatives with free admission to its away-from-home games.

Recruiting at your home or high school

5. It breaks NCAA rules for a university to make an in-person, off-campus recruiting contact with you, your relatives, or your legal guardian before you complete your junior year in high school. You must follow the previous guidelines for contacts.

That's simple enough—no visits before you are a senior. It's simple, yet it's a rule that's often broken by college coaches trying to get an early advantage in the recruiting game. Remember, a college coach who willingly breaks this rule is not stopping by your home because he is friendly or a nice guy. He is threatening your opportunity to play for four years in college. Don't let his desire to get the jump on the competition endanger your eligibility.

6. University boosters (Division I or II) cannot make in-person, off-campus recruiting contacts with you, your relatives, or your legal guardian.

Boosters have ruined the careers of too many athletes. Before 1985, not many illegal booster–athlete relationships were publicly exposed. However, reporters for newspapers and television are now letting the public know about these scandals, so it is much more likely that athletes who receive illegal favors from boosters will be caught and lose their eligibility. Undoubtedly, you will meet many well-meaning and loyal alumni at the school you choose to attend. You will have many opportunities to enjoy friendships with these people when you are in college. High school is not the time.

7. You cannot be contacted at your school without permission from an authorized representative of your high school.

8. You cannot be contacted at your school during an athletic competition. This means:
   - You can't be contacted if you are participating or preparing to participate in a contest or competition.
   - You can't be contacted on the day of the competition before the event and then not until you have completed the competition (including *all* games of a tournament).
   - You must be released by your school authority, dressed, and out of the dressing room before anyone can contact you.

9. If you are practicing for or competing in a high school all-star game of basketball or football, then a coach or staff member of a Division I or II school cannot contact you at the site of the contest unless it is within the contact periods set forth above.

Always let your high school's college recruiting coordinator and coach guide you on when you can and can't be contacted by university recruiters. The spring before your senior year, learn the dates and restrictions in the NCAA guidelines.

Sports camps

10. A coach at an NCAA school cannot participate in any coaching school or sports camp that includes student–athletes who are eligible for admission to a university or who have started classes for the senior year of high school.

11. As a high school athlete, you cannot receive free or reduced-cost admission to any sports camp operated by an NCAA college or by a member of its athletic staff. Also, you cannot take a job at such a camp.

Most college coaches have their own summer sports camps. They can be great places to strengthen your skills. Nonetheless, if you are financially "sponsored" to attend a camp, or if you are employed at one when you are not supposed to be, you can lose your eligibility. Because it is public knowledge that you are at a camp, it is easy for NCAA investigators to find out about it.

If you are one of the top players selected for an All-Star camp, then be especially alert. These camps are often called "meat markets" by college scouts because coaches flock there to get a look at the best talent. It is an easy way for them to see the top players in one place. Use your time at these camps to sharpen your skills by competing with other top players. Don't let overly aggressive recruiters ruin what can be an enjoyable and worthwhile experience. If you've earned the right to be at an All-Star camp then you'll probably get your fill of recruiting after the summer.

On-campus visits

12. Your visit to the campus cannot be publicized by the university that is trying to recruit you.

13. You cannot appear on a radio or television program conducted by a college coach, or one in which the college coach or a staff member is participating, or one in which your appearance was only arranged by the college coach or a staff member.

Don't rush publicity. If you are so good that the coach wants to put you on his show while you are still in high school, there will be plenty of radio and TV appearances in your future.

14. It is strictly forbidden for you to have money spent on you by any agency, group of individuals, or organization outside the university. This includes transportation, entertainment, and gifts or services for you, your relatives, and your friends. Among other things, this means that it is illegal for:

   • Two or more persons to contribute money to recruit a prospect.
   • Company funds to be used to pay the expenses (including providing a company airplane) of transporting you to visit a campus or of any other recruiting cost.

15. The university cannot pay for or arrange the payment of transportation costs for your relatives or friends to visit its campus or anywhere. It also cannot transport them to the campus or elsewhere in a representative's own vehicle.

In addition to your high school coach, your family and friends certainly have your best interest at heart. Understandably, they want to share in your achievements. Just as you should discuss the recruiting rules with your coach, you should also discuss them with your family and friends. It would be a good idea to do this when your high school coach is present, so that he can help explain the rules. Dishonest recruiters will not only pay illegal visiting expenses, they will sometimes also offer your family members jobs, money, and other inducements to make sure that you come to their school. Read the story of Sean Stopperich in the chapter on recruiting to see what can happen if you are not careful.

16. If a university brings you to its campus for a visit, all entertainment for you, your parents, or your spouse must take place within thirty miles of the main campus, and the entertainment must be at the level of normal student life. In Division I or II colleges, boosters may be involved in your entertainment, but only on the campus. Boosters are forbidden to entertain your friends at any site. During the visit, you cannot:
    • Receive cash or the use of an automobile.
    • Be excessively entertained.
17. The university is strictly forbidden to ask you to practice on campus or elsewhere so that they may observe your athletic ability.

No doubt you will want to display your skills during your campus visit. After all, you have gotten this far because you are a competitor. But don't be tempted. Don't innocently get involved in a practice session or a pick-up game with members of the university's team. You have nothing to gain, and a great deal to lose.

Signing your letter-of-intent

18. When you sign up for a university, it cannot hold a press conference, reception, or dinner to make the announcement. It can publicize your acceptance of its offer of financial assistance through its own normal media outlets and through your current and/or former school.
19. If you are a football player going to a Division I-A university, your future head coach cannot be present if you sign a letter-of-intent at an off-campus site.

As you review these guidelines with your parents, coach, or athletic director, keep in mind that it is your responsibility to understand all the NCAA recruiting rules, and to obey them. Many times "ignorance of the law" will not protect you from losing your eligibility and/or your athletic scholarship.

If you knowingly break one or more of the NCAA recruiting rules, you will find yourself in serious difficulty. Don't forget the warning we mentioned earlier: the NCAA has passed a rule that says student–athletes will be held fully responsible for breaking an NCAA recruiting rule that they were aware of.

College coaches throughout the country are strongly in favor of the NCAA regulations. Bob Knight, Indiana's basketball coach and the 1984 United States Olympic Basketball Coach, stated, "when a recruiting rule is broken it's easy to pin all the blame on a school, an alum, or a coach. But many times it's also the kid who's being recruited who is at fault. He knows what the rules are . . . or he should."

Digger Phelps feels that penalties for recruiting violations should be stronger. "Penalize the recruit. Before a high school player can be contacted, make the kid, his parents, and his high school coach sign an affidavit that they have reviewed the recruiting rules. Then if he breaks a rule he loses the rest of his eligibility."

Is it worth it to accept illegal payments from a college coach or an athletic booster? Kenneth Davis, the former All-American running back at Texas Christian University, says no. Davis is a "former" All-American because he lost his eligibility when it was discovered that he had accepted approximately $20,000 from TCU boosters in return for playing at the Texas school.

Davis told the *Fort Worth Star–Telegram,* "The biggest thing I would tell an 18-year-old is that the money they are offering you is not worth the rewards you are going to receive mentally and morally and the way people are going to respond to you."

``

The money was there . . . and I took it. That's the biggest reason I took it. Because it was there. But I was wrong. I was wrong to the extent that every dream in my life that I've had has been thrown away because I was offered money from an alumnus and I took it.

Kenneth Davis
former All-American running back at Texas Christian University who lost his eligibility when it was discovered he had accepted approximately $20,000 from TCU boosters

``

"I would tell someone that the greatest thing about going to a university is to get your degree, be your own man, and don't let someone entice you. Live to your own standards and what you believe in.

"I've thrown it all away. I threw it away when I was 18 years old and made the decision to take the money."

Know the recruiting rules, obey them, and you should have a great college experience. Ignore them, and you may be finished before you even begin. It is as easy—or as hard—as that.

Courtesy of Mazza Marketing and Public Relations

"

Stay in school and get your education. Then work towards other pursuits in life. Education will allow you to attain your goals. Sports can be very rewarding, but always strive to learn something new every day.

Evelyn Ashford
Olympic gold-medal sprinter

"

7 Women as Student–Athletes

On the afternoon of February 3, 1985, the University of Iowa's Carver Arena was packed to the rafters with an overflow crowd. More than 22,000 eager college basketball fans had made the trek to Iowa City to witness a key Big Ten showdown between the hometown Hawkeyes and the league leaders, the Ohio State Buckeyes. The Iowa basketball team has always received tremendous support from fans throughout the state, so the large turnout should have been no surprise. After all, hoop fans from coast to coast are used to sold-out arenas when the best college basketball teams meet head to head.

So what was so special about this particular crowd?

These 22,000-plus fans had not come to watch coach George Raveling's highly touted men's team—they were on hand for the Iowa–Ohio State women's game. This fact made the Sunday afternoon game very special indeed.

Iowa basketball coach Vivian Stringer has counted on a large crowd, but she did not expect the packed house of Hawkeye supporters that greeted her team that day.

"Obviously I was thrilled for our team to have the opportunity to play before such a large crowd," said Stringer. "It was a very big thrill for us, but more importantly, a great day for women's college basketball.

"The fact that the level of the women's game continues to make giant strides forward has gotten people excited about our program. The skeptics who felt people would never be interested in watching women's basketball are being proven wrong."

Statistics support Stringer's claim. Only five years ago, many of the top women's teams had trouble drawing over 100 fans a game. Since then, however, people have begun to sit up and notice the outstanding basketball being played by women throughout the nation. Now women's games often draw thousands of spectators. For example, in February 1986, more than 11,000 fans were on hand to see a key Atlantic Coast Conference match between Virginia and the University of North Carolina. Over 1,500 fans had to be turned away. The 1986 University of Texas women's basketball team played before an average of over 5,000 fans per game. And this trend is not limited to basketball. Attendance records are also being set in women's soccer, softball, and volleyball—games that were thought to be only for men in the past.

The main reason for these new levels of national interest in women's college athletics is the growth of female participation in high school and even earlier. Before 1972, when the Title IX law was passed, only 4,000 high schools in the whole country offered girl's basketball. Today there are 17,000! (Title IX is an important equal opportunity law, which we will discuss later in this chapter.) In 1972 there were 66,000 women participating in college athletics—today there are over 150,000! Between 1972 and 1985, women's participation in high school sports increased almost *500 percent.*

For too many years women could not enjoy and benefit from sports—largely because many administrators insisted that athletics were for men, and that women did not belong on the playing field. However, the efforts of countless women athletes, and their outstanding dedication and abilities, are rapidly erasing these old-fashioned ideas.

The days when competitive athletics were only for men are long gone. Women are being recognized as talented athletes and serious competitors in sports from basketball to soccer. You are very lucky to live in an age when there are plenty of opportunities for young women to compete in both inter-scholastic and intercollegiate athletics. This was not always the case.

Intercollegiate Athletics for Women Since 1970: Fifteen Years of Progress

As we mentioned before, college-level women's athletics have gone through many dramatic changes since the Title IX rule was passed in 1972. This rule is a portion of an educational amendment to the Constitution, and it prohibits sex discrimination in any educational program that receives money from the government. Because almost all high schools and colleges get some federal aid, they have to obey the Title IX rule. In sports, this means that women and men have to be given the same opportunities to play.

Title IX has led to a big increase in women's participation in college sport and to an explosion of public interest. Unfortunately, at the same time, women's athletics have started to suffer from some of the abuses that have plagued men's intercollegiate athletics.

Merilee Dean Baker, the women's athletic director at the University of Minnesota and a past-president of the Association of Intercollegiate Athletics for Women (AIAW), has witnessed the growth of women's college athletics firsthand.

"The passing of Title IX in 1972 brought college athletics for women to a whole new level. In order to be in compliance with Title IX, colleges and universities had no choice but to upgrade existing programs or create new women's teams."

Along with Title IX, 1972 was the year that the AIAW became the national governing body of women's intercollegiate athletics.

"One great thing about the AIAW was that it gave women athletic administrators an opportunity to write rules which would place the well-being of the student–athlete first," commented Baker. "We had a golden opportunity to study some of the problems that existed in men's intercollegiate athletics, and to create legislation that would help insure that women would avoid these pitfalls. Of course we were also able to draw from many of the things that the NCAA did well."

By 1975 women's sports programs were growing in leaps and bounds at schools from New York to California. Also, for the first time, colleges and universities were beginning to award athletic scholarships to women. This helped raise the quality of play in almost all college-level women's sports. In addition, the hope of ath-

Courtesy of the University of Southern California Sports Information Department

"

You have to realize it's no tea party out there. Just because we're women we don't work or struggle or compete or want to win any less than men.

Cheryl Miller
four-time All-American Basketball Player and 1984 Olympic Gold Medalist
in *Sports Illustrated*

"

letic scholarships encouraged girls to participate in sports in high school. Even though women had no professional opportunities in team sports, the chance of a free education through an athletic scholarship was a tempting goal. When parents discovered these opportunities, they began to support their daughters' interests in athletics.

"We [AIAW administrators] viewed the advent of women's athletic scholarships as a mixed blessing," recalled Baker. "While they led to equality and increased opportunities for women athletes, they also opened the door to illegal recruiting and over-emphasis. Once schools started to give athletic scholarships and raise women's program budgets, the pressures to win began to increase dramatically. The emphasis began to switch from healthy participation to win at all costs . . . which was what the AIAW was trying to avoid from its inception."

Examples of Baker's "mixed blessing" theory have shown up in women's intercollegiate athletics throughout the 1980s. In 1982 the NCAA took responsibility for running women's sports at the college level. When the NCAA set up women's championships, women's programs enjoyed increased funding and media attention. That is the good news. Some of the bad news was found at places like Northeast Louisiana University.

In 1985, NLU's women's basketball team made its first trip to the Final Four in the NCAA championships. The team was led by the outstanding play of freshman Chana Perry, who had averaged eighteen points and thirteen rebounds a game. While in high school Perry had been selected as the *USA Today* 1984 National High School Player of the Year. She was hotly pursued by the top basketball programs in the country before she chose NLU.

Early in the 1986 season, NLU was ranked ninth in the country. The team was looking forward to making another bid for the national championship when the dream fell apart.

An NCAA investigation discovered that Perry had been illegally recruited by NLU while she was a high school senior in Brookhaven, Mississippi. Perry was given illegal automobile transportation and lodging in another community by an NLU assistant coach. Also, she was observed by the same assistant coach while she worked out in the NLU gym during her campus visit. When these violations were revealed, Northeast Louisiana's women's basketball program was placed on probation for one year. They were also ruled ineligible to compete in the 1986 NCAA championships.

Perhaps the biggest loser was Chana Perry. She was declared ineligible for the rest of the 1986 season. Perry's fate clearly shows that women athletes, if they don't know the "rules of the game," or don't want to live by them, can suffer the same fate as well-known male athletes.

"

It's beginning to happen and it's very frustrating. The men have been doing it for 30 or 40 years, so the women [who want to cheat] won't need to develop a new system.

Vivian Stringer
basketball coach, University of Iowa

"

Since the NCAA took over women's athletics, three schools have been placed on probation for recruiting violations. Twelve other schools have received official reprimands.

Women's coaches and athletic administrators are very aware of the possible dangers faced by high school athletes who hope to play in college. Merilee Dean Baker warns that "as more money is invested to build women's programs, the pressure to win becomes greater. This pressure has led to abuses in men's programs for years, and now threatens the integrity of women's athletics.

"You would be well advised to eliminate any school whose coach tries to entice you with anything that is in violation of NCAA rules. If you let yourself be bought, you not only risk your athletic future, but more importantly your self-respect. Top women high school athletes are being recruited with great intensity. It is your job to know the rules, and to help yourself by abiding by them.

"It's important to keep your athletic participation in the proper perspective," adds Baker. "One of the big problems for male athletes is the illusion of a possible professional sports career. The odds against becoming a professional athlete for a woman are even greater than they are for a man. Aside from tennis and golf, the opportunities are very limited. Enjoy your athletic experience, but remember that a quality education is your key to a bright future."

Title IX: An Endangered Law?

As we have already pointed out, Title IX was without question a key that opened the door to athletic opportunity for thousands of young women across the United States. As a high school athlete today, you have many sports opportunities that were not available in the past. Before this rule was passed, countless women had no chance at all to participate in organized sport.

At the time of Title IX, the opportunities for women athletes in high school were already on the rise. After Title IX, this growth exploded.

Lisa Garrett, the director of publicity for the Women's Sports Foundation, pointed to two major reasons for this growth. "The passing of Title IX legislation forced many secondary school administrators to provide athletic opportunities for girls," claims Garrett. "But I also think that credit should be given to those high school parents, principals, and athletic directors who realized before Title IX went into effect that not only were many high school girls very interested in organized athletic opportunities, but that participation in inter-scholastic sports could greatly enhance the overall educational experience of girls as well as boys.

"Title IX certainly had a direct effect on participation rates in college athletics," said Garrett. "With the growth of women's college sports programs, more and more high school girls became interested in athletics because suddenly they could see viable participation opportunities (including athletic scholarships) beyond high school, and top women college athletes served as role models."

Unfortunately, opportunities for women athletes are in danger once again. In 1984, a new ruling by the U.S. Supreme Court changed the way that Title IX is applied. Under the old form of Title IX, if a school or university received any money from the government, *all* of its programs had to be equally available to all students. The new ruling, however, says that equal opportunity can be "program specific." This means that equal opportunity only has to be offered by the particular programs that get government money. For example, if State U gets federal aid only for its math program, then all students must be able to use the facilities of the math department. But State U doesn't have to offer equal opportunities in any of its other departments that don't receive federal money.

So, if a college athletic department doesn't get any government funding, it doesn't have to provide equal opportunities for men and women. And most athletic programs get their funds from student fees, alumni donations, and ticket sales. Therefore, these departments could now legally cut back their women's programs.

As a female high school athlete, you should understand the consequences of these recent developments. The new changes in the rule threaten the effectiveness of Title IX and your chances for an equal opportunity to participate in athletics.

Both you and your parents should be aware that bills are currently being introduced to try to put the "teeth" back into Title IX. If these bills are passed, they will protect your opportunity for equal rights on the playing field. It is to your advantage to support this legislation in any way possible.

If you are interested in more information on Title IX, or if you believe that you are not being given an equal opportunity to participate in athletics at your school, check the Help Section at the back of the book.

Myth or Fact?

Despite the tremendous advances in performance and participation in women's sport, many people still hold onto out-dated ideas about the female athlete. Through the years, this prejudice has discouraged many young women from becoming involved in competitive sports. Some girls who enjoyed their particular sport, and could have been top athletes, have been talked into quitting because of the social pressures.

But the times are changing quickly. As more women are seen to be competitive athletes, girls are realizing that participation in sports can be every bit as enjoyable for them as it always has been for boys. Sports are for anyone who wants to give it their best shot!

As a young woman, you may be discouraged from participating in athletics by friends, teachers, or even your parents. They may tell you that women aren't strong enough for competitive sports, or that girls who play sports aren't popular with boys. It is important for you to understand the difference between myth and fact, so that you can give sports your very best effort with a clear mind.

Myth: Because women have smaller, weaker bones than men, they are more likely to suffer a serious injury.

Fact: For the most part, women's bones *are* smaller than men's, but they are not weaker. Therefore, women are *not* more likely to be injured. In fact, because men are usually heavier and faster than women, collisions between male players are normally much harder than between women players. So men are actually more likely to suffer broken bones from contact sports than are women. Very few injuries happen only to women. The injuries that occur to both women *and* men are usually caused by poor physical conditioning, not taking enough precautions against injuries, or not allowing old injuries to fully heal. In other words, if you train properly and take care of your body, you are no more likely to be injured than a boy.

Myth: Normal athletic activity can cause irregularities in the menstrual cycle.

Fact: Normal athletic participation has virtually no effect on menstruation in most women. Young women who take part in extremely demanding sports (marathoning, long-distance swimming, triathalons) may find that menstruation is slightly delayed or may even be skipped at times. This is mainly because such symptoms are common in women with a very low percentage of body fat. No evidence suggests that athletics can lead to significant changes in the menstrual cycle. However, everyone's body reacts differently to exercise. If you have unusual menstrual discomfort or pain, be sure to see a doctor.

Myth: Women should avoid exercise during menstruation.

Fact: Most female athletes don't worry about exercising during menstruation. These sportswomen don't see a connection between menstrual disorders and athletic activities. But if you are involved in very intense sports, you may want to adjust your training program during certain times in the menstrual cycle. This, however, is a matter of personal choice, and depends on your individual needs. Many female athletes plan their training without taking their menstrual cycle into account. Girls should not avoid athletics because of fear of menstrual problems. If problems arise, you should see a doctor.

Myth: Athletics can damage a woman's ability to have children.

Fact: Athletic participation *will not* prevent women from being able to have children. In fact, women who exercise regularly often have fewer problems with pregnancy and childbirth than inactive women.

Myth: Women who participate in sports become masculine.

Fact: This statement is only true for people who believe that women should be mild-mannered and weak. Nowadays, most people know that aggression and competitiveness are characteristics of both men and women. It is quite normal for a woman to be a fierce competitor on the playing field and still remain feminine. All kinds of women are now becoming successful in careers that were once thought to be only for men—and sports is no exception. As more and more women succeed in such careers, the old, outdated theories about women will continue to be broken down. Some of the world's top woman athletes have been able to combine marriage and children with their sports careers. Evonne Goolagong Cawley left the women's professional tennis tour to give birth to her first child. She later returned to the circuit and won her second Wimbledon championship. Long-distance running star Ingrid Kristiansen ran the marathon faster than any woman in history within a year of the birth of her first child. Sprinter Valerie Briscoe-Hooks won two gold medals at the 1984 Olympics while her husband and child looked on with pride.

Portrait of a True Student–Athlete

Throughout this book we have stressed the importance of balancing your athletic dreams with the pursuit of a quality education. You may find that this is easier said than done. It takes a great deal of dedication and hard work for a high school student–athlete to successfully juggle schoolwork, athletic training, and a social life. As you saw in chapter 1, Stefan Humphries is one young man who has been able to succeed both on and off the playing field.

University of Virginia women's basketball coach Debbie Ryan knows another person who has managed to be a top athlete and student.

"I know of no harder working, more dedicated individual than Kim Silloway," remarked Ryan. "To me, she truly epitomizes the student–athlete ideal."

When Debbie Ryan first heard about her, Kim Silloway was a high school basketball star at St. Johnsbury Academy in Vermont. At St. Johnsbury, Kim led the girl's basketball team to two state championships in a row, while averaging over twenty-five points per game. She was named to the *Parade Magazine* High School All-American Team in both her junior and senior years. At the same time she was piling up big numbers on the basketball court, Kim was also making equally impressive statistics in the classroom. She was a straight-A student and was ranked near the very top of her class.

"Obviously Kim's outstanding basketball ability was the major reason behind our initial interest in her," commented coach Ryan. "When we found out that she was also a top-notch student with such outstanding work habits, she became even more appealing in our eyes. The more I got to know Kim, the more I wanted her to attend Virginia."

As a two-time high school All-American selection and honor student, Kim quickly learned that Debbie Ryan was only one of many college coaches interested in recruiting such a well-rounded candidate.

"I was really kind of surprised at all the attention I received from college coaches during the summer before my senior year in high school," recalled Kim. "Vermont was not really a state that produced great basketball players, but I guess college scouts noticed me at summer camps and in Junior Olympic competition. I was contacted by more than 200 schools, and I certainly didn't anticipate that much interest.

"Before I started my senior year I came to the conclusion that it would be really important for me to keep the recruiting process under control and in the proper perspective. I wanted to make sure that my schoolwork wouldn't suffer, and that it wouldn't cut into my basketball practice time. The first thing I did was set up a system whereby all contact from college coaches or representatives would go through my parents or my high school coach. The fact that so many schools were interested in me was really flattering, but the recruiting process can drive you crazy unless you handle it in an organized manner. Thanks to my family, my high school coach, and the guidance people at St. Johnsbury, my recruiting experience was very positive. If I hadn't been organized and received such great support, I might have faced some real problems."

Early in her senior year, Kim realized that it was important to narrow down the number of schools that she would consider attending. Otherwise, she felt she would be overwhelmed by too many choices.

"I knew that I wanted to go to a school that had an excellent pre-med program. That was my number one consideration. As far as basketball was concerned, I was really not interested in programs that were already ranked among the top ten teams in the nation. I was more interested in playing for a school that aspired to have a top ten team. I wanted to be part of a program that would continue to improve until it could be competitive with the top basketball powers in the nation, and I wanted the challenge of helping to influence that growth."

Near the end of her high school career, Kim narrowed down her college choices to three schools; Northwestern University, Notre Dame University, and the University of Virginia.

Kim remembered that, "in many ways I felt it would be almost impossible for me to make a bad choice amongst three such great schools. As I struggled to make my final decision I wanted to make a choice that would serve to increase the possibility that I would be

Courtesy of the University of Virginia Office of Sports Information

"

Before I started my senior year I came to the conclusion that it would be really important for me to keep the recruiting process under control and in the proper perspective. I wanted to make sure that my schoolwork wouldn't suffer, and that it wouldn't cut into my basketball practice time.

Kim Silloway
University of Virginia

"

happy academically, athletically, and socially. After a great deal of soul-searching I decided on Virginia, and four years later I'm glad I did."

Today, the University of Virginia is equally pleased with Kim Silloway's decision. Kim's accomplishments both on and off the basketball court have been quite extraordinary, to say the least.

As a four-year starter for the women's basketball team, Kim played a key role in Virginia's rise to national prominence. She has been a starting guard since her freshman year. Her hustle and leadership have earned the respect of teammates and opponents alike.

"Kim was certainly our top defensive player and we always made sure that she guarded the top scorer on the teams we played," said coach Ryan. "Great defensive players have tremendous determination and are usually very unselfish team-oriented players. Kim possesses those attributes as much as any player I've coached."

In her junior year, Kim was selected to the All-Atlantic Coast Conference Team. She was also a starting guard on the East team at the 1983 National Sports Festival and she earned a try-out for the 1984 Women's Olympic Basketball Team. She finished her playing career at Virginia as the school's career assist leader.

Off the court, Kim's accomplishments are even more impressive. While maintaining a 3.0-plus grade-point average in pre-med, she also found the time to have twelve papers published on various medical subjects. Kim invented a special shoulder pad that is used by lacrosse players throughout the country. She also serves as a special consultant to a surgical equipment company in Connecticut. In the summer between her junior and senior years at Virginia, she lived in Paraguay, where she was an assistant to a plastic surgeon.

Kim won the prestigious Pete Gray Award, which is presented annually to "the most outstanding student of the University of Virginia." This award includes a scholarship to study at Virginia for a fifth year, in any academic area that the winner chooses.

"The Pete Gray Award really meant a lot to me because it recognized the fact that I was able to contribute to Virginia in many different areas," noted Kim. "In retrospect I feel great about my college experience. I worked hard academically and at basketball, and also found time to have a great social experience. The people who say that it can't be done are wrong. If you're willing to work hard you'll be surprised at how much you can accomplish.

"My advice to any high school student–athlete would be to learn to organize your time as soon as possible. When I first arrived at Virginia I had quite a few adjustments to make. Being away from home for the first time and having to start over and make new friends again was tough. Those factors, coupled with very time-consuming academic and athletic commitments, forced me to really be disciplined about planning my time. I was determined to get the most I possibly could out of college and I think I came pretty close to doing just that. I feel as if the work habits I've developed will help me to face new challenges in medical school and in later life."

A New Beginning

Women have been participating in sports for many years, but it has taken far too long for them to even begin to have the same kind of athletic opportunities and public support that male athletes have always enjoyed.

From superstars like Cheryl Miller and Evylen Ashford to the millions of junior high and high school female athletes across the nation, women are making their mark on the playing field.

We urge you to seize the athletic opportunities that are being made available to you. Avoid the problems created in men's sports. You have a chance for a new beginning. Take advantage of your chance to participate in sports and to grow both mentally and physically from your involvement.

The woman athlete is here to stay.

Courtesy of the Boston Bruins

"

Balance athletics with a quality education. If you do, then you'll
be a better person and a better athlete.

Bobby Orr
Former defenseman for the Boston Bruins and three-time
National Hockey League Most Valuable Player

"

8 Help Section

■ *Study Skills*

Time Management

One of the major reasons why Stefan Humphries and Kim Silloway could excel in the classroom and on the playing field is that both of these student–athletes learned how to manage their time while in high school. As a high school athlete, you not only have to keep up with your schoolwork like any other student, but you also face many other demands, like daily practices, team meetings, home and away competitions, and injury rehabilitation sessions. And you probably have family chores, and perhaps even a part-time job. Is it possible to juggle all of these demands and still enjoy a normal social life? The answer is yes—if you're willing to make a schedule to help you manage your time properly, *and* if you're determined to stick to that schedule.

Take some time on Sunday afternoon or evening to draw a schedule for the coming week. First make a list of everything that you *have* to do, such as papers that are due, tests to prepare for, or team practices and games. Then make another list of everything you would *like* to do, such as going to parties or to that great new movie you want to see. Take a few minutes and put these lists in order of importance. In other words, rate all your activities, starting with the most important and working down to the least important. Your schoolwork should be your number one priority. It's not an optional activity.

When all of your activities are listed in order, make a time chart like the one below. Begin to fill in your schedule by plugging in the activities at the top of your priority list. Most of the time, this means your studies. Then fill in time slots for less important activities. Finally, complete your schedule by adding your social activities.

Important Time Scheduling Tips

- Every night and every morning before you leave the house, review your schedule and revise it if necessary. This will mentally prepare you for the day, and will also help you make sure you have all the equipment (textbooks, notes, practice gear, etc.) that you will need to meet your goals for the day. If you planned to study for a math quiz during your study hall period, you won't get much work done if you leave your math book at home. Likewise, you would have to sit out the afternoon's practice session if you suddenly realized that you'd forgotten to bring your knee brace to school.

- Be as realistic as possible about whether you can complete assignments or prepare for tests within the time you schedule for them. Don't be afraid to schedule extra time for any activity that might be difficult to finish. Be flexible. If you need a few more hours to prepare for a big history final, change your schedule. Remember, your priorities can vary from day to day due to circumstances beyond your control.

- Don't waste your free time. Get into the habit of using any unexpected free time to get ahead. If the coach cuts practice short during exam week to give you and your teammates some extra study hours, don't go home and watch television. Spend an extra hour in the library and try to get ahead of the game.

- Plan ahead. If you know that the team is taking a weekend overnight trip in three weeks, be sure to add small amounts of work to your weekly schedule to make up for the time you will be away. Let teachers and employers know about your time conflicts well in advance so that other arrangements can be made. Be sure your teachers know that you are eager to make up any work you missed because of athletic events. Don't expect your teachers to tell you to make up missed work. This is your responsibility.

- Make sure you leave yourself enough time for fun. It's possible to work too much. On some days, you will have to spend a great deal

	MON.	TUES.	WED.	THURS.	FRI.	SAT.	SUN.
8:00 AM	Algebra	→	→	→	→		Prepare for Algebra Test
9:00	English	→	→	→	→	Work on English Paper	→
10:00	Study Hall M–F	Prepare for Spanish Quiz	Library Research History Paper	Read English Assignment	College Review Mtg w/ Guidance Counselor	→	→
11:00	History	→	→	→	→	Pre-Game Meal	
12:00 PM	Lunch	→	Snack	Lunch	→	Taping/Treatment	Lunch
1:00	Spanish	→	→	→	→	→	School Car Wash
2:00	Biology	→	→	→	→	Game – Westfield	
3:00	Taping/Treatment	→	Prepare for Bio Lab Quiz	Taping/Treatment →	→	→	→
4:00	Practice	Practice	Pre-Game Meal	Practice	Practice		
5:00	→	→		→	→	→	
6:00	→	→	Game – Caldwell	→	→	Dinner	Dinner
7:00	Dinner	Dinner	→	Dinner	Dinner	School Dance	Set Schedule for Next Week
8:00	Study	Study	→	Study	Movie	→	
9:00	→	→	→	→	→	→	
10:00	→	→	→	→	→		

of time studying, or practicing, or both. Taking a break from your demanding schedule can often be just what the doctor ordered. The *quality* of the time you put in on your activities can be more important than the *amount* of time you spend.

Reading

Whether you are in junior high, in high school, or getting ready for college, your academic performance will depend a lot on your reading skills. As you go on in school, your reading load will constantly grow, to the point where it is important for you to be an *efficient* reader. Strong reading skills will be a big help to you even after you have completed your education.

Important Reading Tips

- Before you begin to read a textbook, go over the foreword, introduction, and table of contents. This will give you a general idea of what the book is all about. Some textbooks have a short introduction at the beginning of each chapter that can be quite helpful.
- When you read, pay special attention to underlined, darkened, or italic print. Many authors will use special print to emphasize important points. This special print is the writers' way of saying, "read this carefully."
- Concentrate on what you're reading. If something seems unclear, stop and re-read it at a slower pace. Sometimes it is helpful to re-read the paragraph before the section that you are having trouble understanding. The earlier paragraph may help you see the connection between the two sections.
- If you come across a word you don't understand, look it up in the dictionary. The same word may be used throughout the book, and if you don't know what it means you may have trouble understanding the book's information.
- Use a highlighter to mark key concepts. This will help you remember important information, and will make reviewing easier.

• If you start dozing off, take a break. When you're tired you will find it hard to concentrate and probably won't read very carefully.

Listening

In most team sports, you spend a lot of the time playing without the ball. Take basketball, for example. Even superstars like Michael Jordan and Cheryl Miller spend a great deal of time playing defense. When their team has the ball, they work without it to get open and will often act as decoys to help teammates free up for easy shots. Throughout a game they are only doing something *with* the ball about twenty percent of the time.

In the classroom, and in most learning situations, you spend most of your time listening. If you are not willing to be a good listener, you will find it harder to understand and remember important information.

Important Listening Tips

• Be a good listener. Review your notes from the last class and your most recent readings. This will prepare you for that day's lecture and/or class discussion. Try to show up early for class so you can find a good seat and get comfortable. You will also have time to get your books and papers ready before the class starts. You can't very well listen to what is being said if you're looking for a pen or a notebook. Check your syllabus before the class begins to give yourself time to think about the subject that the lecture will cover.

• Concentrate on what your teacher and classmates say. When your coach goes over a new play or tactic, you probably give him your undivided attention so that you can help the team as much as possible. Help yourself by giving your teachers the same amount of attention in the classroom. You have a much better chance of understanding the course material if you train yourself to block out classroom distractions.

• Learn to listen for key phrases and speech patterns. If your teacher uses phrases like "keep in mind" or "an example of this would be," he or she is probably about to make an important point. Many teachers slow down their speech or slightly raise their voices when they are trying to emphasize a point. Learn to listen for these cues.

Note-Taking

The quality of the notes you take in your classes and when reading will have an important effect on your academic performance. If your notes are sloppy or wrong, then you will have much more trouble reviewing the material. Neat, accurate, and comprehensive notes will help you understand complex subjects and will help you do better on assignments and tests.

Important Note-Taking Tips

• When taking notes in class, use the method that works best for *you*. Many students think they need to write down almost everything the teacher says or they'll miss something important. This method can be useful for some people, but don't spend so much time writing that you miss important parts of the lecture. One good way to take notes is to concentrate on writing down the key facts and concepts, and summarizing the main points of the lecture.

• No matter what method you use to take notes, you need to make a habit of reviewing and clarifying your notes daily. As an athlete, you normally review films of a game the day after the game so that what worked and what didn't are fresh in your mind. Likewise, if you review and update your notes shortly after the class (within one day is the recommended time), you'll find it easier to understand and organize your notes.

• If some of the subject matter is unclear after you review your notes, be sure to ask your teacher and/or one of your classmates. It is important to understand the class material early in a grading period so that you can follow the facts or concepts that will come later.

• After you have reviewed and summarized your notes, go back and use a magic marker to underline or star key terms and concepts.

When you review your notes, these important themes and phrases should begin to jump out at you.

Preparing for and Taking Tests

The nervous feeling you get in the pit of your stomach as the big game approaches is a lot like feeling you get when you realize that final exams are only a week away. If you've worked hard to perfect your athletic skills and are in top physical condition, you'll probably feel better about the game than someone who has gone through the motions in practice and who regularly breaks training. By the same token, if you've done a good job of keeping up with your studies, you should be more relaxed about the upcoming test than your classmate who's trying to cram two months' worth of studying into a few nights. Preparing for tests is a continuous process.

Important Test Preparation Tips

- Review your class notes and course materials all through the grading period. The more familiar you are with your notes, the easier they will be to understand and remember. Don't set in a situation where you are forced to *re-learn* information from the first few weeks of the grading period. Ideally, the week before a test you should review material that you have already learned. This will leave you with extra time to spend on concepts that you find particularly hard to understand.

- You may find it helpful to practice for an exam by making up your own test. Anticipate some of the questions that are likely to appear on the exam and try to answer them. Ask someone in your class to "buddy-test" with you. Your classmate may think of some questions that you did not, and you'll probably be able to help each other with the difficult material. Studying with a friend can also be a nice change of pace.

- Ask your teacher for copies of past tests that he or she is willing to give to the class. If you get these tests, try to figure out how the test is organized as well as what topics are covered.

• Answer the questions at the end of each chapter in your textbook. These questions usually cover the most important information in the chapter. Don't throw away quizzes that you take during the grading period. Questions from quizzes will often reappear on major exams.

• There is no substitute for doing all the written assignments and readings. One of the best ways to prepare for a test is simply to keep up with your work. If you're not willing to do that, then the rest of these tips won't be much help.

Important Test-Taking Tips

• As difficult as it may be, try to relax. No matter how prepared— or unprepared—you may be, you will think more clearly and concentrate better if you are as calm as possible when you sit down to take a test. Make sure your watch has the right time, get to class early, and organize any materials you may need while taking the test. Take a deep breath and do the best you can. That's all anyone can expect of you, and all you should expect of yourself.

• *Briefly* read over the test when it is first passed out. This will give you a general idea of how much time you'll need for each section.

• Read the directions carefully. If they are unclear, don't be afraid to ask your teacher for help. Don't answer the questions until you fully understand the directions and have a good sense of exactly what kind of answer is required.

• You may want to answer the questions that you are sure of first. This gives you time to concentrate on more difficult material later and also boosts your confidence and helps you relax. It's a little like hitting that first jump shot. It makes the next shot easier to take, and eases the pressure.

• If you have time, check your answer after you've finished the test. Not only is this a smart way to catch nervous mistakes, but it may help trigger the answer to another question that you thought you didn't know.

• You may want to write a *brief* outline before answering an essay question. This will help you to organize your thoughts and save time in the long run.

■ *Standardized Test Preparation*

There is a lot of argument over the usefulness of study aids and preparation courses for standardized college entrance examinations like the SAT or ACT. Before you decide to use a study aid for these tests, you should consider the following information:

- The best preparation for the SAT or the ACT takes place in the classroom. Staying on top of your studies and developing good work habits in junior high and high school will help prepare you for college entrance tests far more than any self-help book or short review course. Study aids are only useful if you have built a solid academic base over the years.

- You may not have to look farther than your own high school for help with preparing for the college entrance exams. Many schools provide books and software to help you prepare, and also offer courses and other special guidance on test-taking and test techniques. Check with your guidance counselor *at the beginning of your junior year* to see what materials and programs your school offers.

- The three main types of standardized test study aids are sample tests, booklets containing test-taking tips and techniques, and courses that teach you how to take tests. Sample tests and preparation booklets are not expensive, and can be somewhat helpful for familiarizing you with the types of questions and general organization of the SAT and ACT. Although these aids cannot guarantee you will score higher on the test, it is safe to say that they probably cannot hurt your performance. There is disagreement about the usefulness of test coaching schools or courses. These courses can be quite expensive. Before spending your time and money, be sure that these courses can really help improve your test performance.

Be sure to sign up to take the SAT and/or ACT at least once in your junior year and twice in your senior year. The chances are good that your score will improve every time you take the test.

You don't have to wait until your senior year to take the Achievement Tests (ACH). You should take these tests as soon as possible after completing a course on the test subject. For instance, if you take calculus in your junior year, don't wait until your senior year to take the calculus ACH exam. Ideally, you want to take the test while the subject matter is fresh in your mind.

■ College Guides

When you begin thinking about the type of school you might be interested in, a college guide book will be a great help to you. The guides listed here contain general information about admissions, financial aid, programs of study, athletics, student life, and the campus at most of the colleges and universities across the nation. While looking through these guides, you will probably be surprised at the number of schools and the different kinds of educational opportunities that exist in your area alone—much less in other regions. Your high school guidance counselor should be able to get some of these publications, and it would definitely be worthwhile for you to buy one of these guides to use at home.

If you become interested in a particular school, be sure to write to that schools' admissions office for more detailed information.

Some of the more comprehensive college guides are:

Barron's Profiles of American Colleges
Barron's Educational Series, Inc.
113 Crossways Park Drive
Woodbury, NY 11797
$12.95

The College Handbook
The College Board
P.O. Box 886
New York, NY 10101
$15.95

Lovejoy's Guide to College
Prentice-Hall Order Dept.
200 Old Tappan Road
Tappan, NJ 07675
$14.95

Peterson's Guide to Four-Year Colleges
Peterson's Guides
P.O. Box 2123
Princeton, NJ 08543-2123
$12.95

■ *Financial Aid*

Millions of students receive financial aid to help them continue their education. You do not have to be poor to qualify for financial aid, because aid is based on what you and your family are *able to pay*. Even students from families with high incomes are often eligible for aid, especially at higher-cost colleges.

Demonstrated Need

Colleges, state scholarship programs, and other organizations award financial aid on the basis of demonstrated need. They believe that you and your parents have a responsibility to pay as much as you can toward your educational costs. Demonstrated need is the difference between what it costs to attend a college and how much your family can reasonably be expected to contribute.

Total college expense − Family contribution = Demonstrated need

Usually you are eligible for financial aid equal to the amount of your demonstrated financial need. Since what you can afford to pay stays the same whether college costs are high or low, you may be eligible for different amounts of aid at different institutions. Don't rule out

Reprinted with permission from *The College Handbook 1985–86*. Copyright © 1985 by College Entrance Examination Board, New York.

applying to any college that interests you on the basis of its costs alone.

Types of Aid Available

Grants or Scholarships

These are types of aid that do not have to be repaid (sometimes called gift aid).

Loans

These usually have low interest rates and must be repaid, but generally only after you have graduated or left college.

Student Employment

This can be a job that the college finds for you or work you find on your own that is funded through a financial aid program.

Financial aid can come from several different sources: the federal government, state government, colleges themselves, and a wide variety of private organizations and scholarship programs.

Sources of Financial Aid

The major financial aid programs are described here:

Institutional Funds

Most colleges have their own scholarships or grants as well as loan and work programs funded from endowments and operational budgets.

Federal Programs

Please note that financial aid programs listed here as sponsored by the federal government may be changed or eliminated by legislation in Congress at the time this book is being published.

Campus-Based Aid

There are three major federal programs that are campus-based, that is, directly administered by colleges. Nearly all colleges participate in these programs.

• Supplemental Educational Opportunity Grant Program (SEOG) provides grants of up to $2,000 for students with financial need.
• National Direct Student Loan Program (NDSL) provides loans for students with demonstrated need. No interest is paid while you are enrolled in college. When you leave college, you must repay with 4 percent interest.
• College Work-Study Program (CWSP) provides jobs for students with demonstrated need.

Colleges may also administer some other federal programs, including ones to assist students who enter nursing and other health programs.

Pell (Basic) Grants

The federal government also sponsors the Pell Grant program. These grants may be as high as $2,100 in 1985–86 although the maximum may vary from year to year depending on the level set by Congress. The grants are based on your family's financial circumstances and may be used at the college of your choice.

Guaranteed Student Loan

The federally sponsored Guaranteed Student Loan Program (GSL) is an important source of loan funds. These loans are made primarily by banks, savings and loan associations, and credit unions, but some colleges are also lenders.

The federal government pays the full 9 percent interest on these loans while you are enrolled in college. When you graduate or leave a college, you must begin repaying the loan with interest.

Parent Loan Program

The federally sponsored Parent Loans for Undergraduate Students (PLUS) allows parents of students to borrow money to help with their children's college costs. The interest rate is 12 percent, and repayment begins 60 days after the loan is disbursed.

State Funds

All states have scholarship or grant programs to help you attend the college of your choice. The regulations and application procedures for these programs vary from state to state. Ask your guidance counselor for information about your state's program or write to the state department of higher education in your state capital.

Community Funds and Other Sources

Financial aid is also provided by community agencies, foundations, corporations, unions, religious organizations, clubs, and civic, cultural, and fraternal groups. Need is usually considered, but other factors may be taken into account in determining a student's eligibility. Check with your counselor for information on local aid sources.

Comparing Financial Aid

You should compare the types of aid offered by the colleges you are considering. Remember that the percentages listed under grants, loans, and jobs in *The College Handbook* are for the total financial aid dollars distributed by each college in the 1983–84 academic year (or the most recent year for which information was available). If you are eligible for financial aid, you probably will get a combination of gift aid and self-help aid (loans and jobs). This combination is called a *financial aid package.*

Financial Aid Checklist

If you think you need aid to continue your education, your chances of getting it are best if you apply in the right way at the right time.
   Begin a year before you expect to enter college.

- Ask for information about financial aid opportunities and application procedures when writing to the admissions office of each college on your list.
- Search for special sources of aid. Your guidance counselor, high school library, and public library will often have this type of information. You may qualify for a private scholarship, grant, or loan program based on academic achievement, religious affiliation, ethnic or racial heritage, community activities, hobbies or special interests, organizational membership, artistic talents, athletic abilities, other special skills, career plans, or proposed field of study.
- Ask for information on federal student aid programs from your high school counselor.
- Ask about student aid available to residents of your state and how to apply for it.
- Make a financial aid calendar for youself. Include (1) the name of each program you may be eligible for, (2) the deadline for applying to the program, and (3) an earlier deadline *for yourself*—a date by which you must have received and completed the application form and any other requirements in time to file your application by the program deadline.
- Make certain you know what need analysis form to file for federal student aid programs. The two most commonly used forms are the Financial Aid Form (FAF) of the College Scholarship Service and the Family Financial Statement (FFS) of the American College Testing Program. You can get these forms from your high school guidance office or a college financial aid office. The forms are gen-

erally available in November, but they should not be filed until after January 1.

- Plan a time when you can spend several hours on your applications. If you are a dependent of your parents, you should plan the time when they can work with you. Your parent or parents should have a copy of their most recent income tax return available.

- Carefully follow the instructions for filling out your need analysis form. Make sure your answers are complete and correct.

- Apply for a Pell Grant. You can use the FAF or FFS to apply for this important federal program simply by checking the appropriate box on the form. There is no extra fee for this service.

- Apply for a state scholarship or grant. In many states your need analysis form can also be used to apply for state aid. Your guidance counselor knows whether you must fill out additional application forms.

- Mail your completed need analysis form as soon as possible after January 1. Send the form for processing at least four weeks before the earliest financial aid deadline set by the colleges, state scholarship programs, or other grant programs for which you may be eligible (but not before January 1).

- Review the acknowledgment you receive after submitting your need analysis form. Make certain that all colleges and programs you indicated are correct on the acknowledgment. Respond promptly to any request for additional information.

- Check to see if other financial aid forms are required by the colleges to which you are applying. Complete the forms as early as possible and return them to the college.

- If you think you may be eligible for aid through the Veterans Administration, the Social Security Administration, or a vocational rehabilitation or other social service agency, contact the nearest office for information.

- Determine how payments from each aid source will be made to you. Generally, payment of financial aid is made at the time you enroll. Find out if there are additional procedures or forms to file in order to receive the aid.

- Pay close attention to award letters. Notify the college whose offer you are accepting, and inform the other colleges of your decision so that the financial aid reserved for you can be freed for other applicants. If you also receive aid notices from the state or federal programs, read them carefully and be sure to follow any directions they contain so that you can be certain of getting your aid.

- Explore alternatives. If the college of your choice cannot provide you with enough aid to meet your full financial need or if your family cannot contribute what is expected, you may want to consider borrowing. Learn about loans—the interest rates, repayment schedules, and other terms and conditions—*before* you apply. Government-sponsored loans, such as the Guaranteed Student Loan Program, usually have the lowest interest rates and the most flexible repayment arrangements. If you do apply for a Guaranteed Student Loan, give yourself enough time (at least six weeks) to have the loan papers processed.

■ *Contacting College Coaches*

As we discussed in the chapter on recruiting, just because you have not been contacted by an athletic recruiter does not mean that you have to abandon your college sports aspirations.

The following is an example of a "letter of interest" and resumé which you can send to coaches at schools in which you are interested in attending.

Remember, most college coaches will be happy to receive your letter, as they know that they are probably not aware of every prospect.

June 12, 1987

Mr. Joseph Smith
Head Football Coach
Department of Athletics
Tuskooga State University
Tuskooga, Pennsylvania 17658

Dear Coach Smith:

My name is Peter Engelhart and this coming fall I will be entering my senior year at Mogadore High School in Mogadore, Ohio.

I have been the starting tailback for the varsity football team for the past two years, and have been elected as a co-captain for next season. Last year, as a junior, I was the team's second leading rusher (537 yards) and top pass receiver (32 receptions). For my efforts, I was named to the All-County second team.

I am very interested in learning more about Tuskooga State University and your football program. I have enclosed a videotape of our county championship game against Central High School, which I hope you will have a chance to review. Should you require any other information regarding my football background, please contact my high school coach:

>   Mr. John H. Ruttgens
>   Head Football Coach
>   Mogadore High School
>   43 Elm Street
>   Mogadore, Ohio 43267
>
>   Office: (216) 768-4300
>   Home: (216) 768-9874

I plan on visiting the Tuskooga campus with my parents on August 17th and would like to have the opportunity to meet with you or one of your assistants. I will call your office next week to set up an appointment.

I would appreciate it if you could send me any available information concerning your football program.

Thank you for your time, and I will look forward to meeting with you next month.

Sincerely,

Peter Engelhart

P.S. Enclosed please find a brief high school resume. Should you require any further information, please contact me.

Peter Engelhart
24 Cedar Street
Mogadore, Ohio 43267
(216) 768-9345

ACADEMIC INFORMATION

Grade Point Average: 2.75
Class Rank: 104/462

SAT: Verbal...460
      Math.....480

ACH: English.....490
      Math........520
      History.....510
      Spanish.....450

ATHLETIC INFORMATION

Varsity Football: 10, 11, 12

-second on team in rushing (537 yards) and first in receptions (32) in junior year

-second team All-County selection

-co-captain elect for senior year

Varsity Track: 10, 11, 12

-time for 100 meters: 11.2 seconds

-time for 200 meters: 24.7 seconds

-placed third in both events at 1986 Warren County Track and Field Meet

-qualified for the Ohio State Track and Field Meet in both events

EXTRACURRICULAR ACTIVITIES

-Junior Class Vice-President

-Mogadore High School Big Brother Program

-Mogadore Recreation Department Youth Leader

-Ohio State Special Olympics Volunteer

■ *Problems with Drugs and Alcohol*

If you think you have a drug- or alcohol-related problem, you may want to contact one of the important organizations listed below. You can also write to them for information about drug and alcohol prevention and treatment programs.

The National Clearinghouse for Drug Abuse Information (NCDAI)
5600 Fishers Lane
Room 10A–43
Rockville, MD 20857

National Institute on Drug Abuse
Prevention Branch, Room 11A–33
5600 Fishers Lane
Rockville, MD 20857
(800) 638-2045

National Institute on Alcoholism and Alcohol Abuse (NIAAA)
Prevention Branch, Room 16C–14
5600 Fishers Lane
Rockville, MD 20857

Each state has an official agency that helps prevent and treat drug and alcohol problems. The national office of these agencies is in Washington, D.C.:

National Association of State Alcohol and Drug Abuse Directors
444 North Capital Street
Suite 530
Washington, DC 20001
(202) 783-6868

The National Association of State Alcohol and Drug Abuse Directors has an office in every state. The following list gives their addresses.* In the lists, (a) stands for an agency that deals only with alcohol problems; (d) stands for an agency that deals only with drug problems; and (c) stands for agencies that combine both alcohol and drug problems.

Alabama
Ken Wallis, Receiver and Acting
  Commissioner
Department of Mental Health
200 Interstate Park Drive
P.O. Box 3710
Montgomery, AL 36193
(205) 271-9209
(c)

Alaska
Matthew Felix, Coordinator
Office of Alcoholism & Drug Abuse
Department of Health & Social
  Services
Pouch H-05-F
Juneau, AK 99811
(907) 586-6201
(c)

Arizona
Gwen Smith, Program Representative
  for Alcoholism
Office of Community Behav. Health
Arizona Department of Health
  Services
1740 West Adams
Phoenix, AZ 85007
(602) 255-1152
(a)

Ed Zborower, Prog. Rep. for Drug
  Abuse
Office of Community Behav. Health
Arizona Department of Health
  Services
1740 West Adams
Phoenix, AZ 85007
(602) 255-1152
(d)

Akansas
Paul T. Behnke, Director
Arkansas Office on Alcohol and Drug
  Abuse Prevention
1515 W. 7th Avenue, Suite 300
Little Rock, AR 72202
(501) 371-2603
(c)

California
Chauncey Veatch III, Esq., Director
Department of Alcohol and Drug
  Abuse
111 Capitol Mall
Sacramento, CA 95814
(916) 445-0834
(c)

*This list is reprinted courtesy of the National Association of State Alcohol and Drug Abuse Directors.

Colorado
Robert Aukerman, Director
Alcohol and Drug Abuse Division
Department of Health
4210 East 11th Avenue
Denver, CO 80220
(303) 331-8201
(c)

Connecticut
Donald J. McConnell, Executive
    Director
Conn. Alcohol and Drug Abuse
    Commission
999 Asylum Avenue, 3rd Floor
Hartford, CT 06105
(203) 566-4145
(c)

Delaware
Sara Taylor Allshouse, Chief
Bureau of Alcoholism and Drug Abuse
1901 N. DuPont Highway
Newcastle, DE 19720
(302) 421-6101
(c)

District of Columbia
Simon Holliday, Chief
Health Planning and Development
1875 Connecticut Ave., N.W.
Suite 836
Washington, D.C. 20009
(202) 673-7481
(c)

Florida
Linda Lewis, Administrator
Alcohol and Drug Abuse Program
Department of Health and
    Rehabilitative Services
1317 Winewood Blvd.
Tallahassee, FL 32301
(904) 488-0900
(c)

Georgia
Patricia A. (Pam) Redmond, Director
Alcohol and Drug Services Section
878 Peachtree Street, N.E.
Suite 318
Atlanta, GA 30309
(404) 894-6352
(c)

Hawaii
Joyce Ingram-Chinn, Branch Chief
Alcohol & Drug Abuse Branch
Department of Health, P.O. Box 3378
Honolulu, HI 96801
(808) 548-4280
(c)

Idaho
Charles E. Burns, Director
Bureau of Substance Abuse
Department of Health & Welfare
450 West State Street
Boise, ID 83720
(208) 334-4368
(c)

Illinois
William T. Atkins, Director
Illinois Department of Alcoholism and
    Substance Abuse
100 West Randolph Street
Suite 5-600
Chicago, IL 60601
(312) 917-3840
(c)

Indiana
Joseph E. Mills III, Director
Division of Addiction Services
Department of Mental Health
117 East Washington Street
Indianapolis, IN 46204
(317) 232-7816
(c)

Iowa
Mary L. Ellis, Director
Iowa Department of Substance Abuse
Suite 500, Colony Building
507 Tenth Street
Des Moines, IA 50319
(515) 281-3641
(c)

Kansas
Dr. James A. McHenry, Jr.,
   Commissioner
Alcohol and Drug Abuse Services
2700 West Sixth Street
Biddle Building
Topeka, KS 66606
(913) 296-3925
(c)

Kentucky
Michael Townsend, Director
Division of Substance Abuse
Department for Mental Health–
   Mental Retardation Services
275 East Main Street
Frankfort, KY 40621
(502) 564-2880
(c)

Louisiana
Vern C. Ridgeway, Assistant Secretary
Office of Prevention & Recovery from
   Alcohol and Drug Abuse
P.O. Box 53129
Baton Rouge, LA 70892
(504) 922-0730
(c)

Maine
Neill Miner, Director
Office of Alcoholism and Drug Abuse
   Prevention
Bureau of Rehabilitation
State House Station #11
Augusta, ME 04333
(207) 289-2781
(c)

Maryland
John Bland, Director
Alcoholism Control Administration
201 West Preston St., 4th Floor
Baltimore, MD 21201
(301) 225-6542
(a)

Howard B. Silverman
Acting Director
Maryland State Drug Abuse
   Administration
201 West Preston Street
Baltimore, MD 21201
(301) 225-6926
(d)

Massachusetts
Edward Blacker, Ph.D., Director
Massachusetts Division of Alcoholism
150 Tremont Street
Boston, MA 02111
(617) 727-1960
(a)

Dave Mulligan
Division of Drug Rehabilitation
150 Tremont Street
Boston, MA 02111
(617) 727-8614
(d)

Michigan
Robert Brook, Ph.D., Administrator
Office of Substance Abuse Services
Department of Public Health
3500 North Logan Street
Lansing, MI 48909
(517) 373-8603
(c)

Minnesota
Cynthia Turnure, Ph.D., Director
Chemical Dependency Program
   Division
Department of Human Services
4th Floor Centennial Building
658 Cedar
St. Paul, MN 55155
(612) 296-4610
(c)

Mississippi
Anne D. Robertson, Director
Division of Alcohol and Drug Abuse
Department of Mental Health
11th Floor, Robert E. Lee Office
   Building
Jackson, MS 39201
(601) 359-1297
(c)

Missouri
R. B. Wilson, Director
Division of Alcoholism and Drug
   Abuse
Department of Mental Health
2002 Missouri Boulevard
P.O. Box 687
Jefferson City, MO 65101
(314) 751-4942
(c)

Montana
Robert Anderson, Administrator
Alcohol and Drug Abuse Division
State of Montana
Department of Institutions
Helena, MT 59601
(406) 444-2827
(c)

Nebraska
Cecilia Douthy Willis, Ph.D.,
   Director
Division of Alcoholism & Drug Abuse
Department of Public Institutions
P.O. Box 94728
Lincoln, NE 68509
(402) 471-2851, Ext. 5583
(c)

Nevada
Richard Ham, Chief
Bureau of Alcohol and Drug Abuse
Department of Human Resources
505 East King Street
Carson City, NV 89710
(702) 885-4790
(c)

New Hampshire
Geraldine Sylvester, Director
Office of Alcohol & Drug Abuse
   Prevention
Health and Welfare Building
Hazen Drive
Concord, NH 03301
(603) 271-4627
(c)

New Jersey
Riley Regan, Director
New Jersey Division of Alcoholism
129 East Hanover Street
Trenton, NJ 08625
(609) 292-8947
(a)

Richard Russo, MSPH, Director
Division of Narcotic and Drug Abuse
    Control
129 East Hanover Street
Trenton, NJ 08625
(609) 292-5760
(d)

New Mexico
Mela Salazar, Acting Chief
Alcoholism Bureau
Behavioral Health Services Division
P.O. Box 968
Sante Fe, NM 87504
(505) 827-2635
(a)

Ellen Costilla, Chief
Drug Abuse Bureau
Behavioral Health Services Division
P.O. Box 968
Santa Fe, NM 87504
(505) 827-2592
(d)

New York
Robert V. Shear, Director
New York Division of Alcoholism &
    Alcohol Abuse
194 Washington Avenue
Albany, NY 12210
(518) 474-5417
(a)

John S. Gustafson, Deputy Director
Division of Substance Abuse Services
Executive Park South, Box 8200
Albany, NY 12203
(518) 457-7629
(d)

North Carolina
Thomas F. Miriello, Director
Alcohol and Drug Abuse Section
Division of Mental Health and Mental
    Retardation Services
325 North Salisbury Street
Raleigh, NC 27611
(919) 733-4670
(c)

North Dakota
Thomas Hedin, Director
Division of Alcoholism & Drugs
North Dakota Department of Human
    Services
State Capitol
Bismarck, ND 58505
(701) 224-2769
(c)

Ohio
Wayne Lindstrom, Chief
Bureau on Alcohol Abuse & Recovery
Ohio Department of Health
170 North High St., 3rd Floor
Columbus, OH 43215
(614) 466-3445
(a)

Susan L. Srnec, Chief
Office of Special Populations
30 East Broad Street, Room 2495A
Columbus, OH 43215
(614) 466-1102
(d)

Oklahoma
Tom Stanitis, Director
Alcohol and Drug Programs
Department of Mental Health
P.O. Box 53277, Capitol Station
4545 North Lincoln Blvd.
Suite 100 East Terrace
Oklahoma City, OK 73152
(405) 521-0044
(c)

Oregon
Jeffrey Kushner, Assistant Director
Office of Alcohol & Drug Abuse
   Programs
301 Public Service Building
Salem, OR 97310
(503) 378-2163
(c)

Pennsylvania
Luceille Fleming
Deputy Secretary for Drug & Alcohol
   Programs
PA Department of Health
P.O. Box 90
Harrisburg, PA 17108
(717) 787-9857
(c)

Rhode Island
William Pimentel, Assistant Director
Department of Mental Health, Mental
   Retardation & Hospitals
Division of Substance Abuse,
   Substance Abuse Administration
   Building
Cranston, RI 02902
(401) 464-2091
(c)

South Carolina
William J. McCord, Director
South Carolina Commission on
   Alcohol and Drug Abuse
3700 Forest Drive
Columbia, SC 29204
(803) 734-9520
(c)

South Dakota
Lois Olson, Director
Division of Alcohol and Drug Abuse
Joe Foss Building, 523 East Capitol
Pierre, SD 57501
(605) 773-3123
(c)

Tennessee
Robert Currie, Assistant
   Commissioner
Alcohol and Drug Abuse Services
Tennessee Department of Mental
   Health and Mental Retardation
James K. Polk Building, 505
   Deaderick St.
Nashville, TN 37219
(615) 741-1921
(c)

Texas
Ross Newby, Executive Director
Texas Commission on Alcohol and
   Drug Abuse
1705 Guadalupe Street
Austin, TX 78701
(512) 463-5510
(a)

Utah
Leon PoVey, Director
Division of Alcoholism & Drugs
150 West North Temple, Suite 350
P.O. Box 2500
Salt Lake City, UT 84110
(801) 533-6532

Vermont
Richard Powell II, Director
Office of Alcohol and Drug Abuse
   Programs
103 South Maine Street
Waterbury, VT 05676
(802) 241-2170, 241-1000
(c)

Virginia
Wayne Thacker, Director
Office of Substance Abuse Services
State Department of Mental Health &
  Mental Retardation
P.O. Box 1797
109 Governor Street
Richmond, VA 23214
(804) 786-3906
(c)

Washington
Glen Miller, Director
Bureau of Alcoholism & Substance
  Abuse
Washington Department of Social &
  Health Services
Mail Stop OB-44W
Olympia, WA 98504
(206) 753-5866
(c)

West Virginia
Jack Clohan, Jr., Director
Division of Alcohol and Drug Abuse
State Capitol
1800 Washington St., East, Room 451
Charleston, WV 25305
(304) 348-2276
(c)

Wisconsin
Larry W. Monson, ACSW, Director
Office of Alcohol & Other Drug Abuse
1 West Wilson St., P.O. Box 7851
Madison, WI 53707
(608) 266-3442
(c)

Wyoming
Jean DeFratis, Director
Alcohol and Drug Abuse Programs
Hathaway Building
Cheyenne, WY 82002
(307) 777-7115, Ext. 7118
(c)

Guam
Dr. David L. G. Shimizu, Interim
  Director
Department of Mental Health and
  Substance Abuse
P.O. Box 8896
Tamuning, GU 96911
(c)

Puerto Rico
Isabel Suliveres de Martinez,
  Secretary
Department of Addiction Control
  Services
Box B-Y, Rio Piedras Station
Rio Piedras, PR 00928
(809) 764-3795
(c)

Virgin Islands
Corrine A. Allen, Ph.D.
Director, Division of Mental Health,
  Alcoholism and Drug Dependency
Post Office Box 520
St. Croix, VI 00820
(809) 773-1992
(c)

American Samoa
Fualaau Hanipale, Director
Human Services Clinic
Alcohol and Drug Program
LBJ Tropical Medical Center
Pago Pago, AS 96799
(c)

Dr. Lefiga Liaiga, Director
Public Health Services
LBJ Tropical Medical Center
Pago Pago, AS 96799

Trust Territories
Masao Kumangai, M.D., Director
Health Services
Offices of the High Commissioner
Saipan, Trust Territories 96950
(c)

■ *Problems with Gambling*

As you read earlier in the book, involvement with gambling or gambling addiction can be a major threat to you. If you think you have a gambling problem be sure to get help. Listed below are a number of important organizations that may be able to help you with gambling problems.

Gamblers Anonymous National Service Office
Post Office Box 17173
Los Angeles, CA 90017
(213) 386-8789

Gamblers Anonymous has chapters in every major city. To locate the chapter in your area, call or write the Gamblers Anonymous National Service Office. Gamblers Anonymous is a self-help group made up of people who are recovering from addictions to gambling.

National Council on Compulsive Gambling
John Jay College of Criminal Justice
444 West 56th Street
Suite 3207 South
New York, NY 10019
(212) 765-3833

National Center for Pathological Gambling, Inc.
651 Washington Boulevard
Baltimore, MD 21230

Gambling Psycho-Data
651 Washington Boulevard
Baltimore, MD 21230
(301) 576-0312

■ State-by-State Academic Requirements for High School Athletic Eligibility

The following list gives the state-by-state academic requirements for high school athletic eligibility as of 1986. A strong movement at local, state, and national levels is trying to raise current minimum eligibility standards, or to bring in standards where they don't already exist. Because of this, many states are thinking about changing their current systems, and so some of these rules may soon be out of date. At the beginning of the school year, be sure to ask your coach, guidance counselor, or athletic director about the exact eligibility standards that apply to you. Remember, even if your state has no standard (Maine, Maryland, Minnesota, New York, Vermont), your school or school district might.

Alabama: Must pass four units in previous year.

Alaska: Must pass four subjects in previous semester and be enrolled in four in current semester.

Arizona: Must pass four classes in previous semester.

Arkansas: Must pass three full-credit courses in previous semester (four next year).

California: Must pass twenty credits in previous semester and be enrolled in twenty credits in current semester.

Colorado: Must not fail more than one class in previous semester.

Connecticut: Must pass four subjects in previous semester.

Delaware: Must pass at least four courses in previous marking period, including two in science, math, English, or social studies.

District of Columbia: Must pass four credits in previous semester.

Florida: Requires 1.5 GPA on 4.0 scale in previous semester.

Georgia: Must pass four credit courses in previous semester and current semester. Next year: five.

Hawaii: One-year pilot program effective in September 1986 requires 2.0 grade-point average on 4.0 scale in previous semester.

Idaho: Must pass five classes in previous semester.

Illinois: Must pass twenty credit hours in previous semester. Weekly certification of passing work in twenty credit hours in current semester.

Indiana: Must pass four full-credit subjects in previous semester.

Iowa: Must pass three courses in previous semester. Next year: four.

Kansas: Must pass five subjects in previous semester.

Kentucky: Must pass four classes in previous semester, and weekly certification in current semester.

Louisiana: Must pass five subjects, have 1.5 grade-point average on 4.0 scale in previous semester.

Maine: No statewide requirement.

Maryland: No statewide requirement.

Massachusetts: Must pass twenty credits each term.

Michigan: Must pass twenty credits in previous and current semesters.

Minnesota: No statewide requirement.

Mississippi: Must pass three major subjects (English, math, science, social studies) to be eligible following year.

Missouri: Must pass four full-credit courses in previous semester.

Montana: Must pass four credit courses in previous semester.

Nebraska: Must pass fifteen credit hours in previous semester.

Nevada: Must be enrolled in four courses and may not be failing any course while playing sports.

New Hampshire: Must pass three credits in previous period.

New Jersey: Must pass twenty-three credit hours in previous year. Need 11.5 credits from the previous semester for second semester.

New Mexico: Must pass four courses and have a 1.60 on a 4.0 scale in previous grading period.

New York: No statewide requirement.

North Carolina: Must pass four courses and have seventy-five percent attendance in previous semester.

North Dakota: Must pass fifteen credit hours in previous semester.

Ohio: Must pass four full-credit courses in previous grading period.

Oklahoma: Must pass three full-credit courses in previous semester.

Oregon: Must pass at least four subjects in previous semester.

Pennsylvania: Must pass three full-credit courses in previous marking period (four next year).

Rhode Island: Must pass three academic subjects, excluding physical education, in previous marking period.

South Carolina: Must pass all required courses in previous semester.

South Dakota: Must pass twenty hours in previous semester.

Tennessee: Must pass four subjects in previous semester.

Texas: Must maintain grade of 70 in each class during six-week grading period to stay eligible for next six-week period.

Utah: Must not fail more than one class in a grading period and must make up failing grade following semester.

Vermont: No statewide requirement.

Virginia: Must pass four subjects in previous semester.

Washington: Must pass four full-credit subjects in previous semester.

West Virginia: Must have C average in previous semester.

Wisconsin: Must pass four full-credit courses in previous grading period.

Wyoming: Must pass four full-credit subjects in previous semester and be passing in current semester.

■ Rules and Regulations for Collegiate Athletics

As we discussed in the chapter Rules of the Game, it is important for you to have a thorough understanding of the many rules which govern intercollegiate athletics. Failure to abide by these regulations may seriously jeopardize your college athletic career.

There are three major national athletic associations that govern college sports: the National College Athletic Association (NCAA), the National Association of Intercollegiate Athletics (NAIA), and the National Junior College Athletic Association (NJCAA). Each of these associations has its own set of rules and regulations.

The NCAA governs over 400 schools, which are divided into three divisions. Division I and Division II schools are permitted to offer athletic scholarships, while Division III schools are not permitted to award scholarships based on athletic ability or potential. At some NCAA schools, teams in some sports may compete at one divisional level, while teams in other sports may compete at another divisional level.

NCAA Regulations

The *NCAA Guide for the College-Bound Student–Athlete, 1986–87** is a summary of the rules and regulations on recruiting and eligibil-

*This guide is reprinted by permission of the National Collegiate Athletic Association. Permission to reprint this material does not constitute endorsement of the Center for the Study of Sport in Society.

ity that are contained in the NCAA manual. This guide is reprinted on the following pages. The list is not a full explanation of these rules, and the rules are often changed. Additional questions should be sent to the NCAA at the following address:

National Collegiate Athletic Association
Legislative Services Department
P.O. Box 1906
Mission, KS 66201
(913) 384-3220

Introduction

The information contained in this publication is designed to provide a general summary of NCAA rules and regulations in easy-to-read form to prospective student-athletes, high school and junior college officials, representatives of NCAA member institutions, and other interested individuals. These guidelines relate primarily to the recruiting and eligibility of prospective student-athletes as well as to the financial aid they are permitted to receive. Please note that these rules do not apply to an individual's eligibility for high school or junior college participation.

This publication does not include all applicable provisions of NCAA legislation. Also, NCAA legislation may be subject to additional official interpretations when its application to specific situations is not readily apparent. Individuals should contact the NCAA national office if they have any questions about NCAA legislation.

Therefore, this pamphlet should be considered only as a guide to a general understanding of NCAA rules and regulations, with a view to avoiding involvement in a violation of NCAA legislation that might result in the loss of an individual's eligibility or disciplinary action against a member institution.

In addition, collegiate institutions and athletics conferences have rules that affect the recruiting and college eligibility of prospective student-athletes. In some instances, these rules may be more demanding than NCAA requirements. Accordingly, an institution's director of athletics, as well as the chief executive officer of the athletics conference in which an institution holds membership, should be contacted for interpretations of institutional and conference requirements.

WILFORD S. BAILEY
Secretary-Treasurer

JOHN R. DAVIS
President

Professional Rulings

An individual MAY:

1. Take or have taken pay for participation in one sport without affecting the individual's eligibility for intercollegiate competition in another sport.

2. Prior to enrolling in a collegiate institution,

   (a) try out (i.e., practice but not participate against outside competition) with a professional sports team;

   (b) receive actual and necessary expenses from any number of professional sports organizations for one visit per professional organization not in excess of 48 hours, and

   (c) be employed to give instruction in a particular sport.

3. Receive compensation authorized by the United States Olympic Committee to cover financial loss occurring as a result of absence from employment to prepare for or participate in the Olympic Games.

4. Borrow against future earnings potential from an established, accredited commercial lending institution only for the purposes of purchasing insurance (with no cash surrender value) against a disabling career-ending injury, provided no third party is involved in arrangements for securing the loan.

An individual SHALL NOT be eligible for intercollegiate competition in a sport if, in that sport, the individual:

1. Takes or has taken pay, or has accepted the promise of pay, in any form for participation.

2. Has entered into an agreement of any kind to compete in professional athletics or to negotiate a professional contract.

3. Requests that the individual's name be placed on the draft list of a professional sports organization.

4. Has directly or indirectly used athletic skill for pay in any form.

5. Signs or has ever signed a contract or commitment of any kind to play professional athletics, regardless of its legal enforceability or the consideration (if any) received.

6. Plays or has ever played on any professional athletics team.

7. Receives or has received, directly or indirectly, a salary, reimbursement of expenses (except as permitted on one visit prior to enrollment) or any other form of financial assistance from a professional sports organization based upon athletic skill or participation.

Professional Rulings

An individual SHALL NOT be eligible for intercollegiate athletics in any sport if the individual:

1. Agrees or has ever agreed to be represented generally, rather than with regard to a specific sport, by an agent or an organization in the marketing of the individual's athletic ability or reputation.

2. Subsequent to becoming a student-athlete in a collegiate institution, accepts remuneration for or permits the use of the individual's name or picture to directly advertise, recommend or promote the sale or use of a commercial product or service of any kind.

   [NOTE: Under certain limited conditions, a student-athlete involved prior to college enrollment in such promotional activities on the basis of reasons independent of athletics ability may continue to participate in such activities subsequent to enrollment in a member institution. Appropriate authorities of the NCAA or the student-athlete's institution should be contacted to review such as case.]

8. Participates on an outside sports team and receives, directly or indirectly, any salary, division or split of surplus, incentive payment or award, gratuity or comparable compensation, educational expenses or expense allowances other than actual and necessary travel and meal expenses for practice and games.

9. During regular enrollment in a collegiate institution, tries out (i.e., practices but does not participate against outside competition) with a professional sports organization during any part of the regular academic year at the individual's institution.

10. Agrees or has ever agreed to be represented by an agent or an organization in the marketing of the individual's athletic ability or reputation.

11. Is placed for compensation by an individual, agency or organization in a collegiate institution as a recipient of institutional, athletically related financial aid.

Financial Aid

A student MAY:

1. Receive unearned athletically related financial aid administered by the institution for any regular term the student is in attendance, provided it does not exceed that amount equal to tuition and fees, room and board, and required course-related books, and provided the student is not under contract to or currently receive compensation from a professional sports organization.

2. Receive unearned athletically related financial aid awarded only by an institution's regular financial aid committee for a maximum period of one year, it being understood that such aid may be renewed for additional, maximum one-year periods by the institution while the recipient is an undergraduate or a graduate student with remaining eligibility.

3. Receive income from employment during term time or nonathletics grants for educational purposes in combination with unearned athletically related financial aid, provided the total from all sources does not exceed the actual cost of room and board, tuition and fees, and required course-related books. Income from employment during official institutional vacation periods need not be considered in this limit.

4. Receive athletically related financial assistance from an outside organization or agency through an established and continuing program for recognition of outstanding high school graduates on the basis of the recipient's past performance and overall record as measured by established criteria,

provided disbursement of the assistance is through the member institution, the recipient's choice of institution is not restricted by the donor, the donor is not a representative of a member institution's athletics interests, the award does not exceed the actual cost of room and board, tuition and fees, and required course-related books, and the award is provided to the recipient on only one occasion.

A student SHALL NOT:

1. Receive athletically related financial aid from an NCAA member institution to attend its summer term prior to the student's initial enrollment as a regular student during the regular academic year at the institution. This prohibition does not apply to a summer orientation program for which participation (by both athletes and nonathletes) is required and financial aid is administered on the same basis for all participants in the program.

2. Receive financial aid other than that administered by the institution if the aid has any relationship whatsoever to athletic ability. This prohibition shall not apply to earnings from a professional organization in a sport other than the student's collegiate sport.

3. Receive an extra benefit not available to members of the student body in general.

[NOTE: Division III member institutions generally may not award financial aid to student-athletes except on a showing of financial need by the recipient.]

General Principles of Eligibility

A prospective student-athlete SHALL BE SUBJECT TO LOSS OF ELIGIBILITY if the prospect:

1. Following completion of high school eligibility in the sport and prior to graduation from high school, participates in an all-star football or basketball contest that is not specifically approved either by the appropriate state high school athletics association or, if interstate, by the NCAA All-Star High School Games Committee, or participates in more than two approved all-star football contests or more than two approved all-star basketball contests.

2. Following graduation from high school and prior to enrollment in college, participates in an interstate football or basketball contest that was not specifically approved by the NCAA All-Star High School Games Committee.

3. Violates NCAA legislation related to the receipt of financial assistance.

4. Is guilty of fraudulence in connection with an entrance or placement examination.

5. Exhibits dishonesty in evading or violating NCAA regulations.

6. Is knowingly involved in arrangements for fraudulent academic credit or false transcripts.

7. Knowingly furnishes the NCAA or the individual's institution false or misleading information concerning the individual's involvement in or knowledge of a violation of an NCAA regulation.

8. Enrolls in a member institution that violated NCAA regulations in recruiting the individual.

9. Knowingly provides information to assist individuals involved in organized gambling activities concerning intercollegiate athletics competition, solicits a bet on any intercollegiate team, accepts a bet on any team representing the institution or participates in any gambling involving intercollegiate athletics through a bookmaker, a parlay card or any other method employed by organized gambling.

Recruiting Rules and Regulations

DEFINITIONS:

1. An individual, who is not enrolled in the member institution and has not exhausted eligibility for intercollegiate athletics under NCAA regulations, becomes a "prospective" student-athlete if a member institution's athletics staff member or other representative of its athletics interests:

   (a) provides transportation for the individual to visit the campus;

   (b) entertains the individual in any way on the campus, except that the institution may make available to the prospect a complimentary admission to an athletics contest;

   (c) initiates or arranges telephone contact with the individual or a member of the individual's family (or guardian) for the purpose of recruiting;

   (d) visits the individual or a member of the individual's family (or guardian) for the purpose of recruiting, or

   (e) entertains members of the family (or guardian) of the individual on its campus.

2. An individual becomes a "representative of an institution's athletics interests" when an institutional staff member requests the individual to recruit a particular prospect or has knowledge that the individual is recruiting a prospect. Further, an institution's responsibility for the conduct of its intercollegiate athletics program includes responsibility for the acts of an individual when the institution's executive or athletics administration has knowledge that such an individual is promoting the institution's intercollegiate athletics program. Once a person is identified as a representative, it is presumed the person retains that identity.

ATTENTION prospective student-athletes, their parents, high school and junior college coaches:

If an NCAA college coach or a representative of any NCAA member institution's athletics interests attempts to recruit a prospective student-athlete with the offer of gifts, improper aid or other improper inducements, please report the matter to the NCAA. Do not permit prospective student-athletes to jeopardize their collegiate eligibility through involvement in violations of NCAA legislation.

REMEMBER:

1. In recruiting a prospective student-athlete, a representative of an institution's athletics interests is governed by the same requirements as those placed upon institutional athletics staff members; further, an institution is responsible for the actions of its athletics representatives. **Please note that a representative of the athletics interests of a Division I or Division II member institution (as defined in Paragraph No. 2, Page No. 6) is not permitted to make in-person, off-campus recruiting contacts.**

Recruiting Rules and Regulations

2. A prospective student-athlete remains a prospect even after signing a letter of intent or tender to attend a certain institution, and both the institution and the prospect are governed by NCAA recruiting legislation until:

   (a) the prospect reports for regular squad practice at a collegiate institution, and such reporting is certified by the institution's director of athletics; or

   (b) the institution's registrar or director of admissions certifies that the prospect was officially registered and enrolled at the institution on the opening day of classes for any regular term, or

   (c) the prospect attends a class or classes in any regular term.

3. For a prospect to receive one expense-paid visit to a member institution's campus for a period not to exceed 48 hours. Only actual round-trip transportation by direct route between the student's home (or junior college, preparatory school or high school in which the prospect is enrolled) and the institution's campus may be paid. Such a visit may not occur until after the beginning of classes for the prospect's senior year in high school, and a prospect may not accept expense-paid visits to more than a total of five Division I and Division II member institutions. If commercial air transportation is used, the fare may not exceed tourist (or comparable) class.

4. For a member institution to reimburse a prospect for actual and necessary transportation expenses incurred in traveling on his or her one paid visit to an institution's campus in the automobile of the prospect or the prospect's family even though the prospect is accompanied by relatives or friends on the trip.

5. For a member institution to entertain the parents (or legal guardians) or spouse of a prospect one time only on the institution's campus when they accompany the prospect on the prospect's one paid campus visit.

6. For a member institution to house and entertain a prospect, the prospect's parents (or legal guardians) or spouse during the one paid campus visit only in the area within a 30-mile radius of the institution's main campus and only at a scale

In recruiting a prospective student-athlete, it IS PERMISSIBLE:

1. For a bona fide alumni organization of a member institution (which does not necessarily include all athletics booster groups) to entertain prospects at luncheons, teas or dinners at which prospective students (athletes and nonathletes) of that immediate locale are guests.

2. For a member institution to request a prospect to undergo a medical examination through the institution's regular team physician at the time of the prospect's visit to the campus to determine the prospect's medical qualifications for athletic competition.

comparable to that of normal student life.

7. For a member institution's athletics staff member to make a total of three in-person contacts (at sites other than the prospect's educational institution) with a prospect, the prospect's relatives or legal guardian at any location off the collegiate institution's campus for recruiting purposes; however, they shall not expend any funds for entertainment of the prospect, the prospect's relatives or friends.

In sports other than Division I football, three additional in-person, off-campus contacts per prospect shall be permitted by each member institution on the grounds of the prospect's educational institution and with the approval of that institution's executive officer or authorized representative.

Effective August 1, 1986, in Division I football only, one additional in-person, off-campus contact per prospect shall be permitted during each week of the appropriate contact period by each member institution on the grounds of the prospect's educational institution and with the approval of that institution's executive officer. However, a member institution may visit a prospect's educational institution on no more than one occasion during a particular week, regardless of the total number of recruited prospects enrolled in the same institution.

Once a prospective student-athlete has signed a National Letter of Intent with a Division I or II member institution, there shall be no limit (subsequent to the occasion of the signing) on off-campus recruiting contacts with the prospect, the prospect's relatives or legal guardian by the institution with which the prospect has signed.

Any face-to-face encounter that is by prearrangement or that takes place on the grounds of the prospect's educational institution or at the sites of organized competition and practice involving the prospect or the team (i.e., high school, preparatory school, junior college or all-star team) the prospect represents shall be counted toward the limit on permissible in-person, off-campus recruiting contacts, regardless of the conversation that occurs.

A representative of the athletics interests of a Division I or Division II member institution is not permitted to make in-person, off-campus recruiting contacts.

In-person, off-campus contacts with prospects shall be permissible in the sport of football only during the period between December 1 (or the date of the completion of the prospect's final high school or junior college contest, if it occurs thereafter) and March 1, except that no member of a Division I institution's coaching staff shall contact a prospect on or off the institution's campus during the annual convention of the American Football Coaches Association.

In the sport of men's basketball, in-person, off-campus contacts with prospects shall be permis-

Recruiting Rules and Regulations

sible only during the period between September 1 and October 10 and the period between March 1 (or the date of the completion of the prospect's final high school or junior college contest, if it occurs thereafter) and May 15, except that no member of a Division I or Division II institution's coaching staff shall contact a prospect on or off the institution's campus during the period beginning with the Thursday prior to the National Collegiate Division I Men's Basketball Championship game and ending at noon on the Tuesday after the game.

In addition, no in-person contact with a prospect shall be made by a member of a Division I institution's coaching staff in the sport of women's basketball during the period beginning with the Wednesday prior to the National Collegiate Division I Women's Basketball Championship game and ending at noon on the Monday after the game. Further, no in-person contact with a prospect shall be made by a member of a Division I institution's coaching staff in the sports of ice hockey, women's gymnastics and women's volleyball, respectively, during the periods beginning with the Wednesday prior to the Division I championships finals in each of those sports and ending at noon on the Sunday after the ice hockey and gymnastics championships and noon the day after the volleyball championship game, respectively.

[NOTE: The limitations on the number of off- campus recruiting contacts, the prohibition against off-campus recruiting contacts by representatives of athletics interests and the dates of the football and basketball recruiting seasons do not apply to Division III member institutions.]

8. For a prospect to visit a member institution's campus as many times as it is desirable at the prospect's own expense, it being understood that on such visits the institution may only provide a maximum of three complimentary admissions to a campus athletics event in which the institution's intercollegiate team competes to admit the prospect and those accompanying the prospect on the visit. Further, effective September 1, 1986, the institution may provide transportation during such a visit to the prospect, when accompanied by an institutional staff member, only to view off-campus practice and competition sites within a 30-mile radius of the institution's campus. In addition, during such a visit to a Division II or Division III institution, the institution may provide a meal to the prospect in the institution's on-campus student dining facilities. Any entertainment except the three complimentary admissions and the meal at a Division II or Division III institution shall cause the visit to be considered an expense-paid visit, only one of which is permissible to each member institution's campus.

9. For a member institution to pay the actual cost (provided it is necessary and reasonable) of the room and board expenses incurred by a prospect

Recruiting Rules and Regulations

in traveling between the prospect's home and the campus on the prospect's one official expense-paid visit.

10. For an athletics staff member or athletics representative to describe the member institution's grant-in-aid program and recommend a prospect for such aid, it being understood that only an institution's regular financial aid authority can actually award aid; further, this authority must provide the prospect with a written statement setting forth the amount, duration, conditions and terms thereof before the award of aid is official.

11. For a prospect to receive an expense-paid visit to a member institution's campus (in addition to the one athletically related paid visit), provided it is for a purpose having nothing whatsoever to do with athletics recruitment by that institution (e.g., band trip, senior day, fraternity or sorority weekend) and provided the institution's athletics department or athletics representatives are not involved in any way in the arrangements for the visit.

12. Effective August 1, 1986, for a member institution's staff member to provide transportation for the prospective student-athlete to the campus from the bus or train station or major airport nearest the campus on the occasion of the student-athlete's initial arrival at the institution to attend classes.

In recruiting a prospective student-athlete, it is NOT PERMISSIBLE:

1. To give, offer or be involved, directly or indirectly, in making arrangements for a prospect, the prospect's relatives or friends to receive financial aid or equivalent inducements, regardless of whether similar financial aid, benefits or arrangements are available to prospective students in general, their relatives or friends, except as permitted by the NCAA, the institution and the athletics conference of which an institution is a member. Included as improper inducements are such things as cash; the promise of employment after college graduation; special discounts or payment arrangements on loans, employment of the relatives of a prospect, provision of loans to the relatives or friends of a prospect, involvement in arrangements for professional and personal services, purchases or charges; regular or periodic use of an automobile; transportation to or from a summer job or to any site other than the institution's campus on an official visit; signing or cosigning a note for a loan; the loan or gift of money or other tangible items (e.g., clothes, cars, jewelry, electronic equipment); guarantees of bond; purchase of items or services from a prospect or the prospect's family at inflated prices; transportation to enroll; any financial aid other than that administered by a member institution's regular scholarship awards authority, and the promise of financial aid for a period beyond

one year or for a postgraduate education.

2. To make an in-person, off-campus recruiting contact with a prospective student-athlete, the prospect's relatives or legal guardian before the completion of the prospect's junior year in high school.

3. To make in-person recruiting contacts with a prospect, the prospect's relatives or legal guardian other than those specifically permitted as set forth in Paragraph No. 7 beginning on Page No. 8.

   [NOTE: The limitations on the number of off-campus recruiting contacts and the dates of the football and basketball recruiting seasons do not apply to Division III member institutions.]

4. For a Division I member institution to make (effective August 1, 1986) an in-person, off-campus recruiting contact with a high school nonqualifier enrolled during the first year of junior college.

5. For a representative of the athletics interests (as defined in Paragraph No. 2, Page No. 6) of a Division I or Division II member institution to make in-person, off-campus recruiting contacts with a prospect or the prospect's relatives or legal guardian.

6. To contact a prospect at the prospect's school (high school, preparatory school or junior college) without permission from the institution's executive officer or an authorized representative.

7. To contact a prospect at the site of the prospect's school's (high school, preparatory school or junior college) athletics competition if the prospect is participating or preparing to participate in a contest or competition. No such contact shall be made with the prospect prior to the competition on the day of competition and then not until the prospect has completed the competition (including all games of a tournament or event extended over several days) and then has been released by the prospect's school authority, dresses and departs the dressing room or meeting room facility.

8. For a member of a Division I or Division II institution's coaching staff to contact a prospect in the sports of football or basketball on or off its campus at the site of practice or competition for a high school all-star game outside the permissible contact periods set forth in Paragraph No. 7 beginning on Page No. 8.

9. To publicize or arrange publicity of the commitment of a prospect to attend an institution, other than to publicize a prospect's acceptance of its tender of financial assistance through the normal media outlets of the institution and the prospect's current and former educational institutions. Press conferences, receptions, dinners, or similar meetings held for the purpose of making such announcements are expressly prohibited.

Recruiting Rules and Regulations

10. For the head football coach of a Division I-A member institution to be present when an off-campus site is utilized to obtain the prospect's signature on a National Letter of Intent or signed acceptance of the institution's or conference's financial aid statement or written tender of financial assistance.

11. To publicize or arrange publicity of the visit of a prospect to the institution's campus.

12. For a prospect or the prospect's high school, college preparatory school or junior college coach to appear on a radio or television program conducted by a college coach, a program in which the college coach is participating, or a program for which a member of the athletics staff of a collegiate institution has been instrumental in arranging the appearance of the prospect or the prospect's coach, or related program material.

13. For any agency, group of individuals or organization outside the NCAA member institution to administer or expend funds for recruiting prospects in any way, including the transportation and entertainment of and the giving of gifts or services to a prospect, the prospect's relatives or friends.

14. For two or more persons to pool resources for recruiting a prospect.

15. For company funds to be used to pay expenses (including the provision of a company airplane) incurred in transporting a prospect to visit a campus or for any other recruiting expenses.

16. For a member institution to conduct or have conducted in its behalf on its campus or elsewhere, any athletics practice session, tryout or test in which a prospect reveals, demonstrates or displays athletic ability.

17. For a coach of an NCAA member institution to participate in any coaching school or sports camp that includes as a participant any individual who is eligible for admission to a member institution or has started classes for the senior year of high school.

18. For a high school, preparatory school or junior college athletics award winner to be employed by or receive free or reduced-cost admission to any sports camp operated by an NCAA member institution or member of its athletics staff.

19. For a prospect to receive more than one expense-paid visit to the institution's campus.

20. For a Division I member institution to provide (effective August 1, 1986) an expense-paid visit to its campus to a high school nonqualifier enrolled during the first year of junior college.

21. For a member institution or athletics representative to pay or arrange the payment of transportation costs incurred by relatives or friends of a prospect to visit an institution's campus or elsewhere.

22. For a member institution's athletics representative to transport the relatives or friends of a prospect to visit the campus or elsewhere in the representative's own vehicle.

Recruiting Rules and Regulations

23. For a member institution to entertain a prospect, the prospect's parents or spouse anywhere except one time within a 30-mile radius of the institution's main campus at a scale comparable to student life. A Division I or Division II member institution's athletics representative may be involved in a prospect's entertainment only on the institution's campus.

24. For a member institution or athletics representative to entertain the friends of a prospect at any site.

25. For a member institution or its athletics representatives to offer, provide or arrange financial assistance for a prospect to pay in whole or in part the costs of the prospect's educational or other expenses for any period prior to the prospect's regular enrollment or to obtain a postgraduate degree.

26. For a prospect to receive cash or the use of an automobile during a campus visit.

27. For a prospect to be excessively entertained during a campus visit or at any other time.

28. For a member institution or its athletics representative to pay any costs incurred by an athletics talent scout or representative of its athletics interests in studying or recruiting a prospect.

29. For a member institution or its athletics representatives to reimburse the coach of a prospect for expenses incurred in transporting a prospect to visit the campus.

30. For a member institution or its athletics representative to entertain high school, preparatory school or junior college coaches at any location except on the institution's campus, or in the community in which the institution is located. Such permissible entertainment shall be limited to two tickets to home athletics contests, but shall not include food and refreshments, room expenses or the cost of transportation to and from the campus.

31. For a member institution or its athletics representatives to provide free admission to its away-from-home athletics contests to prospects, their friends or relatives.

Eligibility

NCAA Bylaws 5-1 and 5-6-(b) [initial eligibility standard]

High School Students:

Effective August 1, 1986, in order to be eligible for practice, participation in regular-season competition and athletically related financial aid during the first academic year in residence, a student entering a Division I NCAA member institution directly out of high school must have:

(i) Graduated from high school with a minimum grade-point average of 2.000 (based on a maximum of 4.000) in a core curriculum of at least 11 academic full-year courses, including at least three in English, two in mathematics, two in social science and two in natural or physical science (including at least one laboratory class, if offered by the high school) as well as a 700 combined score on the SAT verbal and math sections or a 15 composite score on the ACT; or:

(ii) Presented more than the minimum standard set forth in the preceding paragraph for either the core-curriculum grade-point average or required test score, in which case eligibility may be established during the specified time periods on the basis of the following eligibility indices:

For those freshmen entering subsequent to August 1, 1986, and prior to August 1, 1987:

GPA	SAT	ACT
2.200-above	660	13
2.100-2.199	680	14
2.000-2.099	700	15
1.900-1.999	720	16
1.800-1.899	740	17

For those freshmen entering subsequent to August 1, 1987, and prior to August 1, 1988:

GPA	SAT	ACT
2.100-above	680	14
2.000-2.099	700	15
1.900-1.999	720	16

Junior College Transfer Students:

1. In order to be eligible for practice, regular-season competition and athletically related financial aid during the first academic year in residence at a Division I NCAA member institution, a junior college transfer student who graduated from high school having met the requirements noted in paragraphs (i) or (ii), must satisfy the transfer and eligibility requirements of the institution as well as its athletics conference. For such a student who entered a junior college prior to August 1, 1984, to be immediately eligible for competition at a Division I NCAA member institution, the student must be a junior college graduate or present a minimum of 24 semester hours or 36 quarter hours of transferable degree credit with an accumulative minimum grade-point average of 2.000 and have spent at least two semesters or three quarters in residence at the junior college (excluding summer sessions).

In addition, such a student who entered a junior college subsequent to August 1, 1984, must meet the aforementioned requirements and must have completed satisfactorily an average of at least 12

Eligibility

semester hours or quarter hours of credit during each academic term of attendance.

For such a student first entering a junior college subsequent to August 1, 1985, in order to be immediately eligible at a Division I institution, the student must: (1) be a junior college graduate and have completed satisfactorily a minimum of 48 semester or 72 quarter hours of transferable degree credit acceptable toward any baccalaureate degree program at the certifying institution, or (2) present a minimum of 24 semester hours or 36 quarter hours of transferable degree credit with an accumulative minimum grade-point average of 2.000, have completed satisfactorily an average of at least 12 semester or quarter hours of transferable degree credit acceptable toward any baccalaureate degree program at the certifying institution during each academic term of attendance and have spent at least two semesters or three quarters in residence at the junior college (excluding summer sessions).

2. In order to be eligible for practice, competition and athletically related aid during the first year in residence at a Division I NCAA member institution, a junior college transfer student who, upon graduation from high school, failed to meet the initial eligibility standard noted on Page 14, must graduate from a junior college with an associate or equivalent degree in an academic curriculum and, for those students first entering junior college subsequent to August 1, 1984, must have satisfactorily completed a minimum of 48 semester or 72 quarter hours of transferable degree credit acceptable toward any baccalaureate degree program at the certifying Division I institution.

3. To be immediately eligible for competition at a Division II or Division III NCAA member institution (regardless of the student's high school academic record), the junior college transfer student must graduate from the junior college or present a minimum of 24 semester hours or 36 quarter hours of transferable degree credit with an accumulative minimum grade-point average of 2.000 and have spent at least two semesters or three quarters in residence at the junior college (excluding summer sessions).

4. A student who transfers to an NCAA member institution from a junior college after transferring from any four-year college must complete one calendar year of residence at the NCAA member institution in order to be eligible for competition, unless the student has completed a minimum of 24 semester or 36 quarter hours at the junior college following the student's transfer from the four-year college and also has graduated from the junior college, and one calendar year has elapsed since the transfer from the first four-year college. Such a student transferring to a Division III member institution need not graduate from the junior college but must meet the other requirements set forth in this paragraph.

Eligibility

5. When a student has been in residence at two or more junior colleges, the terms of residence at all junior colleges may be combined in order to satisfy the residence requirements described in Paragraph Nos. 1, 2 and 3 of this section. All grades earned by the student in courses that would be transferable to the NCAA member institution must be included in determining whether the student has earned the required average.

6. A transfer student from a junior college is not eligible for competition in a sport if the student-athlete has competed at the junior college in that sport during the same academic year.

7. A transfer student from a junior college is not subject to the residence requirement for NCAA championships or postseason football competition if the NCAA Eligibility Committee concludes that the student changed institutions in order to continue participation in a sport because the student's junior college dropped the sport from its intercollegiate program or never sponsored the sport on the intercollegiate level while the student was in attendance at the institution, provided the student never attended any other collegiate institution that offered intercollegiate competition in that particular sport and provided the student earned at least a minimum 2.000 grade-point average at the junior college.

8. A transfer student from a junior college to a Division II or Division III member institution is not subject to the residence requirement for competition in a particular sport if the student-athlete was not recruited, has not received athletically related financial aid, has neither practiced nor competed in intercollegiate athletics prior to transfer and was eligible for admission to the certifying institution prior to initial enrollment in the junior college.

9. A transfer student from a junior college to a Division III member institution is not subject to the residence requirement for competition in a particular sport if the student has not competed in that sport at the previous institution or has not competed in that sport for a period of one year immediately prior to the date on which the student begins participation (practice or competition) in that sport at the certifying institution and the student has entered the certifying institution prior to the start of the regular-season competition in that sport and provided the student earned at least a minimum 2.000 grade-point average at the junior college.

[NOTE: Divisions II and III member institutions do not apply Bylaw 5-6-(b) [initial eligibility standard] to the eligibility of either freshmen or junior college transfer students for practice, regular-season participation or athletically related financial aid and therefore such eligibility is determined on the basis of institutional and conference regulations.

In order to be eligible for practice, participation in regular-season competition and athletically related financial aid, an entering freshman as well as a junior college transfer student must also satisfy the transfer and eligibility rules of the member institution in which the individual enrolls and the athletics conference in which the institution holds membership as well as possibly numerous other NCAA individual eligibility rules.]

Division I Only:

For students enrolling in Division I institutions only, any participation by a student as an individual or as a representative of any team in organized competition in a sport during each 12-month period after the student's 20th birthday and prior to matriculation at a member institution shall count as one year of varsity competition in that sport unless such participation occurs during time spent in the U.S. armed services.

NOTE: High school students who will enter Division I member institutions after August 1, 1986, and are interested in obtaining additional information concerning high school academic requirements for initial athletics eligibility and receipt of athletically related financial aid at Division I member institutions may wish to write to the NCAA national office and request the "Guide to the new college freshman eligibility requirements for NCAA Division I institutions."

NOTE: Prior to participating in intercollegiate competition during each academic year in which the student-athlete is enrolled in an NCAA member institution, the student-athlete must sign a statement in which information related to the student-athlete's eligibility, recruitment, financial aid and amateur status under the governing legislation of the NCAA is reported. Accordingly, a prospective student-athlete should take care not to jeopardize collegiate eligibility through involvement in violations of NCAA legislation.

NOTE: Student-athletes who are considering a professional athletics career may wish to obtain a copy of the booklet "A Career in Professional Sports: Guidelines that Make Dollars and Sense" by writing to the NCAA national office.

Inasmuch as NCAA eligibility rules are oftentimes complex as they might apply to certain students, this guide should not be relied upon exclusively and the NCAA national office should be contacted for proper interpretations in specific cases. Inquiries should be addressed to the NCAA legislative services staff at the address that appears on the inside front cover.

Non-NCAA Regulations

The NAIA governs over 500 colleges, while the NJCAA governs most of the nation's junior college athletic programs. Once again, it is important for you to keep in mind that the NAIA and the NJCAA have their own separate sets of rules and regulations.

Should you require any information concerning recruiting rules or eligibility requirements for schools within the NAIA or NJCAA, you can contact these organizations at the addresses listed below.

National Association for Intercollegiate Athletics (NAIA)
1221 Baltimore Avenue
Kansas City, MO 64104
(816) 842-5050

National Junior College Athletic Association (NJCAA)
P.O.Box 1586
Hutchinson, KS 67504
(316) 665-3500

■ Title IX: Information and Assistance

If you are a female athlete, you can write to the following organizations for help with a sex discrimination complaint. These organizations will also answer your questions about equal opportunities in sports or in education.

United States Department of Education
Office for Civil Rights
Mary E. Switzer Building
330 C. Street, S.W.
Washington, DC 20202
(202) 245-3192

Women's Equity Action League
805 15th Street NW
Washington, DC 20005
(202) 898-1588

Women's Law Center
1616 P Street NW
Suite 100
Washington, DC 20036
(202) 328-5160

Women's Sports Foundation
195 Moulton Street
San Francisco, CA 94123
(415) 563-6266

■ Women's Scholarship Guide

This guide comes from the Women's Sports Foundation.* It gives a state-by-state list of the colleges and universities that offer scholarships. Each entry includes the school's name, address, and telephone number; the name and title of the person to contact for scholarship information; and the sports in which scholarships are available.

*This material is reprinted courtesy of the Women's Sports Foundation.

KEY TO SPORTS ABBREVIATIONS

ARCH	Archery	**RD**	Rodeo
BAD	Badminton	**SKI**	Skiing
BB	Basketball	**SOC**	Soccer
B	Bowling	**SB**	Softball
CREW	Crew	**S**	Swimming
CC	Cross-country	**S&D**	Swimming and diving
FENC	Fencing		
FH	Field hockey	**SYNC**	Synchronized swimming
G	Golf		
GYM	Gymnastics	**TEN**	Tennis
IH	Ice hockey	**T**	Track
LAX	Lacrosse	**T&F**	Track and Field
RIFLE	Rifle	**VB**	Volleyball

ALABAMA

ALABAMA A&M UNIVERSITY, Betty Kelly Austin, Assistant Athletic Director, Athletic Dept., Huntsville, AL 35762, (205) 859-7362. NCAA. 12 **BB**, 7 **S&D**, 14 **T&F**, 10 **VB**: partial.

ALABAMA CHRISTIAN COLLEGE, Barbara Main, Coach, 5345 Atlanta Hwy., Montgomery, AL 36193, (205) 272-5820. NAIA. 6 **TEN**: full.

ALABAMA STATE UNIVERSITY, Hoyt Taylor, Director of Athletics, 915 S. Jackson St., Montgomery, AL 36195, (205) 293-4472. NCAA. 13 **BB**, 4 **TEN**, 14 **T&F**, 8 **VB**: full.

AUBURN UNIVERSITY, Joe Ciampi, Assistant Athletic Director, Box 351, Auburn, AL 36849, (205) 826-4750. NCAA, SEC, I. 15 **BB**, 6 **G**, 10 **GYM**, 13 **S&D**, 8 **TEN**, 16 **T&F**: full.

BIRMINGHAM-SOUTHERN COLLEGE, Ann Dielen, Coach, 800 Eighth Ave. West, Birmingham, AL 35254, (205) 956-6840. NAIA, Southern States. 5 **TEN**: full.

35632, (205) 766-4100 ext. 397. NCAA. 9 **BB**, 3 **TEN**, 5 **VB**: full.

UNIVERSITY OF SOUTH ALABAMA, Joe Gottfried, Athletic Director, Mobile, AL 36688, (205) 460-7121. NCAA. 1 **BB**, 5 **TEN**, 3 **T&F**, 9 **VB**: partial. 10 **BB**, 1 **TEN**: full.

ALASKA

UNIVERSITY OF ALASKA (ANCHORAGE), Ron Petro, Director of Athletics, 3211 Providence Dr., Anchorage, AK 99508, (907) 786-1230. NCAA, CD, II. 11 **BB**, 2 **RIFLE**, 8 **SKI**, 2 **CC**, 3 **GYM**, 5 **VB**: partial. 3 **GYM**: partial. 3 **GYM**, 2 **VB**: full.

UNIVERSITY OF ALASKA (FAIRBANKS), Karen J. Morris, Assistant Athletic Director, 105 Patty Bldg., Fairbanks, AK 99775-0240, (907) 474-7205. NCAA, Continental Divide, II. 3 **RIFLE**, 6 **SKI**, 4 **S&D**: partial. 8 **BB**, 6 **VB**: full.

ARIZONA

ARKANSAS

ARKANSAS COLLEGE, Van Compton, Coach, Batesville, AR 72501, (501) 793-9813. NAIA. 12 **BB**: full.

ARKANSAS STATE UNIVERSITY, Bill Davidson, Associate Athletic Director, Box 1000, State University, AR 72467, (501) 972-2082. NCAA. 15 **BB**, 2 **SB**, 4 **TEN**, 4 **T&F**, 4 **VB**: full.

ARKANSAS STATE UNIVERSITY (BEEBE), Napolean Cross, Coach, Beebe, AR 72012, (501) 882-6452. NJCAA. 5 **BB**: full.

ARKANSAS TECH UNIVERSITY, Jime Dicherson, Coach, Hwy. 7, Russellville, AR 72801, (501) 968-0285. NAIA. 12 **BB**, 12 **VB**: full.

HARDING UNIVERSITY, Harry Olree, Athletic Director, Box 765, Searcy, AR 72143, (501) 268-6161 ext. 249. NAIA, AIC, I. 12 **BB**, 12 **VB**: partial. **CC**, **T&F**: non-scholarship.

HENDERSON STATE UNIVERSITY, Bettye Wallace, Women's Athletic Director, Box 7572, Arkadelphia, AR 71923, (501) 246-5511 ext. 320. NAIA, AIC. 12 **BB**, 12 **VB**: full. **TEN**: non-scholarship.

HENDRIX COLLEGE, Bob Courtway, Athletic Director, Conway, AR 72032, (501) 450-1313. NAIA. 6 **VB**: partial.

SOUTHERN ARKANSAS UNIVERSITY, W.T. Watson, Athletic Director, Magnolia, AR 71753, (501) 234-5120 ext. 360. NAIA. 12 **BB**, 12 **VB**: full.

SOUTHERN ARKANSAS UNIVERSITY (Tech Branch), Ira Green, Athletic Director, Sau-Tech Station, Camden, AR 71701, (501) 574-4543. NJCAA. 10 **GYM**: full.

SOUTHERN BAPTIST COLLEGE, Carol Halford, Women's Athletic Director, Box 387, Walnut Ridge, AR 72476, (501) 886-6741 ext. 153. NJCAA. 12 **BB**: partial to full.

UNIVERSITY OF ARKANSAS (FAYETTE-VILLE), Ruth Cohoon, Women's Athletic

CALIFORNIA POLYTECHNIC STATE UNIVERSITY (SAN LUIS OBISPO), Marilyn McNeil, Primary Women's Administrator, San Luis Obispo, CA 93407, (805) 546-2923. NCAA. 6 **BB**, 1 **SB**, 6 **T&F**, 10 **VB**: full.

CALIFORNIA STATE POLYTECHNIC UNIVERSITY (POMONA), Darlene May, Sports Coordinator, 3801 W. Temple, Pomona, CA 91768, (714) 598-4611. NCAA. 12 **BB**, 4 **GYM**, 3 **SOC**, 6 **SB**, 6 **TEN**, 6 **T&F**, 6 **VB**: partial.

CALIFORNIA STATE UNIVERSITY (BAKERSFIELD), Gloria Friedman, Assistant Athletic Director, 9001 Stockdale Hwy., Bakersfield, CA 93309, (805) 833-2189. NCAA. **CC**, **SB**, **S&D**, **TEN**, **T&F**, **VB**: partial to full.

CALIFORNIA STATE UNIVERSITY (DOMINGUEZ HILLS), Susan Carberry, Athletic Director, 100 E. Victoria St., Dominguez Hills, CA 90747, (213) 516-3893. NCAA. 12 **BB**, 12 **SOC**, 15 **SB**, 6 **T&F**, 12 **VB**: partial.

CALIFORNIA STATE UNIVERSITY (FULLERTON), Coach of Specific Sport, 800 N. State College St., Fullerton, CA 92634, (714) 773-3050. NCAA. 14 **BB**, 5 **CC**, 5 **G**, 18 **SB**, 5 **TEN**, 12 **VB**: partial to full. 10 **GYM**: full.

CALIFORNIA STATE UNIVERSITY (LONG BEACH), Kay Don, Primary Women's Administrator, 1250 Bellflower Bl., Long Beach, CA 90840, (213) 498-4655. NCAA, PCAA, I. 1 **CC**, 2 **G**, 3 **GYM**, 2 **SOC**, 1 **SB**, 1 **S&D**, 1 **TEN**: partial. 3 **BB**, 2 **SB**, 1 **S&D**, 2 **TEN**, 2 **T&F**, 3 **VB**: full.

CALIFORNIA STATE UNIVERSITY (LOS ANGELES), Carol M. Dunn, Associate Athletic Director, 5151 State University Dr., Los Angeles, CA 90032, (213) 224-3254. NCAA. 6 **BAD**, 3 **S&D**, 3 **TEN**, 7 **T&F**, 30 **VB**: partial. 6 **BAD**, 2 **S&D**, 2 **TEN**, 7 **T&F**, 5 **VB**: full.

CALIFORNIA STATE UNIVERSITY (NORTHRIDGE), Judith M. Brame, Athletic Director, 18111 Nordhoff, Northridge, CA

JACKSONVILLE STATE UNIVERSITY, Jerry Cole, Athletic Director, Physical Education Dept., Jacksonville, AL 36265, (205) 435-9820 ext. 365. NCAA. 10 BB: full. 10 GOLF, 6 TEN, 12 VB: partial.

LIVINGSTON UNIVERSITY, Dr. Jim Pate, Director of Athletics, Station 23, Livingston, AL 35470, (205) 652-9661. NCAA, Gulf South Conference, II. 7.5 BB, 1.3 SB, 1.3 TEN, 1.3 VB: full.

SPRING HILL COLLEGE, Drayton Miller, Athletic Director, 4000 Dauphin St., Mobile, AL 36608, (205) 460-2346. NAIA, Gulf Coast Athletic. 3 BB, 2 TEN: partial. 4 BB: partial.

TALLADEGA COLLEGE, James Adams, Athletic Director, 627 W. Battle St., Talladega, AL 35160, (205) 362-0206 ext. 290. NAIA. 9 BB: full.

TROY STATE UNIVERSITY, Joyce Sorrell, Women's Athletic Coordinator, Davis Field House, Troy, AL 36082, (205) 566-3000 ext. 480. NCAA. 5 G, 12 T&F, 8 VB: partial. 8 BB: full.

TUSKEGEE INSTITUTE, Tiny Laster, Women's Athletic Coordinator, Logan Hall, Tuskegee, AL 36088, (205) 727-8855/8849. NCAA, SIAC, II. 6 BB, 2 TEN, 4 T&F, 4 VB: partial.

UNIVERSITY OF ALABAMA, Sarah Patterson, Assistant Athletic Director, Box 6449, University, AL 35486, (205) 348-7077. NCAA, Southeastern Conference, I. 15 BB, 6 G, 10 GYM, 14 S&D, 8 TEN, 16 T&F: full.

UNIVERSITY OF ALABAMA (HUNTSVILLE), Paul Brand, Athletic Director, 205 Spragins Hall, Room 205, Huntsville, AL 35899, (205) 895-6144. NAIA. 3 CREW: partial. 13 BB: full.

UNIVERSITY OF MONTEVALLO, Beverly Warren, Women's Athletic Director, Station 181, Montevallo, AL 35115, (205) 665-2521. NAIA. 10 BB, 10 VB: full.

UNIVERSITY OF NORTH ALABAMA, Bill Jones, Athletic Director, Florence, AL

ARIZONA WESTERN COLLEGE, Charlie Dine, Athletic Director, Box 929, Yuma, AZ 85364, (602) 726-1000. NJCAA, ACCAC. 12 SB, 8 TEN, 12 VB: partial.

ARIZONA STATE UNIVERSITY, Associate Athletic Director, University Activity Center, Tempe, AZ 85287, (602) 965-3382. NCAA, PAC 10 & PAC West. I. 6 ARCH, 6 BAD: partial. 15 BB, 6 G, 10 GYM, 11 SB, 14 S&D, 8 TEN, 16 T&F, 12 VB: full.

CENTRAL ARIZONA COLLEGE, Lin L. Laursen, Coach, Woodruff Rd., Coolidge, AZ 85228, (602) 836-8243 ext. 304. NJCAA, ACCAC, Jr. College. 12 BB, 6 RD, 15 SB, 12 VB: partial to full.

COCHISE COLLEGE, Dick Wilkinson, Athletic Director, Hwy. 80 W., Douglas, AZ 85607, (602) 364-7943. NJCAA. 6 BB, 4 RD, 5 VB: partial to full.

EASTERN ARIZONA COLLEGE, Jeannette Williams, Women's Athletic Director, 626 Church St., Thatcher, AZ 85552, (602) 428-1133 ext. 414. NJCAA, ACCAC. 7 BB, 9 SB, 9 VB: full.

GRAND CANYON COLLEGE, Keith Baker, Sports Information Director, 3300 W. Camelback Rd., Phoenix, AZ 85019, (602) 249-3300, ext. 382. 6 TEN: partial. 1 VB: full.

NORTHERN ARIZONA UNIVERSITY, Dave Brown, Assistant Athletic Director, Box 15400, Flagstaff, AZ 86011, (602) 523-5353. NCAA. BB, SB, S&D, TEN, T&F, VB: partial to full.

PHOENIX COLLEGE, Donna Rebadow, Women's Athletic Director, 1202 W. Thomas Rd., Phoenix, AZ 85013, (602) 264-2492 ext. 314. NJCAA, ACCAC. 8 ARCH, 12 BB, 6 CC, 15 SB, 6 TEN, 15 T&F, 12 VB: partial.

UNIVERSITY OF ARIZONA, Mary Roby, Associate Athletic Director, 233 McKale Center, Tucson, AZ 85721, (602) 621-2473. NCAA, PAC-WEST, I. BB, CC, G, GYM, SB, S&D, TEN, T&F, VB: partial to full.

Director, Barnhill Arena, Fayetteville, AR 72701, (501) 575-4959. NCAA, SC, I. 15 BB, 8 TEN, 9 S&D, 16 T&F: full.

UNIVERSITY OF ARKANSAS (LITTLE ROCK), Richard Turner, Assistant Athletic Director, 2605 S. Fillmore, Little Rock, AR 72204, (501) 569-3304. NCAA, I. 15 BB, 10 S&D, 7 TEN, 10 VB: partial. CC, G: non-scholarship.

UNIVERSITY OF ARKANSAS (MONTICELLO), Alvy Early, Coach, Box 2555-UAM, Monticello, AR 71655, (501) 367-6811 ext. 57. NAIA. 12 BB, 12 T&F: full.

UNIVERSITY OF ARKANSAS (PINE BLUFF), Rosalyn Landes, Coach, Box 4096, Pine Bluff, AR 71601, (501) 541-6591. NAIA. 6 BB, 6 VB: partial to full.

UNIVERSITY OF CENTRAL ARKANSAS, Sallie V. Dalton, Coach, Box 1764 U, Conway, AR 72032, (501) 450-3154. NAIA. 12 BB, 12 VB: full.

CALIFORNIA

AZUSA PACIFIC UNIVERSITY, Cliff Hamlow, Athletic Director, Azusa, CA 91702, (818) 969-3434 ext. 3382. NAIA. BB, CC, SB, T&F, VB: partial.

BIOLA UNIVERSITY, Betty Norman, Women's Athletic Director, 13800 Biola Ave., La Mirada, CA 90638. (213) 944-0351 ext. 3426. NAIA. TEN: partial. BB, VB: partial to full.

CALIFORNIA BAPTIST COLLEGE, Dave King, Athletic Director, 8432 Magnolia Ave., Riverside, CA 92504, (714) 689-5771. NAIA. 10 BB, 6 VB: partial.

CALIFORNIA LUTHERAN COLLEGE, Carey J. Snyder, Athletic Director, 60 Olsen Rd., Thousand Oaks, CA 91360, (805) 492-2411. NAIA, District III, II. BB, SB, TEN, T&F, VB: partial.

91330, (213) 885-3208. NCAA, California Collegiate Athletic Association, II. 12 BB, 6 GYM, 20 SB, 12 S&D, 8 TEN, 14 T&F, 12 VB: partial.

CALIFORNIA STATE UNIVERSITY (SAN DIEGO), Judy Somers, Student-Athlete Coordinator, Athletic Dept., San Diego, CA 92182, (619) 265-4152. NCAA, PCAA, I. 15 BB, 4 G, 12 WB, 8 TEN: full. 3 SB, 5 T&F: partial to full.

CALIFORNIA STATE UNIVERSITY (SAN JOSE), Carolyn Lewis, Associate Athletic Director, One Washington Square, San Jose, CA 95192-0064, (408) 277-3141. NCAA, NOR PAC, I. 12 BB, 6 FH, 6 G, 3 GYM, 3 SB, 3 S&D, 3 TEN, 12 VB: full.

CHAPMAN COLLEGE, Penny Brush, Associate Athletic Director, 333 N. Glassel, Orange, CA 92666, (714) 997-6691. NCAA, CCAA, II. 6 BB, 6 SB, 6 VB: partial. CC, SOC, TEN, T&F: non-scholarship.

FRESNO STATE UNIVERSITY, Jack Lengyel, Athletic Director, Athletic Dept., Fresno, CA 93706, (209) 294-3178. NCAA, NORPAC. 15 BB, 11 SB, 6 S&D, 4 TEN, 10 T&F/CC, 12 VB: full.

LOYOLA MARYMOUNT UNIVERSITY, Margaret P. Olaveson, Assistant Athletic Director/Coordinator Women's Sports, 7101 W. 80th St., Los Angeles, CA 90045, (213) 642-2765. NCAA, West Coast Athletic Conference, I. 3.5 BB, 1 CC, 3 TEN, 5 VB: full. CREW, SB, S&D: non-scholarship.

UNITED STATES INTERNATIONAL UNIVERSITY, Al J. Palmiotto, Athletic Director, 10455 Pomerado Rd., San Diego, CA 92131, (619) 693-4584. NCAA. 12 BB, 7 G, 12 SB, 7 TEN, 14 T&F, 12 VB: full.

UNIVERSITY OF CALIFORNIA (BERKELEY), Luella J. Lilly, Women's Athletic Director, 177 Hearst Gym, Berkeley, CA 94720, (415) 642-2098. NCAA, NORPAC, I. 3 BB, 3 FH, 2 GYM, 8 SOC, 3 SB, 4 S&D, 6 T&F, 2 VB: partial. 12 BB, 8 FH, 8 GYM, 8 SB, 10 S&D, 1 SOC, 8 TEN, 10 VB: full.

UNIVERSITY OF CALIFORNIA (IRVINE), Robert Halvaks, Assistant Athletic Director, Crawford Hall, Irvine, CA 92717, (714) 856-6202. NCAA, PCAA, I. 5.25 BB, .75 S&D, 3 TEN, 2 T&F, 5.25 VB: partial. SOC: non-scholarship.

UNIVERSITY OF CALIFORNIA (LOS ANGELES), Dr. Judith R. Holland, Sr. Associate Director, 405 N. Hilgard Ave., Los Angeles, CA 90024, (213) 206-6780. NCAA, Pacific West, I. 15 BB, 6 G, 10 GYM, 11 SB, 14 S&D, 8 TEN, 16 T&F/CC, 12 VB: full. CREW: non-scholarship.

UNIVERSITY OF CALIFORNIA (RIVERSIDE), Nancy Paris, Assistant Athletic Director, Physical Education Dept., Riverside, CA 92521, (714) 787-5432. NCAA, CCAA, II. 10 BB, 10 VB: partial. 0 CC, 0 SB, 0 TEN, 0 T&F.

UNIVERSITY OF CALIFORNIA (SANTA BARBARA), Alice Henry, Associate Athletic Director, Athletic Dept., Santa Barbara, CA 93106, (805) 961-2247. NCAA. BB, GYM, SOC, SB, S&D, TEN, T&F, VB: partial to full.

UNIVERSITY OF THE PACIFIC, Coach of Specific Sport, 3601 Pacific Ave., Stockton, CA 95211, (209) 946-2471. NCAA, PCAA, I. 12 BB, 4 FH, 9 SB, 8 S&D, 5 TEN: partial. 12 VB: full.

UNIVERSITY OF THE REDLANDS, Pam Walker, Associate Director of Athletics, 1200 Colton Ave., Redlands, CA 92374, (714) 793-2121. NCAA, Southern California Intercollegiate Athletic Conference, III. 15 BB, 7-10 CC, 20 SOC, 20 SB, 15 S&D, 12-15 TEN, 10 T&F, 15-20 VB: partial.

UNIVERSITY OF SAN DIEGO, Coach of Specific Sport, Alcala Park, San Diego, CA 92110, (619) 293-4803. NCAA, WCAC, I. 12 BB, 2 S&D, 4.5 TEN, 6 VB: full. CREW, CC, SB: non-scholarship.

UNIVERSITY OF SAN FRANCISCO, Sandee L. Hill, Associate Athletic Director, Athletic Dept., San Francisco, CA 94117, (415) 666-6623. NCAA, WCAC, I. 10 BB, 2

NCAA, NAIA, II, District vII, Continental Divide. 10 BB, 5 CC (coed), 5 SOC, 5 SB, 2 S&D, 3 TEN, 11 VB: partial.

REGIS COLLEGE, Barb Schroeder, Athletic Director, W. 50th Ave. & Lowell Blvd., Denver, CO 80221, (303) 458-4070. NCAA, NAIA. 12 BB, 2 S&D, 2 TEN, 10 VB: partial.

UNITED STATES AIR FORCE ACADEMY, Fred Casotti, Associate Athletic Director, Campus Box 368, Boulder, CO 80309, (303) 492-7931. NCAA. 8 SKI, 4 TEN, 12 T&F: partial. 15 BB, 1 TEN, 5 T&F: full.

UNIVERSITY OF DENVER, Helen McGraw, Administrative Assistant, Athletic Dept., Field House Room 225, Denver, CO 80208, (303) 871-3399. NCAA. 5.2 BB, 5 GYM, 2 SOC, 1 S&D, 6.66 TEN, 2 VB: partial. 3 BB, 4 GYM: full.

UNIVERSITY OF NORTHERN COLORADO, Rosemary Fri, Associate Athletic Director, Butler-Hancock 227, Greeley, CO 80639, (303) 351-2523. NCAA, Continental Divide, II. 10 BB, 11 GYM, 8 S&D, 7 TEN, 14 T&F, 10 VB: partial. 2 BB, 3 VB: full.

UNIVERSITY OF SOUTHERN COLORADO, Jessie F. Banks, Assistant Athletic Director, Robert Muller, Athletic Director, 2200 Bonforte, Pueblo, CO 81001, (303) 549-2660. NAIA. 4.6 BB, 3 GYM, 2.1 TEN, 2.4 T&F, 3.9 VB: partial.

UNITED STATES AIR FORCE ACADEMY, Lt. Col. Micki King Hogue, Assistant Director of Athletics, US Air Force Academy, Colorado Springs, CO 80840, (303) 472-4008. NCAA, Continental Divide, II. BB, CC, FN, F: partial to full.

Dover, DE 19901, (302) 736-4928. NCAA. 15 BB, 15 T&F: partial to full.

UNIVERSITY OF DELAWARE, Mary Ann Hitchens, Assistant Athletic Director, Delaware Field House, Newark, DE 19716, (302) 451-2496. NCAA, East Coast Conference, I. 15 BB, 11 equivalency FH: partial to full. CC, LAX, SB, S&D, TEN, T&F, VB: non-scholarship.

DISTRICT OF COLUMBIA

THE AMERICAN UNIVERSITY, Robert H. Frailey, Athletic Director, Athletic Dept., Washington, DC 20016, (202) 686-2560. NCAA. BB, FH, S&D, TEN: partial.

GEORGE WASHINGTON UNIVERSITY, Lynn George, Women's Athletic Director, 600 22nd St. NW, Washington, DC 20052, (202) 676-6283. NCAA, Atlantic 10, I. GYM, SOC, S&D, TEN, VB: partial. BB: full.

GEORGETOWN UNIVERSITY, Nathalie Paramskas, Assistant Athletic Director, McDonough Arena, Washington, DC 20057, (202) 625-4021. NCAA. 2 TEN, 8 T&F, 7 VB: partial. 12 BB: full.

HOWARD UNIVERSITY, Sandra Norrell-Thomas, Associate Athletic Director, Sixth and Girard NW, Washington, DC 20059, (202) 636-7140. NCAA. S&D, T&F, VB: partial to full. BB: full.

UNIVERSITY OF THE DISTRICT OF COLUMBIA, Emma Best, Assistant Athletic Director, 4200 Connecticut NW, Washington, DC 20008, (202) 282-2748/49. NCAA. 6 TEN, 12 T&F, 12 VB: partial. 12 BB: partial to full.

CONNECTICUT

FAIRFIELD UNIVERSITY, Dianne Nolan, Coordinator of Women's Athletics, N. Benson Rd., Fairfield, CT 06430, (203) 254-4040. NCAA, MAAC, I. 15 BB: full. 3 FH, 2 SB, 2 VB: partial. CC, FN, G, S&D, TN: non-scholarship.

FLORIDA ATLANTIC UNIVERSITY, Jack Mehl, Athletic Director, 500 N.W. 20th St., Boca Raton, FL 33431, (303) 393-3710. NCAA, Independent, II. 5 BB, 1 CC, 3 FN, 3 S&D, 5 TEN: partial. 6 BB, 3 G, 1 S&D: full.

FLORIDA INTERNATIONAL UNIVERSITY, Nancy J. Olson, Athletic Director, Tamiami Trail, Miami, FL 33162, (305) 554-2756. NCAA. 9 BB, 10 G, 3 TEN, 6 T&F, 12 VB: partial.

FLORIDA SOUTHERN COLLEGE, Lois Webb, Assistant Athletic Director, Lakeland, FL 33802, (813) 680-4248. NCAA, Sunshine State Conference, II. 4.5 BB, 3.25 SB, 2.5 TEN, 5.25 VB: full. CC: non-scholarship.

FLORIDA STATE UNIVERSITY, Barbara Palmer, Associate Athletic Director, 100 Tully Gym, Tallahassee, FL 32306, (904) 644-1901. NCAA. 15 BB, 6 G, 11 SB, 14 S&D, 8 TEN, 16 T&F, 12 VB: full.

GULF COAST COMMUNITY COLLEGE, Steve Dubrieul, Athletic Director, 5230 W. Hwy. 98, Panama City, FL 32401, (904) 769-1551. NJCAA. 15 SB: partial to full.

HILLSBOROUGH COMMUNITY COLLEGE, Dr. R.G. Lawman, Director of Athletics & Intramurals, Box 30030, Tampa, FL 33603, (813) 879-7222 ext. 444. NJCAA, Florida Suncoast, VIII. 15 SB, 8 TEN, 12 VB: partial.

INDIAN RIVER COMMUNITY COLLEGE, Bob Bottger, Coordinator of Athletics, 3209 Virginia Ave., Ft. Pierce, FL 33454, (305) 464-2000. NJCAA, FCCAA. 12 BB, 18 S&D, 8 TEN, 8 VB: partial.

JACKSONVILLE UNIVERSITY, Paul S. Griffin, Athletic Director, University Blvd., Jacksonville, FL 32211, (904) 744-3950. NCAA. 5 TEN, 6 VB: partial. 2 VB: full.

LAKE CITY COMMUNITY COLLEGE, Jean Williams, Coach, Rte. 7, Box 378, Lake City, FL 32055, (904) 752-1822 ext. 295. NJCAA. 15 SB: partial.

MIAMI-DADE COMMUNITY COLLEGE

SB, 1 TEN, 4 VB: full.

UNIVERSITY OF SANTA CLARA, Marygrace Colby, Director Women's Athletics, Santa Clara, CA 95053, (408) 554-4078. NCAA, I. .5 BB, .5 TEN, .5 T&F: partial. 6 BB, 2 TEN, 6 T&F: full. CREW, SOC, SB, CC: non-scholarship.

UNIVERSITY OF SOUTHERN CALIFORNIA, Barbara Hedges, Associate Athletic Director, USC Athletic Department, Heritage Hall 203 A, Los Angeles, CA 90089-0602, (213) 743-0793. NCAA, PAC-WEST, I. 15 BB, 6 G, 7 GYM, 14 S&D, 5 TEN, 14 T&F, 10 VB: full.

WESTMONT COLLEGE, Coach of Specific Sport, 955 La Paz Rd., Santa Barbara, CA 93108, (805) 969-5051 ext. 541. NAIA, Dist. III. CC, SOC, TEN, T&F, VB: partial.

COLORADO

ADAMS STATE COLLEGE, Bob Boerigter, Athletic Director, Alamosa, CO 81102,, (303) 589-7401. NAIA. 9 BB, 5 GYM, 6 SB, 10 T&F, 7 VB: partial.

COLORADO COLLEGE, Richard Taber, Athletic Director, Colorado Springs, CO 80903, (303) 473-2233. NCAA. 7 SOC: partial. 7 SOC: full.

COLORADO SCHOOL OF MINES, Gail Klock, Coach, Golden, CO 80401, (303) 273-3371. NCAA, NAIA, Rocky Mountain Athletic, II. 6 BB, 3 SB, 3 S&D, 3 T&F, 5 VB: partial.

COLORADO STATE UNIVERSITY, Nancy J. O'Connor, Women's Athletic Director, Moby Gym, Athletic Dept., Ft. Collins, CO 80523, (303) 491-7352/5326. NCAA. 15 BB, 11 SB, 14 S&D, 16 T&F, 12 VB: full.

MESA COLLEGE, Coach of Specific Sport, Grand Junction, CO 81501, (303) 248-1278. NAIA. 10 BB, 5 SB, 1 TEN, 6 VB: partial.

METROPOLITAN STATE COLLEGE, Bill Helman, Athletic Director, 1006 11th St., Denver, CO 80204, (303) 556-8300.

MITCHELL COLLEGE, Daniel B. Mara, Assistant Athletic Director, 437 Pequot Ave., New London, CT 06320, (203) 443-2811. NJCAA. 15 BB, 20 FH, 20 SOC, 20 SB: partial.

QUINNIPIAC COLLEGE, Lauren A. Fraser, Women's Athletic Director, Mt. Carmel Ave., Hamden, CT 06518, (203) 288-5251. NCAA. 2 CC, 4 SB, 3 TEN: partial.

SACRED HEART UNIVERSITY, Dave Bike, Athletic Director, Box 6460, Bridgeport, CT 06606, (203) 371-7827. NCAA, ECAC, NECC, II. VB: partial. BB, SB: partial to full. CC: non-scholarship.

TRINITY COLLEGE, Robin Sheppard, Women's Athletic Director, Ferris Athletic Center, Hartford, CT 06106, (802) 658-0337. NCAA, ECAC, NESCAC, III. BB, CREW, FEN, FH, G (coed), LAX, SOC, SB, S&D, TEN, T&F, VB, Squash.

UNIVERSITY OF BRIDGEPORT, Ann V. Fariss, Women's Athletic Director, Bridgeport, CT 06497, (203) 576-4059. NCAA. 12 BB, 6 GYM, 10 SB: partial to full.

UNIVERSITY OF CONNECTICUT, John L. Toner, Athletic Director, U-78, Storrs, CT 06268, (203) 486-4858. NCAA, Big East, Yankee Conference, I. BB, CC, FH, GYM, SOC, SB, S&D, TEN, T&F, VB: partial to full.

UNIVERSITY OF HARTFORD, Gordon McCullough, Athletic Director, 200 Bloomfield Ave., W. Hartford, CT 06117, (203) 243-4650. NCAA. BB, SOC, SB, TEN, T&F, VB: full.

UNIVERSITY OF NEW HAVEN, Deborah Chin, Associate Athletic Director, 300 Orange Ave., W. Haven, CT 06516, (203) 932-7020. NCAA, NECC, II. 2 TEN: partial. 7 BB, 4 SB, 6 VB: full.

DELAWARE

DELAWARE STATE COLLEGE, Coach of Specific Sport, 1200 N. Dupont Hwy.,

BREVARD COMMUNITY COLLEGE, Robert A. Anderson, Dean of Collegewide Student Services, 1519 Clearlake Rd., Cocoa, FL 32922, (305) 632-1111 ext. 3750. NJCAA. 11 BB, 5 CC, 10 SB, 7 S&D, 5 T&F, 7 VB: full.

BROWARD COMMUNITY COLLEGE, Rex Brumley, Athletic Director, 225 E. Las Olas Blvd., Ft. Lauderdale, FL 33301, (305) 761-7488. NJCAA, FCCAA, Southern Conference. 12 BB, 15 SB, 10 S&D, 8 TEN, 12 VB: partial.

CENTRAL FLORIDA COMMUNITY COLLEGE, Michael J. McGinnis, Athletic Director, Box 1388, Ocala, FL 32678, (904) 237-2111. NJCAA, Mid-Florida, JC. 12 BB: partial.

DAYTONA BEACH COMMUNITY COLLEGE, Tom Schlageter, Athletic Director, Box 1111, Daytona Beach, FL 32015, (904) 255-8131. NJCAA. 14 S&D, 6 TEN: partial.

ECKERD COLLEGE, Celia Bloodworth, Women's Athletic Coordinator, 4200 54th Ave., S., St. Petersburg, FL 33733, (813) 867-1166 ext. 295. NCAA. 10 BB, 10 SB, 5 TEN, 10 VB: partial.

EDISON COMMUNITY COLLEGE, Melissa DeMarchi, Women's Athletic Coordinator, College Pkwy., Ft. Myers, FL 33936, (813) 489-9300 ext. 238. NJCAA, Southern Conference. 10 BB, 12 SB, 10 VB: partial-tuition & books.

EDWARD WATERS COLLEGE, John Lee, Athletic Director, 1658 Kings Rd., Jacksonville, FL 32209, (904) 355-3030 ext 298. NAIA, II. 14 BB, 14 SB: partial. 3 BB, 3 SB: full.

FLORIDA A&M UNIVERSITY, Sarah E. Hill, Women's Athletic Director, Box 982, Tallahassee, FL 32307, (904) 599-3272/3528. NCAA, New South Women's Athletic Conference, I. 3 BB, 7 CC, 7 SB, 3 S&D, 2 TEN, 5 T&F, 9 VB: partial. 12 BB, 4 SB, 1 SD, 6 TEN, 9 T&F, 3 VB: full.

(NORTH), Dr. Ron Warnok, Assistant Athletic Director, 11380 N.W. 27th Ave., Miami, FL 33167, (305) 347-1362. NJCAA, FCCAA. 12 BB, 12 SB, 5 S&D, 8 TEN, 12 VB: partial.

MIAMI-DADE COMMUNITY COLLEGE (SOUTH), Jim Cox, Physical Education & Athletics Administrator, 11011 S.W. 104th St., Miami, FL 33176, (305) 347-2140. NJCAA, Florida Community College Activities Association-Southern Conference. 12 BB, 12 SB, 5 S&D, 6 TEN, 12 VB: full in-state tuition and books.

MIAMI-DADE NEW WORLD CENTER, Jeanine Smith, Administrative Assistant, 300 N.E. 2nd Ave., Miami, FL 33132, (305) 577-6839. NJCAA. 13 SB, 8 TEN, 11 VB: partial.

ROLLINS COLLEGE, Gloria E. Crosby, Athletic Business Manager, Athletic Dept., Winter Park, FL 32789, (305) 646-2429. NCAA. 6 BB, 3 G, 5 TEN, 5 VB: partial to full.

ST. LEO COLLEGE, Norm Kaye, Athletic Director, Box 2038, St. Leo, FL 33574, (904) 588-8221. NCAA. Sunshine State Conference, II. BB, TEN, VB: partial. CC, SB: non-scholarship.

ST. JOHNS RIVER COMMUNITY COLLEGE, Bill Tuten, Softball Coach, 5000 St. Johns Ave., Palatka, FL 32077, (904) 328-1571 ext. 60. NJCAA, Florida CC Activities Association-Mid Florida. 10 SB: partial.

SANTA FE COMMUNITY COLLEGE, Stan Mitchell, Student Activities Director, 3000 N.W. 83rd St., Gainesville, FL 32602, (904) 395-5000. NJCAA. 12 BB, 15 SB, 8 TEN: partial.

SEMINOLE COMMUNITY COLLEGE, Joe Sterling, Athletic Director, Sanford, FL 32771, (305) 323-1450 ext. 380. NJCAA, Mid-Florida Conference, Region VIII. 10 BB, 10 SB: partial.

STETSON UNIVERSITY, Nancy Nichols, Coordinator of Women's Athletics, Box

8359, Deland, FL 32720, (904) 734-4121. NAIA. 10 **BB**, 1 **SB**, 2 **TEN**, 2 **VB**: full.

UNIVERSITY OF MIAMI, Corey Johnson, Assistant Athletic Director, Hecht Athletic Center, Coral Gables, FL 33124, (305) 284-3822. Independent, I. 12 **BB**, 6 **G**, 11 **S&D**, 8 **TEN**, 4 **T&F**: full.

UNIVERSITY OF NORTH FLORIDA, Bruce A. Grimes, Athletic Director, Box 17074, Jacksonville, FL 32216, (904) 646-2833. NAIA. 4 **G**, 7 **TEN**, 12 **T&F**: partial.

UNIVERSITY OF SOUTH FLORIDA, Barbara Sparks-McGlinchy, Assistant Athletic Director, 4202 E. Fowler Ave., Tampa, FL 33620, (813) 974-2125. NCAA. Sun Belt, I. 15 **BB**, 6 **G**, 10 **SB**, 9 **S&D**, 8 **TEN**, 11 **VB**: full.

UNIVERSITY OF TAMPA, Robert Birrenkott, Athletic Director, 401 W. Kennedy Blvd., Tampa, FL 33606, (813) 253-8861. NCAA. 11 **S&D**: partial. 6 **BB**, 5 **VB**: full.

UNIVERSITY OF WEST FLORIDA, Kathy Davis, Coach, University Blvd., Pensacola, FL 32514-0101, (904) 477-9366. NAIA. Southern States. **BB, CC, SB, TEN**: partial.

VALENCIA COMMUNITY COLLEGE, Phyllis Shemelya, Athletic Director, Box 3028, Orlando, FL 32802, (305) 299-5000 ext. 1408. NJCAA. Mid-Florida Conference. 12 **BB**, 15 **SB**, 12 **VB**: partial.

GEORGIA

ARMSTRONG STATE COLLEGE, Betty J. Ford, Coach, Athletic Dept., 11935 Abercorn Ext., Savannah, GA 31419-1997, (912) 927-5336. NAIA. 10 **SB**, 6 **TEN**: partial. 10 **BB**: full.

AUGUSTA COLLEGE, Marvin Vanover, Marietta, GA 30061, (404) 429-7431. NAIA. District 25, I. 5 **BB**, 5 **SB**, 3 **T&F**: partial. 5 **BB**: full. **CC**: non-scholarship.

MORRIS BROWN COLLEGE, Vista H. Bryant, Women's Athletic Director, 643 Martin L. King Dr. S.W., Box 524, Atlanta, GA 30314, (404) 525-7831. NCAA. 5 **BB**: full.

NORTH GEORGIA COLLEGE, Lynn Jarrett, Women's Athletic Coordinator, Dahlonega, GA 30597, (404) 864-3391. NAIA. 4 **BB**: full.

SHORTER COLLEGE, Richard Cowan, Athletic Director, Shorter Hill, Rome, GA 30161, (404) 291-2121. NAIA. 10 **BB**, 5 **TEN**: partial.

TIFT COLLEGE, Laurie Jossey, Athletic Director, Tift College Dr., Forsyth, GA 31029, (912) 994-5454. NAIA. 8 **BB**, 3 **TEN**: partial. 1 **TEN**: full.

UNIVERSITY OF GEORGIA, Liz Murphey, Women's Athletic Director, Box 1472, Athens, GA 30613, (404) 542-5817. NCAA. Southeastern Conference, I. 15 **BB**, 6 **G**, 10 **GYM**, 14 **S&D**, 8 **TEN**, 16 **T&F**, 12 **VB**: full.

WEST GEORGIA COLLEGE, Barbara Brown, Women's Athletic Coordinator, Carrolton, GA 30118, (404) 834-1232. NAIA. 6 **BB**, 4 **VB**: partial to full.

HAWAII

BRIGHAM YOUNG UNIVERSITY (HAWAII), Ted Chidester, Athletic Director, 55-220 Kuluni, Laie, HI 96762, (808) 293-3760. NCAA, NAIA, I. 4 **CC**, 5 **TEN**, 8 **VB**: partial.

HAWAII LOA COLLEGE, Albert Minn, Athletic Director, 45-045 Kam Hwy., Kaneohe, HI 96744, (808) 235-3641. NAIA. 5 **VB**: partial.

HAWAII PACIFIC COLLEGE, Athletic Department, 1060 Bishop St. PH, Honolulu, HI 96813, (808) 544-0221. NAIA,

ILLINOIS

BELLEVILLE AREA COLLEGE, Jay Harrington, Athletic Director, 2500 Carlyle Rd., Belleville, IL 62221, (618) 235-2700. NJCAA. 6 **BB**, 5 **SB**, 2 **TEN**, 6 **VB**: partial.

BRADLEY UNIVERSITY, Ron Ferguson, Director of Athletics, Athletic Department, Peoria, IL 61625, (309) 676-7611 ext. 321. NCAA, Gateway Collegiate Athletic Conference, I. 10 **CC**, 12 **SB**, 6 **TEN**, 10 **T&F**, 12 **VB**: partial. 12 **BB**: full.

CHICAGO STATE UNIVERSITY, Bruce Herron, Athletic Director, 95th at King Dr., Chicago, IL 60628, (312) 995-2290. NAIA. 4 **SB**, 4 **T&F**: partial. 8 **BB**, 8 **VB**: full.

COLLEGE OF ST. FRANCIS, Rich Luenemann, Assistant Athletic Director, 500 Wilcox Ave., Joliet, IL 60435, (815) 740-3407. NAIA, Chicagoland and Collegiate Athletic Conference. 24 **BB**, 12 **CC**, 30 **SB**, 15 **TEN**, 28 **VB**: partial.

DePAUL UNIVERSITY, Jean M. Lenti Ponsetto, Associate Athletic Director, 1011 W. Belden Ave., Chicago, IL 60614, (312) 321-8549. NCAA, North Star Conference, I. 5 **SB**, 4 **TEN**, 14 **T&F**, 9 **VB**: partial. 15 **BB**: full.

EASTERN ILLINOIS UNIVERSITY, Coach of Specific Sport, 262 Lantz, Charleston, IL 61920, (217) 581-2106. NCAA, Gateway Collegiate Athletic Conference, I. 15 **BB**, 7.5 **CC**, 6 **SB**, 7.5 **T&F**, 8 **VB**: full. 6 **TEN**: partial.

BELLEVILLE AREA COLLEGE (GRANITE CITY CAMPUS), Terry Collins, Athletic Director, 4950 Maryville Rd., Granite City, IL 62040, (618) 931-0600. NJCAA, Independent. **BB, VB**: partial.

ILLINOIS STATE UNIVERSITY, Donna Taylor, Assistant Athletic Director, 211 Horton Field House, Normal, IL 61761, (309) 426-2677. NCAA, Gateway, I. 15 **BB**, 4 **G**, 8 **GYM**, 11 **SB**, 9 **S&D**, 4 **TEN**, 14 **T&F/CC**, 12 **VB**: full.

NORTHERN ILLINOIS UNIVERSITY, Susie Pembroke-Jones, Director of Women's Intercollegiate Athletics, 101 Evans Field House, DeKalb, IL 60115, (815) 753-1494. NCAA, Mid-American Conference, I-A. 2 **TEN**: partial. 15 **BB**, 9 **FH**, 4 **G**, 10 **GYM**, 11 **SB**, 10 **S&D**, 6 **TEN**, 12 **VB**: full.

NORTHWESTERN UNIVERSITY, Sandy Barbour, Assistant Athletic Director, 1501 Central St., Evanston, IL 60201, (312) 491-7893. NCAA, Big Ten, I. **BB, CC, FH, SB, S&D, TEN, T&F, VB**: partial to full. **FN, LAX**: non-scholarship.

QUINCY COLLEGE, Sharlene A. Peter, Women's Athletic Director, Quincy, IL 62301, (217) 222-8020. NAIA. 10 **BB**, 10 **SB**, 6 **TEN**, 10 **VB**: partial.

ROSARY COLLEGE, Bill Brucks, Athletic Director, 7900 W. Division, River Forest, IL 60305, (312) 366-2490. NAIA, Chicagoland Collegiate Athletic Conference. 12 **BB**, 6 **TEN**, 12 **VB**: partial.

ST. AMBROSE COLLEGE, Jim Fox, Athletic Director, Rock Island, IL 61201, (319) 383-8727. NAIA. 7 **BB**, 8 **SB**, 3 **TEN**, 8 **VB**: partial to full.

ST. XAVIER COLLEGE, Lynn O'Lenski, Women's Athletic Director, 3700 W. 103rd St., Chicago, IL 60655, (312) 779-3300. NAIA. 4 **SB**, 4 **VB**: partial to full.

SANGAMON STATE UNIVERSITY, Aydin Gonulsen, Athletic Director, Sheppard Rd., Springfield, IL 62708, (217) 786-6674. NAIA, District 20. 8 **TEN**: partial.

SOUTHEASTERN ILLINOIS COLLEGE, Don Gines, Women's Athletic Coordinator, R.R. 4, Harrisburg, IL 62946, (618) 252-6376. NJCAA. 6 **BB**, 6 **SB**: partial to full.

SOUTHERN ILLINOIS UNIVERSITY (CARBONDALE), Charlotte West, Athletic Director, Intercollegiate Athletics for Women, Carbondale, IL 62901, (618) 536-5566. NCAA, Gateway Collegiate Athletic Conference, I. 3 **FH**, 2 **G**, 4 **SB**, 4 **S&D**, 2 **GYM**, 2 **TEN**, 4 **T&F**: partial.

Athletic Director, 2500 Walton Way, Augusta, GA 30910, (404) 737-1626. NAIA. 12 **SB**, 8 **TEN**, 6 **XC**: partial. 12 **BB**: partial to full.

BERRY COLLEGE, Bob Pearson, Box O, Mount Berry, GA 30149, (404) 232-5374. NAIA. 16 **BB**, 10 **TEN**, 10 **T&F**: partial.

BRENAU COLLEGE, Jean Harris, Athletic Director, Prior St., Gainesville, GA 30501, (404) 534-6237. NAIA. 10 **S&D**, 8 **TEN**: partial.

COLUMBUS COLLEGE, Herbert Greene, Athletic Director, Columbus, GA 31993, (404) 568-2204. NAIA. 6 **SB**, 6 **TEN**: partial.

FORT VALLEY STATE COLLEGE, Doug Porter, Athletic Director, 805 State College Dr., Ft. Valley, GA 31030, (912) 825-6208/6209. NCAA. 7 **T&F**: partial. 12 **BB**: full.

GEORGIA COLLEGE, Dr. Mike Peeler, Athletic Director, HPER Dept., Milledgeville, GA 31061, (912) 453-4072. NAIA, Georgia Intercollegiate. **BB, GYM**: partial to full. **SB, TEN**: partial.

GEORGIA INSTITUTE OF TECHNOLOGY, Bernadette McGlade, Assistant Athletic Director, 150 Third St., Atlanta, GA 30332, (404) 894-5416. NCAA, Atlantic Coast Conference, I. **BB, CC, TEN, T&F, VB**: partial to full.

GEORGIA SOUTHERN COLLEGE, David B. Wagner, Athletic Director, Box 8115, Statesboro, GA 30460, (912) 681-5376. NCAA. 5 **SB**, 5 **S&D**, 5 **TEN**: partial. 15 **BB**: full. **CC, VB**: non-scholarship.

GEORGIA SOUTHWESTERN COLLEGE, Bob C. Clark, Athletic Director, Americus, GA 31709, (912) 928-1262. NAIA. 1 **SB**: partial. 3 **BB**: full.

GEORGIA STATE UNIVERSITY, Sherman R. Day, Athletic Director, University Plaza, Atlanta, GA 30303, (404) 658-2772. NCAA. 14 **SB**, 5 **S&D**, 7 **TEN**, 12 **T&F**: partial. 6 **CC**: partial to full

KENNESAN COLLEGE, Ronda Seagraves, Administrative Assistant, Box 444,

District 29. **CC, G, TN**: partial. **BB, VB, C**: full.

UNIVERSITY OF HAWAII (HILO), Joey Estrella, Director of Athletics, Hilo, HI 96720-4091, (808) 961-9520. NAIA, NAIA, Dist. 29. 3 **CC**, 6 **TEN**, 4 **VB**: partial. 6 **VB**: full.

UNIVERSITY OF HAWAII (MANOA), Cindy Boerner Mazda, Women's Athletic Director, 1337 Lower Campus Rd., Honolulu, HI 96822, (808) 948-7347. NCAA, PCAA, I. **BB, G, SB, S&D, TEN, VB**: partial to full.

IDAHO

BOISE STATE UNIVERSITY, Carol J. Ladwig, Women's Athletic Director, 1910 University Dr., Boise, ID 83725, (208) 385-1655. NCAA, Mountain West Conference, I. 1 **TEN**: partial. 13 **BB**, 5 **GYM**, 2 **TEN**, 10 **T&F**, 8 **VB**: full.

IDAHO STATE UNIVERSITY, Dr. Kathy Hildreth, Director of Women's Athletics, Box 8173, Pocatello, ID 83209, (208) 236-2771. NCAA, Mountain West Athletic Conference, I. 15 **BB**, 8 **TEN**, 20 **T&F/CC**, 12 **VB**: partial to full.

LEWIS-CLARK STATE COLLEGE, Richard R. Hannan, Athletic Director, 6th St. & 8th Ave., Lewiston, ID 83501, (208) 746-2273. NAIA. 12 **BB**, 12 **VB**: partial to full.

NORTH IDAHO COLLEGE, Daralyn Mattei, Women's Athletic Coordinator, 1000 W. Garden Ave., Coeur d'Alene, ID 83814, (208) 667-7422. NJCAA. 16 **BB**, 6 **T&F**, 14 **VB**: full.

RICKS COLLEGE, Glenn Dalling, Athletic Director, Rexburg, ID 83440; (208) 356-2104. NJCAA. 8 **BB**, 8 **T&F**, 8 **VB**: partial.

UNIVERSITY OF IDAHO, Kathy Clark, Assistant Athletic Director, 223 KAC, Moscow, ID 83843, (208) 885-0200. NCAA, Mountain West Conference, I. 4 **TEN**, 14 **T&F/CC**, 3 **VB**: partial. 12 **BB**, 4 **TEN**, 14 **T&F/CC**, 9 **VB**: full.

JOHN A. LOGAN COLLEGE, John Sala, Athletic Director, Carterville, IL 62918, (618) 985-3741. NJCAA, GRAC, I. 9 **BB**, 5 **SB**, 4 **VB**: partial. 5 **BB**: full.

JUDSON COLLEGE, Steve Burke, Athletic Director, 1151 N. State St., Elgin, IL 60120, (312) 695-2500. NAIA, NCCAA. 7 **BB**, 7 **VB**: partial.

KISHWAUKEE COLLEGE, Gregg Gierke, Athletic Director, Malta, IL 60150, (815) 825-2086 ext. 240. NJCAA, Arrowhead. 6 **BB**, 9 **SB**, 6 **VB**: full.

LEWIS UNIVERSITY, Paul Ruddy, Athletic Director, Rte. 53, Romeoville, IL 60441, (815) 838-0500 ext. 247. NCAA. 6 **BB**, 3 **SB**, 2 **TEN**, 6 **VB**: partial to full.

LINCOLN COLLEGE, Joyce Paige, Financial Aid Director, 300 Keokuk St., Lincoln, IL 62656, (217) 732-3155 ext. 237. NJCAA. **BB, CC, G, SB, S&D, TEN, VB**: partial.

LOYOLA UNIVERSITY (CHICAGO), Carolyn Vellos, Assistant Athletic Director, 6525 N. Sheridan Rd., Chicago, IL 60626, (312) 508-2560. NCAA, North Star, I. **CC, VB**: partial. **BB**: full. **SB, T&F**: non-scholarship.

McKENDREE COLLEGE, Harry Statham, Athletic Director, 701 College Rd., Lebanon, IL 62254, (618) 537-4481. NAIA. **BB, SB, VB**: partial.

MUNDELEIN COLLEGE, Brenda Weare, Athletic Director, 6363 N. Sheridan Rd., Chicago, IL 60660, (312) 262-8100. NJCAA. 10 **BB**, 10 **VB**: partial.

NATIONAL COLLEGE, Patti McLean, Director of Athletics, 2840 Sheridan Rd., Evanston, IL 60201, (312) 256-5150, ext. 313. NAIA, Chicago Land, II. **SB, VB**: partial. **BB**: full. **G**: non-scholarship.

NORTHEASTERN ILLINOIS UNIVERSITY, Betty Fields, Women's Athletic Coordinator, 5500 N. St. Louis Ave., Chicago, IL 60625, (312) 583-4050 ext. 480. NAIA. 6 **BB**, 12 **VB**: partial. 6 **SB**, 4 **TEN**: full.

15 **BB**, 8 **FH**, 4 **G**, 8 **GYM**, 8 **SB**, 10 **S&D**, 6 **TEN**, 12 **T&F**, 12 **VB**: full.

SOUTHERN ILLINOIS UNIVERSITY (EDWARDSVILLE), Cindy Jones, Assistant Athletic Director, Box 129, Edwardsville, IL 62026, (618) 692-2871. NCAA, Independent, II. 12 **BB**, 10 **SOC**, 8 **SB**, 6 **TEN**, 4 **T&F**: full. **VB**: non-scholarship.

SPOON RIVER COLLEGE, Ed Georgieff, Athletic Director, R.R. 1, Canton, IL 61520, (309) 647-4645 ext. 275. 7 **BB**, 5 **SB**, 4 **VB**: partial.

UNIVERSITY OF ILLINOIS (CHAMPAIGN-URBANA), Karol Ann Kahrs, 235J-505 E. Armory, Champaign, IL 61820, (217) 333-0171. NCAA, Big Ten, I. 15 **BB**, 6 **G**, 10 **GYM**, 16 **S&D**, 8 **TEN**, 16 **T&F**, 12 **VB**: full.

UNIVERSITY OF ILLINOIS (CHICAGO), Tom Russo, Associate Athletic Director, 901 W. Roosevelt Rd., Chicago, IL 60608, (312) 996-2498. NCAA. 8 **BB**, 7 **GYM**, 7 **SB**, 7 **S&D**, 3 **TEN**, 7 **T&F**, 8 **VB**: full.

WABASH VALLEY COLLEGE, Paul Schnarre, Athletic Director, 2200 College Dr., Mount Carmel, IL 62863, (618) 262-8641. NJCAA. 12 **BB**, 4 **SB**, 4 **VB**: partial.

WESTERN ILLINOIS UNIVERSITY, Dr. Helen Smiley, Women's Athletic Director, Brophy Hall, Macomb, IL 61455, (309) 298-1964. NCAA, Gateway, I. 12 **BB**, 11 **SB**, 7 **S&D**, 4 **TEN**, 12 **T&F**, 11 **VB**: full.

INDIANA

BALL STATE UNIVERSITY, Andrea Seger, Director of Athletics/Women, Muncie, IN 47306, (317) 285-1671. NCAA, Mid-America Conference, I-A. 15 **BB**, 7 **FH**, 6 **GYM**, 11 **SB**, 9 **S&D**, 5 **TEN**, 8 **T&F**, 12 **VB**: full.

BUTLER UNIVERSITY, Mary Ann Rohleder, Associate Director of Athletics, 4600 Sunset Ave., Indianapolis, IN 46208,

(317) 283-9375. NCAA, North Star, I. 2 CC, 5 SB, 5 S&D, 5 TEN, 8 VB: partial. 8 BB, 2 VB: full.

GRACE COLLEGE, Terry Weinberger, Women's Athletic Coordinator, 200 Seminary Dr., Winona Lake, IN 46590, (219) 267-8191 ext. 176. NAIA. BB, SB, VB: partial.

HUNTINGTON COLLEGE, Mike Frame, Sports Information Director, 2303 College Ave., Huntington, IN 46750, (219) 356-6000 ext. 176. NAIA, NCCAA, MCC-Mid Central. 12 BB, 12 SB, 8 TEN, 12 VB: partial.

INDIANA CENTRAL UNIVERSITY, William Bright, Athletic Director, 1400 E. Hanna, Indianapolis, IN 46227, (317) 788-3248. NCAA, Great Lake Valley Conference, I. 5 BB, .5 CC, 1 G, 2 SB, 2 S&D, 1 TEN, 2 T&F, 1.75 VB: equivalency full.

INDIANA INSTITUTE OF TECHNOLOGY, Dan Kline, Athletic Director, 1600 E. Washington St., Fort Wayne, IN 46803, (219) 422-5561. NAIA. 12 BB: partial to full.

INDIANA STATE UNIVERSITY (EVANSVILLE), Mark Coomes, Athletic Director, 8600 University Blvd., Evansville, IN 47712, (812) 464-1846. NCAA. 12 BB, 8 SB, 3 TEN, 6 VB: partial to full.

INDIANA STATE UNIVERSITY (TERRE HAUTE), Alpha Cleary, Associate Athletic Director, Terra Haute, IN 47809, (812) 237-4089. NCAA, Gateway, I. 5 B, 4 GYM, 10 SB, 3 TEN, 11 T&F: partial. 15 BB, 4 GYM, 6 SB, 3 TEN, 7 T&F/CC, 12 VB: full.

INDIANA-PURDUE UNIVERSITY (FORT WAYNE), Arnie Ball, Assistant to Administration Director, 2102 Coliseum Blvd. E., Fort Wayne, IN 46805, (219) 482-5351. NCAA, I. 14 BB, 13 VB: partial. CC, SB, TEN: non-scholarship.

INDIANA-PURDUE UNIVERSITY (INDIANAPOLIS), Robert Lovell, Athletic Director, 901 W. New York St., Indianapolis, IN 46223, (317) 264-2725. NAIA, Independent. 11 BB, 11 SB, 10 VB: full.

IOWA

BRIARCLIFF COLLEGE, Jim Eilwanger, Director of Athletics, 3303 Rebecca, Sioux City, IA 51104, (712) 279-1656. NAIA, La-Kota. 1 BB, .5 G, .5 SB, 1 VB: partial.

DRAKE UNIVERSITY, Betty Miles, Associate Athletic Director, Des Moines, IA 50311, (515) 271-2734. NCAA. 2 SB, 4 TEN, 14 T&F, 8 VB: partial to full. 12 BB: full.

ELLSWORTH COMMUNITY COLLEGE, M. Dittmer, Athletic Director, Iowa Falls, IA 50126, (515) 648-4611. NJCAA, Iowa Athletic Conference. 6 BB, 5 SB, 3 VB: partial.

GRACELAND COLLEGE, Tom Powell, Athletic Director, Clesson Center, Lamoni, IA 50140, (515) 784-5311. NAIA. 13 BB, 22 VB: partial.

GRAND VIEW COLLEGE, David Sisam, Athletic Director, 1200 Grandview Ave., Des Moines, IA 50316, (515) 263-2897. NAIA. 15 BB, 8 G, 10 SB, 8 TEN: partial.

IOWA STATE UNIVERSITY, Dave Cox, Assistant Athletic Director, Olsen Bldg., Ames, IA 50011, (515) 294-3662. NCAA, Big Eight, I. BB, G, GYM, SB, S&D, TEN, T&F, VB: partial.

IOWA WESLEYAN COLLEGE, Betty J. Sammons, Athletic Director, Mt. Pleasant, IA 52641, (319) 385-8021. NAIA. BB, FH, SB, S&D, T&F, VB: partial.

IOWA WESTERN COMMUNITY COLLEGE (COUNCIL BLUFFS), Julie Woine, Athletic Director, 2700 College Rd., Box 4C, Council Bluffs, IA 51502, (712) 325-3200. NJCAA. 3 SB, 2 VB: partial.

KIRKWOOD COMMUNITY COLLEGE, Gregg Bosch, Athletic Director, Box 2068, Cedar Rapids, IA 52406, (319) 398-5462. NJCAA. 8 BB, 6 SB: partial. 2 BB, 2 SB: full.

MARSHALLTOWN COMMUNITY COLLEGE, Jon Renner, Athletic Director, 3700 S. Center, Marshalltown, IA 50158, 353-7265. NCAA, Big Ten, I. 15 BB, 11 FH, 6 G, 10 GYM, 11 SB, 14 S&D, 8 TEN, 16 T&F, 12 VB: full.

UNIVERSITY OF NORTHERN IOWA, Dr. Sandra C. Williamson, Associate Director of Athletics, Dome West, Cedar Falls, IA 50614, (319) 273-6033. NCAA, Gateway Collegiate AC, I 12 BB, 3 G, 9 SB, 1 S&D, 1 TEN, 10 T&F, 11 VB: full.

WESTMAR COLLEGE, Milton Martin, Athletic Director, LeMars, IA 51031, (712) 546-7081. NAIA. 10 BB, 9 SB, 10 VB: partial.

KANSAS

ALLEN COUNTY COMMUNITY COLLEGE, Hugh Haire, Dean/Registrar, 801 N. Cottonwood, Iola, KS 66749, (316) 365-5116. NJCAA, Kansas Jayhawk Comm. College Conference. 12 BB, 6 CC, 6 RD, 13 SB, 2 TEN, 6 T&F, 7 VB: partial. ARCH: non-scholarship.

BENEDICTINE COLLEGE, Larry Wilcox, Athletic Director, Box 68N, Atchison, KS 66002, (913) 367-5340. NAIA, Independent. 12 BB, 12 SB, 10 TEN, 12 VB: partial.

BETHEL COLLEGE, George Rogers, Athletic Director, N. Newton, KS 67117, (316) 283-2500 ext. 277. NAIA. 5 BB, 3 TEN, 4 T&F, 5 VB: partial.

COFFEYVILLE COMMUNITY COLLEGE, Coach of Specific Sport, 11th and Willow, Coffeyville, KS 67337, (316) 251-9482. NJCAA. 15 BB, 6 TEN, 15 VB: partial.

COLBY COMMUNITY COLLEGE, Victor Oelke, Athletic Director, 1255 S. Range, Colby, KS 67701, (913) 462-3984. NJCAA. 12 BB, 8 T&F, 12 VB: partial.

COWLEY COUNTY COMMUNITY COLLEGE, Linda Hargrove, Director of Admissions, 125 S. Second, Arkansas City, KS 67005, (316) 442-0430. NJCAA, Jayhawk, Eastern. 15 BB, 18 SB, 12 VB: partial.

DODGE CITY COMMUNITY COLLEGE, House, Manhattan, KS 66506, (913) 532-6910. NCAA. 6 G, 11 SB, 6 TEN, 16 T&F, 12 VB: partial to full. 15 BB: full.

KANSAS WESLEYAN UNIVERSITY, Tracy Rietzke, Coach, 100 E. Claflin, Salina, KS 67401, (913) 827-5541. NAIA. BB, SB, T&F, VB: partial.

MARYMOUNT COLLEGE OF KANSAS, Todd Reynolds, Athletic Director, Box 2000, E. Iron Ave., Salina, KS 67401, (913) 825-2101. NAIA. SB, T&F: partial. BB, VB: partial to full.

McPHERSON COLLEGE, Paul N. Graber, Athletic Director, McPherson, KS 67460, (316) 241-0731. NAIA. BB, TEN, T&F, VB: partial.

MID-AMERICA NAZARENE COLLEGE, Gordon DeGraffenreid, Athletic Director, 2030 Collegeway, Olathe, KS 66061, (913) 782-3750. NAIA, Heart of American Athletic Conf. BB, CC, SB, T&F, VB: partial.

OTTAWA UNIVERSITY, Bob Cole, Athletic Director, 9th & Cedar, Box I, Ottawa, KS 66067, (913) 242-5200 ext. 324. NAIA. BB, CC, TEN, T&F, VB: partial.

PITTSBURG STATE UNIVERSITY, David Suenram, Athletic Director, Pittsburg, KS 66762, (316) 231-7000 ext. 295. NAIA. 12 BB, 11 SB, 10 VB: partial.

PRATT COMMUNITY COLLEGE, Glen Piper, Dean of Students, Hwy. 61, Pratt, KS 67124, (316) 672-5641. NJCAA. 15 BB, 10 RD, 10 T&F, 20 VB: partial.

ST. JOHN'S COLLEGE, Neil Lohmeyer, Winfield, KS 67156, (316) 221-4000. NAIA. 15 BB, 18 SB, 12 VB: partial.

ST. MARY OF THE PLAINS, Coach of Specific Sport, Dodge City, KS 67801, (316) 225-4171. NAIA. 10 BB, 10 SB, 10 VB: partial.

SOUTHWESTERN COLLEGE, Gerald Raines, Coach, 100 College St., Winfield, KS 67156, (316) 221-4150 ext. 217. NAIA, KCAC, III. 10 BB, 10 CC, 10 SB, 10 T&F,

partial.

INDIANA UNIVERSITY, Isabella Hutchison, Associate Athletic Director, Assembly Hall, Bloomington, IN 47405, (812) 335-8261. NCAA, Big Ten, I. 15 **BB**, 6 **G**, 10 **GYM**, 10 **SB**, 12 **S&D**, 8 **TEN**, 14 **T&F/CC**, 11 **VB**: full.

INDIANA UNIVERSITY SOUTHEAST, Linda C. Ruf, Coordinator of Women's Sports/Coach, 4201 Grant Line Rd., New Albany, IN 47150, (812) 945-2731. NAIA, Independent. 6 **BB**: partial. **TEN**, **VB**: non-scholarship.

OAKLAND CITY COLLEGE, Jill Padgett, Assistant Athletic Director, Oakland City, IN 47660, (812) 749-4781 ext. 47. NAIA. 12 **BB**, 12 **VB**: partial.

PURDUE UNIVERSITY, Dr. Carol Mertler, Associate Athletic Director, Mackey Arena, West Lafayette, IN 47907, (317) 494-3209. NCAA, Big Ten, I. 15 **BB**, 11 **FH**, 6 **G**, 14 **S&D**, 8 **TEN**, 16 **T&F/CC**, 12 **VB**: full.

ST. FRANCIS COLLEGE, Thelma Morgan, Athletic Director, 2701 Spring St., Fort Wayne, IN 46808, (219) 432-3551. NAIA, **TEN**, **VB**: partial.

ST. JOSEPH'S COLLEGE, Bill Hogan, Athletic Director, Box 875, Rensselaer, IN 47978, (219) 866-7111. NCAA. **SB**, **TEN**, **T&F**: partial. 5 **BB**, 4 **VB**: partial to full.

UNIVERSITY OF EVANSVILLE, Linda Wambach, Assistant Athletic Director, 1800 Lincoln Ave., Evansville, IN 47714, (812) 479-2756. NCAA, North Star, I. 1.5 **CC**, 2 **G**, 3.5 **SB**, 3 **S&D**, 3 **TEN**, 1.5 **T&F**, 5.5 **VB**: partial. 8.5 **BB**: full.

VALPARAISO UNIVERSITY, Cindy Young, Women's Athletic Coordinator, Valparaiso, IN 46383, (219) 464-5460. NCAA. 4 **BB**, 8 **FH**, .8 **GYM**, .8 **SB**, .8 **S&D**, 8 **TEN**, 3 **VB**: full.

VINCENNES UNIVERSITY, Wanda J. Schwartz, Women's Basketball Coach, Vincennes, IN 47591, (812) 885-4511. NJCAA. **B**, **BB**, **S&D**, **T&F**, **VB**: partial to full.

(515) 752-7106. NJCAA. 5 **BB**, 5 **SB**: partial.

MARYCREST COLLEGE, Kim T. Vieira, Athletic Director, 1607 W. 12th, Davenport, IA 52804, (319) 326-9584. NAIA, Independent, I. **BB**, **VB**: partial. **SB**: non-scholarship.

MORNINGSIDE COLLEGE, Roberta Boothby, Women's Athletic Director, 1501 Morningside Ave., Sioux City, IA 51106, (712) 274-5317. NAIA. **BB**, **SB**, **VB**: partial to full.

MUSCATINE COMMUNITY COLLEGE, Paul Mayes, Coach, 152 Colorado, Muscatine, IA 52761, (319) 263-8250. NJCAA, Eastern Iowa JUCO. 6 **BB**: full.

NORTHWESTERN COLLEGE, Paula Beach, Assistant Professor Physical Education, Orange City, IA 51041, (712) 737-4821 ext. 304. NAIA, Io-Kota. 2.4 **BB**, .25 **G**, 1.5 **SB**, .25 **TEN**, 1.2 **T&F**, 2.4 **VB**: partial.

ST. AMBROSE COLLEGE, Jim Fox, Athletic Director, 518 W. Locust, Davenport, IA 52803, (319) 383-8727. NAIA. 8 **BB**, 8 **SB**, 3 **TEN**, 8 **VB**: partial to full.

SIOUX EMPIRE COLLEGE, Brian Engleman, Athletic Director, Box 312, Hawarden, IA 51023, (712) 552-2260. NJCAA. 12 **BB**, 15 **SB**, 12 **VB**: partial to full.

SOUTHEASTERN COMMUNITY COLLEGE, Jim Wyatt, Athletic Director, Hwy. 406 and Gear, West Burlington, IA 52655, (319) 752-2731 ext. 170. NJCAA. 5 **BB**, 5 **VB**: partial.

SOUTHWESTERN COMMUNITY COLLEGE, Ron Clinton, Athletic Director, Townline Rd., Creston, IA 50801, (515) 782-7081. NJCAA. 10 **BB**, 10 **SB**, 6 **VB**: partial.

UNIVERSITY OF IOWA, Linda C. Hackett, Athletic Director, 340F Carver Hawkeye Arena, Iowa City, IA 52242, (319)

Max Van Laningham, Athletic Coordinator, 2501 N. 14th, Dodge City, KS 67801, (316) 225-1321 ext. 255. NJCAA, Kansas Jayhawk CCC. **BB**, **CC**, **RD**, **TEN**, **T&F**, **VB**: partial.

EMPORIA STATE UNIVERSITY, William Quayle, Athletic Director, 1200 Commercial, Emporia, KS 66801, (316) 343-1200. NAIA. 3 **B**, 3 **G**, 6 **TEN**: partial. 8 **BB**, 4 **SB**, 7 **T&F**, 6 **VB**: full.

FORT HAYS STATE UNIVERSITY, Nancy Popp, Associate Athletic Director, 600 Park St., Hays, KS 67601-4099, (913) 628-4050. NAIA. 12 **BB**, 7 **GYM**, 7 **SB**, 4 **TEN**, 12 **T&F**, 14**VB**: partial.

FRIENDS UNIVERSITY, Ron Heller, Athletic Director, 2100 University Ave., Wichita, KS 67213, (316) 264-9627. NAIA. 15 **BB**, 24 **SB**, 15 **VB**: partial.

GARDEN CITY COMMUNITY COLLEGE, Betty Jo Johns, 801 Campus Dr., Garden City, KS 67846, (316) 276-7611. NJCAA, Jayhawk. 10 **BB**, 6 **TEN**, 10 **T&F**, 12 **VB**: partial. **SB**: non-scholarship.

HUTCHINSON COMMUNITY COLLEGE, Ruby Munzer, Assistant Athletic Director, 1300 N. Plum, Hutchinson, KS 67501, (316) 665-3586. NJCAA. 12 **BB**, 6 **TEN**, 12 **T&F**, 12 **VB**: partial.

INDEPENDENCE COMMUNITY COLLEGE, Coach of Specific Sport, Box 708, Independence, KS 67301, (316) 331-4100. NJCAA. 12 **BB**, 5 **TEN**, 12 **VB**: partial.

KANSAS NEWMAN COLLEGE, Patrick Thomas, Coach, 3100 McCormick, Wichita, KS 67213, (316) 942-4291. NAIA, Independent. **BB**, **VB**: partial.

JOHNSON COUNTY COMMUNITY COLLEGE, J.M. Yasko, Athletic Director, 12345 College at Quivira, Overland Park, KS 66210 (913) 469-3819. Kansas Jayhawk Conference, Eastern Division. 14 **BB**, 12 **SOC**, 4 **SB**: partial.

KANSAS STATE UNIVERSITY, Larry Travis, Athletic Director, Ahearn Field

10 **VB**: partial.

TABOR COLLEGE, Del Reimer, Athletic Director, 400 S. Jefferson, Hillsboro, KS 67063, (316) 947-3121 ext. 326. NAIA. 8 **BB**, 4 **SB**, 3 **TEN**, 6 **VB**: partial.

UNIVERSITY OF KANSAS, Pat Collinson, Administrative Assistant, Allen Field House, Lawrence, KS 66045, (913) 864-3681. NCAA, Big 8, I. 6 **G**, 11 **SB**, 14 **S&D**, 8 **TEN**, 16 **T&F**, 12 **VB**: partial to full. 15 **BB**: full.

WASHBURN UNIVERSITY, Steve Anson, Assistant Athletic Director, 1700 College, Topeka, KS 66621, (913) 295-6334. NAIA, Central States Intercollegiate. 12 **BB**, 13 **SB**, 8 **TEN**, 11 **VB**: partial. 3 **BB**, 3 **SB**: full.

KENTUCKY

BELLARMINE COLLEGE, James R. Spalding, Athletic Director, 2000 Norris Pl., Louisville, KY 40205, (502) 452-8380. NCAA, Great Lakes Valley, II. 7 **CC**, 12 **SB**, 6 **TEN**, 9 **VB**: partial. 12 **BB**: full.

EASTERN KENTUCKY UNIVERSITY, Martha Mullins, Assistant Athletic Director, AC128-EKU, Richmond, KY 40475, (606) 622-5108. NCAA, Ohio Valley Conference, I. 6 **FH**, 8 **S&D**, 1 **T&F**, 4 **VB**: partial. 12 **BB**, 6 **FH**, 4 **TEN**, 12 **T&F/CC**, 6 **VB**: full.

GEORGETOWN COLLEGE, Jim Reid, Athletic Director, College St., Georgetown, KY 40324, (502) 863-8055. NAIA. 12 **BB**, 6 **TEN**, 10 **VB**: partial.

KENTUCKY STATE UNIVERSITY, Kenneth Gibson, Athletic Director, E. Main St., Frankfort, KY 40601, (502) 227-6014/6011. NCAA, NAIA. 6 **BB**, 8 **SB**, 6 **T&F**, 6 **VB**: partial.

LINDSEY WILSON COLLEGE, Dean Adams, Athletic Director, 210 Lindsey Wilson St., Columbia, KY 42728, (502) 384-2126. NJCAA, KJCAC. **BB**: partial to full.

MIDWAY COLLEGE, Denise Beuke, Athletic Director, Midway, KY 40347, (606) 846-4421 ext. 286. 12 **BB**, 8 **RIDING**, 10 **SB**, 12 **VB**: partial.

MOREHEAD STATE UNIVERSITY, G.E. Moran, Jr., Director of Athletics, Academic Center, Morehead, KY 40351, (606) 783-2386. NCAA, Ohio Valley, I. 10 **SB**, 4 **TEN**: partial. 12 **BB**, 12 **VB**: full. **CC, SOC, S&D**: non-scholarship.

MURRAY STATE UNIVERSITY, Johnny Reagan, Athletic Director, University Station, Murray, KY 42071, (502) 762-6184. NCAA. 12 **BB**, 4 **TEN**, 12 **T&F**: partial to full.

NORTHERN KENTUCKY UNIVERSITY, Jane Meier, Women's Athletic Coordinator, Albright Health Center, Highland Heights, KY 41076, (606) 572-5193. NCAA, Great Lakes Valley Conference, II. 8 **BB**, 3 **SB**, 1 **TEN**, 3 **VB**: full. **CC**: non-scholarship.

SUE BENNETT COLLEGE, Diane L. Campbell, Dean of Students, 101 College St., London, KY 40741, (606) 864-2236. NJCAA, KWIC, KJCAC. 12 **BB**: partial.

THOMAS MORE COLLEGE, Peg Hofmann, Assistant Athletic Director. Crestville Hills, KY 41017, (606) 341-3336. NAIA, KWIC, KIAC, small college. **BB, SB, VB**: partial.

TRANSYLVANIA UNIVERSITY, Pat Deacon, Associate Athletic Director, 300 N. Broadway, Lexington, KY 40508, (606) 233-8194. NCAA, KY Women I.C. 8 **BB**, 2 **FH**, 1 **SB**, 6 **S&D**, 6 **TEN**: partial.

UNION COLLEGE, Tamra Cash, Head Basketball & Softball Coach, Box 430 College St., Barbourville, KY 40906, (606) 546-4151 ext. 235. NAIA, KIAC. 15 **BB**, 18 **SB**: partial.

UNIVERSITY OF KENTUCKY, Susan B. Feamster, Assistant Athletic Director/ Womens, Lexington, KY 40506-0019, (606) 257-8604. NCAA, SEC, I. 15 **BB**, 6 **G**, 10 **GYM**, 16 **S&D**, 5 **TEN**, 16 **T&F**, 12 **VB**: full.

NORTHEAST LOUISIANA UNIVERSITY, Lenny Fant, Administrative Assistant, Malone Stadium, Monroe, LA 71209, (318) 342-3100. NCAA, Southland Women's Conference, I. 15 **BB**, 11 **SB**, 6 **S&D**, 8 **TEN**, 8 **T&F/CC**, 6 **VB**: full.

NORTHWESTERN LOUISIANA UNIVERSITY, Patricia N. Pierson, Women's Athletic Director, Prather Coliseum, Natchitoches, LA 71497, (318) 357-5891. NCAA. 15 **BB**, 6 **SB**, 5 **TEN**: full.

SOUTHEASTERN LOUISIANA UNIVERSITY, Maria K. Ferguson, Women's Athletic Director, Box 309, Hammond, LA 70402, (504) 549-2253. NCAA. 15 **BB**, 5 **TEN**, 8 **VB**: full.

SOUTHERN UNIVERSITY, Richard Hill, Athletic Director, Box 4492, Baton Rouge, LA 70813, (504) 771-3170. NCAA. 15 **BB**, 14 **T&F**, 5 **VB**: partial to full.

UNIVERSITY OF NEW ORLEANS, F. Joseph Favaloro, Women's Athletic Coordinator, Lakefront, New Orleans, LA 70148, (504) 286-6239. NCAA. 10 **BB**, 4 **S&D**, 3 **TEN**, 6 **VB**: full.

UNIVERSITY OF SOUTHWESTERN LOUISIANA, Sherry LeBas, Assistant Athletic Director, 201 Reinhardt Dr., Lafayette, LA 70506-4297, (318) 231-5720. NCAA. 15 **BB**, 7 **SB**, 8 **TEN**, 5 **T&F**, 12 **VB**: full.

XAVIER UNIVERSITY OF LOUISIANA, Denny Alexander, Director of Athletics, 7325 Palmetto St., New Orleans, LA 70125, (504) 486-7411. NAIA, II. 9 **BB**: partial.

MAINE

UNITY COLLEGE, Vivian Kanezevich, Dean of Students, Rt. 78, Box 1, Unity, ME 04988, (207) 948-3131. NAIA. **VB**: partial.

UNIVERSITY OF MAINE (ORONO), Ellen Chessa, 303 Memorial Gym, Orono, ME

MASSACHUSETTS

AMERICAN INTERNATIONAL COLLEGE, Robert E. Burke, Associate Athletic Director, 1000 State St., Springfield, MA 01109, (413) 737-7000. NCAA, ECAC, NECAC; Northeast-8 Conference, II. 4.5 **BB**, 2.5 **SB**, 1.5 **VB**: full.

ASSUMPTION COLLEGE, Rita Castagna, Assistant Athletic Director, 500 Salisbury St., Worcester, MA 01609, (617) 752-5615. NCAA. 6 **BB**: full.

BENTLEY COLLEGE, Paula M. Mullen, Assistant Athletic Director, Dana Athletic Center, Waltham, MA 02254, (617) 891-2256. NCAA, NE-8, II. 10 **BB**: full. **CC, FH, SB, TEN, T&F, VB**: non-scholarship.

BOSTON COLLEGE, Mary Miller Carson, Assistant Athletic Director, Roberts Center, Chestnut Hill, MA 02167, (617) 552-4528. NCAA, ECAC, Big East, I. **BB, FH, LAX, SOC, SB, S&D, TEN, T&F, VB**: partial to full. **FEN, G, SKI, SAILING**.

BOSTON UNIVERSITY, Averill C. Haines, Assistant Athletic Director, 285 Babcock St., Boston, MA 02215, (617) 353-4683. NCAA, ECAC, Seaboard, Gr. Bost., I. **CREW**: partial. **CC, FH, S&D, TEN, T&F**: partial to full. **BB**: full. **LAX, SAILING**: non-scholarship.

GORDON COLLEGE, Steven Larson, Athletic Director, 255 Grapevine Rd., Wenham, MA 01984, (617) 927-2300 ext. 4335. NAIA, Independent. **BB, FH, SB, TEN, VB**: partial.

HOLY CROSS COLLEGE, Diane S. Holt, Athletic Coordinator, College Hill, Worcester, MA 01610, (617) 793-2628. NCAA, Metro Atlantic, I. 3 **BB, FH, LAX, SOC, S&D, TEN, VB**: partial. **CC, T&F**: partial to full. 12 **BB**: full. **CREW, SB**: non-scholarship.

MERRIMACK COLLEGE, Robert DeGregoria Jr., Director of Athletics, N. Andover, MA 01845, (617) 683-7111 ext. 341/342. NCAA, ECAC, Northeast Eight

GRAND VALLEY STATE COLLEGE, Joan Boand, Women's Athletic Coordinator, 187 Field House, Allendale, MI 49401, (616) 895-3233. NCAA, WLIAC, II. **BB, SB, VB**: partial to full.

HILLSDALE COLLEGE, Jack McAvoy, Athletic Director, 201 Oak St., Hillsdale, MI 49242, (517) 437-7364. NAIA, NCAA. 6 **BB**, 3.5 **TEN**, 4 **T&F**, 5.5 **VB**: full.

LAKE MICHIGAN COLLEGE, Liz Miller, Athletic Director, 2755 E. Napier, Benton Harbor, MI 49022, (616) 927-3571. NJCAA. 10 **BB**, 10 **SB**, 10 **VB**: partial.

LAKE SUPERIOR STATE COLLEGE, Ronald Cooper, Athletic Director, Norris Physical Education Center, Sault Ste Marie, MI 49783, (906) 635-2366. NCAA. 8 **BB**, 4 **SB**, 4 **TEN**, 4 **VB**: partial to full.

MADONNA COLLEGE, Raymond Sobocinski, Athletic Director/Coach, 36600 Schoolcraft Rd., Livonia, MI 48150, (313) 591-5138. **BB, G, SB**: partial. **ARCH, BAD, BOW, CREW, CC, FEN, FH, GYM, IH, LAX, RIDING, RIFLE, RODEO, SKI, SOC, S&D, SS, TEN, T&F**: non-scholarship.

MICHIGAN CHRISTIAN COLLEGE, Bill Shinsky, Athletic Director, 800 W. Avon Rd., Rochester, MI 48063, (313) 656-1924. Independent. 8 **SB**: partial.

MICHIGAN STATE UNIVERSITY, Coach of Specific Sport, Jenison Field House, East Lansing, MI 48824-1025, (517) 355-9710. NCAA, Big Ten, I. **FH, G, SB, S&D, TEN, T&F**: partial. **BB, GYM, VB**: full.

NORTHERN MICHIGAN UNIVERSITY, Barbara J. Patrick, Associate Athletic Director, Marquette, MI 49855, (906) 227-2109. NCAA. 8 **BB**, 5 **GYM**, 5 **SB**, 8 **S&D**, 6 **VB**: full.

OAKLAND UNIVERSITY, Paul Hartman, Athletic Director, Lepley Sports Center, Rochester, MI 48063, (313) 371-3196. NCAA, GLIAC, II. 12 **S&D**, 4 **VB**: partial. 9 **BB**: full.

SAGINAW VALLEY STATE COLLEGE, Marsha Reall, Women's Athletic

UNIVERSITY OF LOUISVILLE, Jack Tennant, Assistant Athletic Director, Louisville, KY 40292, (502) 588-5732. NCAA. 8 **FH**, 10 **S&D**, 8 **TEN**, 12 **T&F**: partial to full. 13 **BB**, 12 **VB**: full. **SOC**: non-scholarship.

WESTERN KENTUCKY UNIVERSITY, Pam Herriford, Coordinator of Women's Athletics, Athletic Department, Bowling Green, KY 42101, (502) 745-3542. NCAA. Sun Belt Conference. I. 4 **G**, 4 **TEN**, 8 **T&F/CC**, 12 **VB**: full.

LOUISIANA

CENTENARY COLLEGE OF LOUISIANA, Walter C. Stevens, Athletic Director, Box 4188, Shreveport, LA 71134-0188, (318) 869-5275/5034. NAIA. 2 **CC**, 2 **G**, 1 **RIFLE**, 2 **GYM**: partial. 5 **GYM**, 4 **TEN**: full. **VB**: non-scholarship.

LOUISIANA COLLEGE, Frank W. Schneider, Coach, Box 1047, Pineville, LA 71359, (318) 487-7482. NAIA. 9 **BB**: partial to full.

LOUISIANA STATE UNIVERSITY, Larry Jones, Assistant Athletic Director, Baton Rouge, LA 70893, (504) 388-8212. NCAA. 15 **BB**, 6 **G**, 10 **GYM**, 14 **S&D**, 8 **TEN**, 16 **T&F**, 12 **VB**: partial to full.

McNEESE STATE UNIVERSITY, Cheryl Manual, Coach, Women's Athletics, Lake Charles, LA 70609, (318) 477-6045. NCAA. 10 **BB**, 8 **SB**, 5 **TEN**, 5 **VB**: partial to full.

NEWCOMB COLLEGE/TULANE UNIVERSITY, Elizabeth Delery, Director of Women's Athletics, New Orleans, LA 70118, (504) 865-5735. NCAA, I. 1 **CC**, 1 **T&F**: partial. 12 **BB**, 4 **S&D**, 8 **TEN**, 12 **VB**: full.

NICHOLLS STATE UNIVERSITY, Marion S. Curtis, Assistant Athletic Director, Box 2032, NSU, Thibodaux, LA 70310, (504) 446-8111 ext. 518. NCAA. Gulf Star. 15 **BB**, 1 **CC**, 9 **SB**, 5 **TEN**, 1 **T&F**, 9 **VB**: full.

04469, (207) 581-1059. NCAA. 2 **FH**, 4 **S&D**, 2 **VB**: partial. **SB**: partial to full. 4 **BB**: full.

MARYLAND

LOYOLA COLLEGE, Anne McCloskey, Assistant Athletic Director, 4501 N. Charles St., Baltimore, MD 21210, (301) 323-1010 ext. 2270. NCAA, ECAC, I. 9 **BB**, 4 **FH**, 9 **LAX**, 4 **VB**: full.

MORGAN STATE UNIVERSITY, LaRue Fields, Assistant Athletic Director, Coldspring Ln. and Hillen Rd., Baltimore, MD 21239, (301) 444-3485. NCAA. 6 **BB**, 6 **T&F**, 2 **VB**: full.

MOUNT ST. MARY'S COLLEGE, Lynne M. Phelan, Women's Athletic Coordinator, Emmitsburg, MD 21727, (301) 447-6122 ext. 296. NCAA, Mason-Dixon, II. 10 **BB**, 1.5 **TEN**, 4.5 **T&F**: partial to full. **CC**, **FH**, **LAX**, **SOC**, **SB**: non-scholarship.

PRINCE GEORGE'S COMMUNITY COLLEGE, Ronald Mann, Athletic Coordinator, 301 Largo Rd., Largo, MD 20772, (301) 322-0513. NJCAA. .5 **GYM**, .5 **TEN**: partial.

TOWSON STATE UNIVERSITY, Nance Reed, Assistant Athletic Director, 8000 York Rd., Towson, MD 21204, (301) 321-3159. NCAA. **BB**, **FH**, **GYM**, **LAX**, **SB**, **VB**: partial to full.

UNIVERSITY OF MARYLAND, Gothard Lane, Assistant Athletic Director, Box 295, College Park, MD 20740, (301) 454-5854. NCAA, Atlantic Coast, I. 15 **BB**, 11 **FH**, 10 **GYM**, 11 **LAX**, 9 **S&D**, 6 **TEN**, 10 **T&F**, 7 **VB**: full.

UNIVERSITY OF MARYLAND (BALTIMORE COUNTY), Rick Moreland, Sports Information Director, 5401 Wilkens Ave., Catersville, MD 21228, (301) 455-2197. NCAA. **BB**, **GYM**, **T&F**: partial.

Conference, II. 6 **BB**: full. **CC**, **G**, **SOC**, **SB**, **TEN**, **VB**: non-scholarship.

NORTHEASTERN UNIVERSITY, Jeanne Rowlands, Women's Athletic Director, Arena Annex, Boston, MA 02115, (617) 437-2703. NCAA. **BB**, **CREW**, **FH**, **GYM**, **IH**, **LAX**, **S&D**, **TEN**, **T&F**, **VB**: partial to full.

STONEHILL COLLEGE, Paula Sullivan, Assistant Athletic Director, 320 Washington St., N. Easton, MA 02357, (617) 238-1081. NCAA. 7 **BB**: full.

UNIVERSITY OF LOWELL, Denise Legault, South Campus, Lowell, MA 01854, (617) 452-5000 ext. 2461. NCAA, NECC, II. **FH**, **SB**, **TEN**, **T&F**, **VB**: partial. **BB**: partial to full.

UNIVERSITY OF MASSACHUSETTS (AMHERST), Coach of Specific Sport, Boyden Gym., Amherst, MA 01003, (413) 545-2439. NCAA. 14 **BB**, 4 **FH**, 2 **GYM**, 4 **LAX**, 4 **SOC**, 4 **SB**, 3 **T&F**, 3 **VB**: partial to full.

MICHIGAN

CENTRAL MICHIGAN UNIVERSITY, Fran Koenig, Director of Women's Athletics, Mt. Pleasant, MI 48859, (517) 774-6663. NCAA, Mid American, I. 15 **BB**, 9 **FH**, 7 **GYM**, 11 **SB**, 13 **T&F**, 12 **VB**: full.

EASTERN MICHIGAN UNIVERSITY, Lucy N. Parker, Women's Athletic Director, 200 Bowen Field House, Ypsilanti, MI 48197, (313) 487-1330. NCAA, Mid American, I. 15 **BB**, 4 **FH**, 4 **GYM**, 11 **SB**, 6 **S&D**, 5 **TEN**, 8 **T&F**, 12 **VB**: full.

FERRIS STATE COLLEGE, Dean Davenport, Athletic Director, Big Rapids, MI 49307, (616) 796-0461. NCAA. 1 **G**, 4 **TEN**: partial. 11 **BB**, 8 **VB**: full.

GRAND RAPIDS BAPTIST COLLEGE, Dr. John D. Bratcher, Director of Athletics, 1001 E. Beltline NE, Grand Rapids, MI 49505, (616) 949-5300 ext. 306. NCAA, I. **BB**, **SB**, **VB**: partial.

Coordinator, University Center, MI 48710, (517) 790-4118. NCAA, NAIA. 9 **BB**, 5 **SB**, 2 **TEN**, 6 **T&F**, 2 **VB**: full.

SCHOOLCRAFT COLLEGE, Dr. Marvin Gans, Athletic Director, 18600 Haggerty Rd., Livonia, MI 48152, (313) 591-6400 ext 480. 10 **BB**, 7 **CC**, 15 **SOC**, 10 **VB**: partial.

SIENA HEIGHTS COLLEGE, Fred Smith, Athletic Director, 1247 E. Siena Heights Dr., Adrian, MI 49221, (517) 263-0731 ext. 233. NAIA. **BB**, **CC**, **SB**, **TEN**, **VB**: partial.

SOUTHWESTERN MICHIGAN COLLEGE, Ronald Gunn, Dean of Sports Education, Cherry Grove Rd., Dowagiac, MI 49047, (616) 782-5113. NJCAA, Western Collegiate. 5 **BB**, 5 **SB**, 5 **T&F**, 5 **VB**: partial to full.

UNIVERSITY OF DETROIT, Brad Kinsman, Athletic Director, 4001 W. McNicholls Rd., Detroit, MI 48221, (313) 927-1150. NCAA, North Star, I. 4 **CC**, 5 **FENC**, 2 **RIFLE**, 6 **SB**: partial. 14 **BB**: full.

UNIVERSITY OF MICHIGAN (ANN ARBOR), Phyllis M. Ocker, Associate Athletic Director, 1000 S. State St., Ann Arbor, MI 48109, (313) 763-2159. NCAA, Big Ten, I. **BB**, **FH**, **G**, **GYM**, **SB**, **S&D**, **TEN**, **T&F**, **VB**: partial to full.

UNIVERSITY OF MICHIGAN (DEARBORN), Jim DuFresne, Sports Information Director, U of M-D, Dearborn, MI 48128, (313) 593-5540. NAIA, Independent. 2 **BB**, 2 **FENC**, 4 **T&F**: partial.

WAYNE STATE UNIVERSITY, Chris Petrouleas, Assistant Athletic Director, 101 Matthaei, Detroit, MI 48202, (313) 577-4280. NCAA. 7.95 **BB**, 3.5 **FENC**, 3.51 **SB**, 2.03 **TEN**, 4.47 **VB**: partial to full.

WESTERN MICHIGAN UNIVERSITY, Christine W. Hoyles, Associate Athletic Director, Division of Intercollegiate Athletics, Kalamazoo, MI 49008, (616) 383-1930. NCAA, Mid-American, I. 15 **BB**, 7 **GYM**, 11 **SB**, 5 **TEN**, 11 **T&F/CC**, 12 **VB**: full.

MINNESOTA

BEMIDJI STATE UNIVERSITY, Pat Rosenbrock, Director of Women's Athletics, Bemidji, MN 56001, (218) 755-2766. NCAA, NAIA, Northern Sun Conference, II. 9 **BB**, 4 **TEN**, 7 **T&F**, 8 **VB**: partial. **CC, G, SB, FH**: non-scholarship.

BETHANY LUTHERAN COLLEGE, Ron Younge, Athletic Director, 734 Marsh St., Mankato, MN 56001, (507) 625-2977. NJCAA, MCCC. 10 **BB**, 4 **TEN**, 10 **VB**: partial.

MANKATO STATE UNIVERSITY, Georgene Brock, Women's Athletic Director, Mankato, MN 56001, (507) 389-2018. NCAA, North Central Conference, II. 5 **FENC**, 5 **G**, 8 **SB**, 8 **S&D**, 5 **TEN**, 12 **T&F**, 10 **VB**: partial. 9 **BB**: full.

MOORHEAD STATE UNIVERSITY, Mary C. Curtis, Women's Athletic Director, Moorhead, MN 56560, (218) 236-2135. NAIA. 2 **BB**, 1 **G**, 2 **SB**, 2 **TEN**, 3 **T&F**, 2 **VB**: partial.

ST. CLOUD STATE UNIVERSITY, Gladys Ziemer, Director Women's Athletics, Halenbeck Hall, St. Cloud, MN 56301, (612) 255-2182. NCAA, North Central Conference, II. 4 **BB**, 4 **SB**, 8 **S&D**, 10 **T&F**, 6 **VB**: partial. 6 **BB**, 3 **VB**: full.

SOUTHWEST STATE UNIVERSITY, Dr. Jeri Madden, Women's Athletic Director, Hwy. 19 and 23, Marshall, MN 56258, (507) 537-7125. NAIA, NIC. 12 **BB**, 6 **SB**, 8 **TEN**, 8 **T&F**, 12 **VB**: partial.

UNIVERSITY OF MINNESOTA (DULUTH), Linda M. Larson, Coordinator Women's Athletics, 10 University Dr., Duluth, MN 55812, (218) 726-7230. NCAA, Northern Sun Conference, II. 8 **BB**, 3 **SB**, 5 **TEN**, 8 **VB**: partial. 1 **BB**, 1 **VB**: full.

UNIVERSITY OF MINNESOTA (MINNEAPOLIS-ST. PAUL), Coach of Specific Sport, 238 BFAB, 516 15th Ave. SE, Minneapolis, MN 55455, (612)

MISSISSIPPI VALLEY STATE UNIVERSITY, Joseph W. Curtis, Athletic Director, Box 310, Itta Bena, MS 38941, (601) 254-9041 ext. 6359. NCAA. 15 **BB**, 12 **T&F**: partial.

UNIVERSITY OF MISSISSIPPI, Jeanne Taylor, Assistant Athletic Director, Athletic Dept., University, MS 38677, (601) 232-7241. NCAA. 3 **BB**, 2 **TEN**, 5 **VB**: full.

WILLIAM CAREY COLLEGE, Katie Eaton, Women's Basketball Coach, Box 182, Hattiesburg, MS 39401, (601) 582-5051 ext. 223. NAIA, Gulf Coast Athletic Conference. 6 **BB**: partial. 6 **BB**: full.

MISSOURI

AVILA COLLEGE, J. Scott Royal-Ferris, Athletic Director, 11901 Wornall Rd., Kansas City, MO 64115, (816) 942-8400 ext. 235. NAIA. **BB, VB**: partial to full.

CENTRAL MISSOURI STATE UNIVERSITY, Jerry Hughes, Athletic Director, Garrison 106, Warrensburg, MO 64093, (816) 429-4250. NCAA. 12 **BB**, 4 **SB**, 7 **T&F**, 8 **VB**: full.

COLUMBIA COLLEGE, Art Siebels, Director of Athletics, 10th and Rodgers, Columbia, MO 65216, (314) 875-7410. NAIA, Ozark Collegiate. 14 **SB**, 10 **VB**: partial.

CROWDER COLLEGE, Bill Presley, Coach, Neosho, MO 64850, (417) 451-5530. NJCAA. 10 **BB**, 10 **SB**: full.

CULVER-STOCKTON COLLEGE, Gene Hall, Athletic Director, Canton, MO 63435, (314) 228-5221. NAIA. **BB, SB, TEN, VB**: partial.

DRURY COLLEGE, Barb Lawson, Coach, 900 N. Benton, Springfield, MO 65802, (417) 865-8731 ext. 363. NAIA. 1 **TEN**, 6 **VB**: partial.

EVANGEL COLLEGE, David Stair, Athletic Director, 1111 N. Glenstone, Springfield, MO 65802, (417) 865-2811. NAIA. 4.2 **BB**,

785-4236. NCAA, MO Intercollegiate Athletic Association, II. 3 **TEN**: partial. 12 **BB**, 6 **SB**, 6 **S&D**, 6 **T&F/CC**, 4 **VB**: full. **G, SOC**: non-scholarship.

NORTHWEST MISSOURI STATE UNIVERSITY, Sherri Reeves, Women's Athletic Director, Martindale Gym, Maryville, MO 64468, (816) 562-1298. NCAA, MIAA, II. 12 **BB**, 5.5 **SB**, 1 **TEN**, 5.66 **T&F/CC**, 5.66 **VB**: full.

PARK COLLEGE, Jim A. Erber, Women's Cross Country Track Coach, Box 66, Pa'kville, MO 64152, (816) 741-2000 ext. 148. NAIA, Ozark, I. 15 **BB**, 5 **TEN**, 20 **T&F/CC**, 12 **VB**: full.

ROCKHURST COLLEGE, Frank Diskill, Athletic Director, 5225 Troost, Kansas City, MO 64110, (816) 926-4000. 10 **BB**, 10 **VB**: partial.

ST. LOUIS UNIVERSITY, Coach of Specific Sport, 3672 W. Pine Blvd., St. Louis, MO 63108, (314) 658-3177. NCAA. **BB, FH, SB, VB**: partial to full.

SCHOOL OF THE OZARKS, Bob Powers, Coach, Pt. Lookout, MO 65726, (417) 334-6411 ext. 387. NAIA. 15 **S&D**, 15 **T&F**, 15 **VB**: partial to full.

SOUTHEAST MISSOURI STATE UNIVERSITY, Marvin Rosengarten, Athletic Director, 900 Normal Ave., Cape Girardeau, MO 63701, (314) 651-2229. NCAA. 12 **BB**, 4.5 **GYM**, 3 **SB**, 2 **TEN**, 6 **T&F**, 4.5 **VB**: partial to full.

SOUTHWEST BAPTIST UNIVERSITY, Rex Brown, Athletic Director, 1601 S. Springfield, Bolivar, MO 65613, (417) 326-5281. NAIA. 12 **BB**, 15 **SB**, 6 **TEN**, 12 **VB**: partial.

SOUTHWEST MISSOURI STATE UNIVERSITY, Mary Jo Wynn, Women's Athletic Director, 901 S. National, Springfield, MO 65804, (417) 836-5246. NCAA, Gateway Collegiate Athletic, I. 3.8 **FH**, 2.2 **G**, 8 **SB**, 2.9 **TEN**, 6.7 **T&F/CC**: partial to full. 15 **BB**, 12 **VB**: full.

TARKIO COLLEGE, Jeff Moore, Athletic

Kondelis, Financial Aid Officer, W. Park St., Butte, MT 59701, (406) 496-4213. NAIA. 9 **BB**, 9 **VB**: partial to full.

MONTANA STATE UNIVERSITY, Ginny Hunt, Women's Athletic Director, Brick Breeden Field House, Bozeman, MT 59717, (406) 994-3945. NCAA, Mountain West, I. 15 **BB**, 10 **GYM**, 7 **SKI**, 6 **TEN**, 16 **T&F**, 12 **VB**: partial. 8 **BB**, 5 **GYM**, 3 **TEN**, 8 **T&F**, 7 **VB**: full.

NORTHERN MONTANA COLLEGE, Loren Baker, Athletic Director, Havre, MT 59501, (406) 265-7821 ext. 3291. NAIA. 5 **T&F**: partial. 10 **BB**, 10 **VB**: partial to full.

ROCKY MOUNTAIN COLLEGE, Gail Patton, BB Coach/Clarece Ball, T&F Coach, 1511 Poly Dr., Billings, MT 59102, (406) 657-1038. NAIA. 8 **BB**, 12 **T&F**: partial. 4 **BB**, 1 **T&F**: full.

UNIVERSITY OF MONTANA, Dr. Barbara Hollmann, Associate Athletic Director, Missoula, MT 59812, (406) 243-5331. NCAA, Mountain West Athletic Conference, I-AA. 10 **GYM**, 8 **TEN**: partial. 13 **BB**, 11 **T&F/CC**, 9 **VB**: full.

WESTERN MONTANA COLLEGE, Nyles Humphrey, Athletic Director, 710 S. Atlantic, Dillon, MT 59725, (406) 683-7572. NAIA, Frontier, II. 10 **BB**, 2 **T&F**, 4 **VB**: partial to full.

NEBRASKA

BELLEVUE COLLEGE, Karen Nicodemus, Assistant Athletic Director, Wrightway at Galvin Rd., Bellevue, NE 68005, (402) 291-8100. NAIA. 5 **G**, 10 **VB**: partial.

CHADRON STATE COLLEGE, Pat Colgate, Athletic Director, 10th & Main, Chadron, NE 69337, (308) 432-6344. NAIA. 7 **BB**, 1 **CC**, 2 **RD**, 5 **T&F**, 5 **VB**: partial.

COLLEGE OF ST. MARY, Dee Romine, Athletic Director, 1901 S. 72nd St., Omaha, NE 68124, (402) 399-2607. NAIA, II. 15 **BB**, 15 **SB**, 15 **VB**: full.

CONCORDIA COLLEGE, John W. Knight,

373-2255. NCAA, 6 G, 11 SB, 14 S&D, 16 T&F: partial to full. 15 SB, 10 GYM, 8 TEN, 12 VB: full.

WINONA STATE UNIVERSITY, Dr. Toni Poli-Sorensen, Women's Athletic Director, 136 Memorial Hall, Winona, MN 55987, (507) 457-5211/5210. NCAA, NAIA, Northern Sun, II. 8 BB, 4 G, 3 GYM, 3 SB, 2 TEN, 3 T&F/CC, 7 VB: partial.

MISSISSIPPI

BLUE MOUNTAIN COLLEGE, Johnnie Armstrong, Athletic Director, Box 336, Blue Mountain, MS 38610, (601) 685-4771 ext. 46. NAIA, Tenn. Collegiate Athletic Association. 6 BB: partial. 6 BB: full. TEN: non-scholarship.

DELTA STATE UNIVERSITY, Dr. Brad Hovious, Athletic Director, Box A-3, DSU, Cleveland, MS 38733, (601) 846-4300. NCAA, Gulf South, II. 11.5 BB, 3 SB, 2 S&D, 3 TEN: full.

JACKSON STATE UNIVERSITY, Walter Reed, Athletic Director, 1325 Lynch St., Jackson, MS 39217, (601) 968-2291. NCAA, 6 CC, 6 TEN, 5 VB: partial. 15 BB, 21 T&F, 7 VB: full.

MISSISSIPPI COLLEGE, Glenda Holleyman, Women's Athletic Coordinator, Box 4245, Clinton, MS 39058, (601) 924-1989. NCAA, 2 SB, 2 TEN, 2 T&F: partial. 15 BB: full.

MISSISSIPPI STATE UNIVERSITY, Charley Scott, Athletic Director, Drawer 5327, Mississippi State, MS 39762, (601) 325-2808. NCAA, 2 BB, 1 G, 1 SB, 1 TEN, 1 VB: partial. 1 BB, 1 SB, 1 VB: full.

MISSISSIPPI UNIVERSITY FOR WOMEN, Dorothy Burdeshaw, Athletic Director & HPER Chrm., W-1400, Columbus, MS 39701, (601) 329-4750 ext. 225. NCAA, Independent, II. 12 BB, 8 SB, 3 TEN, 8 VB: full.

1.5 TEN, 2 VB: full.

FONTBONNE COLLEGE, Lee O'Donnell, Athletic Director, 6800 Wydown Blvd., St. Louis, MO 63105, (314) 889-1432. NLCAA. 10 BB, 10 VB: partial.

HARRIS STOWE STATE COLLEGE, Ted Savage, Jr., Athletic Director, 3026 Laclede St., St. Louis, MO 63103, (314) 533-3366. NAIA, II. 6 BB, 6 T&F, 6 VB: full.

JEFFERSON COLLEGE, Harold Oetting, Athletic Director, Box 1000, Hillsboro, MO 63050, (314) 789-3951. NJCAA, Midwest Comm. College. 8 BB, 8 VB: partial. 2 BB, 4 VB: full.

LINCOLN UNIVERSITY, Yvonne Hoard, Associate Athletic Director, Jefferson City, MO 65101, (314) 751-2325 ext. 337. NCAA. 2 BB, 3 SB, 3 TEN, 3 T&F, 3 VB: partial. 10 BB, 4 SB, 3 TEN, 7 T&F, 4 VB: full.

LINDENWOOD COLLEGE, Marilyn Morris, Athletic Director, Box 737, St. Charles, MO 63301, (314) 946-6912 ext. 222. NAIA. 5 BB, 7 SOC: partial. 5 BB, 11 SOC: full.

MINERAL AREA COLLEGE, JoAnn Owen, VB Coach/Bill Bradley, BB Coach, Flat River, MO 63601, (314) 431-4593. NJCAA. 8 BB, 9 VB: partial. 4 BB: full.

MISSOURI SOUTHERN STATE COLLEGE, Sallie Beard, Women's Athletic Director, Newman and Duquesne Rds., Joplin, MO 64801, (417) 625-9316. NAIA, Central State Intercollegiate Conf. 6 SB, 9 VB: full.

MISSOURI VALLEY COLLEGE, Kenneth Gibler, Athletic Director, Marshall, MO 65340, (816) 886-6924 ext. 118. NAIA. BB, SB, T&F, VB: partial.

MISSOURI WESTERN STATE COLLEGE, Ed B. Harris, Director of Athletics, 4525 Downs Dr., St. Joseph, MO 64507, (816) 271-4482. NAIA, CSIC, I. 12 BB, 5 SB, 1.5 TEN, 12 VB: full.

NORTHEAST MISSOURI STATE UNIVERSITY, Ken Gardner, Director of Athletics, Kirksville, MO 63501, (816)

Director, 13th and McNary, Tarkio, MO 64491, (816) 736-4131. NAIA. 10 BB, 10 SOC, 15 SB, 20 T&F, 10 VB: partial.

UNIVERSITY OF MISSOURI (COLUMBIA), Coach of Specific Sport, 395 Hearnes Bldg., Columbia, MO 65201, (314) 882-6501. NCAA. 15 BB, 6 G, 10 GYM, 11 SB, 14 S&D, 16 T&F, 12 VB: partial to full.

UNIVERSITY OF MISSOURI (KANSAS CITY), Bruce Carrier, Athletic Director, 51st and Holmes, Kansas City, MO 64110, (816) 276-2713. NAIA. 6 VB: partial. 10 BB: full.

UNIVERSITY OF MISSOURI (ROLLA), Coach of Specific Sport, Multi-purpose Bldg., Rolla, MO 65401, (314) 341-4175. NCAA, SOC, SB, TEN, T&F: partial. BB: partial to full.

UNIVERSITY OF MISSOURI (ST. LOUIS), Coach of Specific Sport, 8001 Natural Bridge, St. Louis, MO 63121, (314) 553-5641. NCAA, SOC, 12 SB, 12 VB: partial. 12 BB: partial to full.

WILLIAM WOODS COLLEGE, Roger Ternes, Athletic Director, Fulton, MO 65251, (314) 642-2251. NAIA. 15 BB, 18 SB, 15 S&D, 12 TEN, 15 VB: partial.

MONTANA

CARROLL COLLEGE, Bob Petrino, Athletic Director, Physical Education Bldg., Helena, MT 59625, (406) 442-3450. NAIA. 10 BB, 10 VB: partial.

COLLEGE OF GREAT FALLS, Steve Aggers, Athletic Director, 1301 20th St. S., Great Falls, MT 59405, (406) 761-8210. NAIA. 6 BB: partial to full.

EASTERN MONTANA COLLEGE, Woody Hahn, Athletic Director, 1500 N. 30th St., Billings, MT 59101-0798, (406) 657-2369. NCAA. 5 G, 5 TEN, 5 T&F: partial. 12 BB: partial to full.

MONTANA COLLEGE OF MINERAL SCIENCE AND TECHNOLOGY, Frank

Athletic Director, Reward, NE 68434, (402) 643-3651. NAIA. 12 BB, 4 G, 10 SB, 5 TEN, 20 T&F, 12 VB: partial.

CREIGHTON UNIVERSITY, Mary Higgins, Women's Athletic Director, 2500 California St., Omaha, NE 68178, (402) 280-2720. NCAA, High Country Conference/Softball only, I. 12 BB, 11 SB: partial to full. CC, G, S&D, TEN: non-scholarship.

DOANE COLLEGE, Linda Papik, Financial Aid Director, 10114 Boswell Ave., Crete, NE 68333, (402) 826-2161. NAIA. 20 BB, 21 T&F, 26 VB: partial.

HASTINGS COLLEGE, Lynn Farrell, Athletic Director, Seventh and Turner, Hastings, NE 68901, (402) 463-2402. NAIA. 15 BB, 8 TEN, 30 T&F, 15 VB: partial.

KEARNEY STATE COLLEGE, Allen H. Zikmund, Athletic Director, Cushing Coliseum, Kearney, NE 68849, (308) 234-8332. NAIA, CSIC, NAC, I. BB, CC, SB, S&D, TEN, T&F, VB: partial.

PERU STATE COLLEGE, Maxine L. Mehus, Athletic Director, Peru, NE 68421, (402) 872-3815. NAIA, NE College Conf., II. 5 BB, 3 CC, 2 SB, 5 T&F, 5 VB: partial. 2 BB, 2 VB: full.

UNIVERSITY OF NEBRASKA (LINCOLN), June B. Davis, Women's Athletic Director, 103 S. Stadium, Lincoln, NE 68588, (402) 472-2366. NCAA. 15 BB, 6 G, 10 GYM, 11 SB, 14 S&D, 8 TEN, 16 T&F, 12 VB: partial to full.

UNIVERSITY OF NEBRASKA (OMAHA), Connie Claussen, Women's Athletics Coordinator, 60th & Dodge Sts., Omaha, NE 68182, (402) 554-2300. NCAA, North Central Conference, II. 12 BB, 6-8 CC, 9-12 SB, 9-12 VB: partial.

WAYNE STATE COLLEGE, Ron Jones, Athletic Director, 200 E. 10th St., Wayne, NE 68787, (402) 375-2200 ext. 301. NAIA. 5 BB, 5 SB, 5 T&F, 5 VB: partial.

YORK COLLEGE, Mike Pruitt, Athletic Director, York, NE 68467, (402) 362-4441 ext. 285. NJCAA. 5-10 BB, 6 VB: partial.

NEVADA

UNIVERSITY OF NEVADA (LAS VEGAS), Christina Kunzer, Assistant Athletic Director, Thomas and Mack Center, Las Vegas, NV 89154, (702) 739-3240. NCAA. 12 SB, 1 S&D: partial. 14 BB, 2 SB, 4 S&D, 12 T&F: full.

UNIVERSITY OF NEVADA (RENO), Anne Hope, Women's Athletic Director, Intercollegiate Athletics, Reno, NV 89557, (702) 584-4681. NCAA, West Coast Athletic Conference. I. 4 CC, 6 SKI, 5 SB, 6 S&D, 4 TEN, 4 VB: partial. 10 BB, 2 CC, 7 SB, 2 S&D, 2 TEN, 7 VB: full.

NEW HAMPSHIRE

FRANKLIN PIERCE COLLEGE, James George Curcio, Women's Athletic Coordinator, Rindge, NH 03461, (603) 899-5111 ext. 332. NAIA. 6 BB, 2.5 FH, 2 SB: full.

KEENE STATE COLLEGE, Dr. Joanne A. Fortunato, Athletic Director, 229 Main St., Keene, NH 03431, (603) 352-1909 ext. 333. NCAA, ECAC, II. 4 BB, 4 SOC, 1 VB: partial. 3 BB, 1 SOC: full. SKI, S&D, T&F: non-scholarship.

NEW HAMPSHIRE COLLEGE, Nancy Ann Rowe, Women's Athletic Coordinator, 2500 North River Rd., Manchester, NH 03104, (603) 668-2211 ext. 263. NCAA, New England Collegiate Conference. II. 5 SOC, 3 SB, 3 VB: partial. 10 BB: full.

UNIVERSITY OF NEW HAMPSHIRE, Gail A. Bigglestone, Women's Athletic Director, Durham, NH 03824, (603) 862-1822. NCAA, ECAC, Seaboard, I. BB, CC, FH, GYM, IH SKI SD, TEN, T&F: partial to full.

NEW JERSEY

BLOOMFIELD COLLEGE, Nancy Bottge, Blvd., Jersey City, NJ 07306, (201) 333-4400 ext. 368. NCAA, Metro Atlantic Athletic Conference, I. 4 CC, 3 SB, 4 S&D, 2 TEN, 4 VB: partial. 15 BB: full.

SETON HALL UNIVERSITY, Sue Dilley, Assistant Athletic Director, South Orange Ave., South Orange, NJ 07079, (201) 761-9498. NCAA, Big East, I. 6 SB, 8 S&D, 6 TEN, 6 T&F, 6 VB: partial. 13 BB: full.

UNION COUNTY COLLEGE, Wynn Phillips, Director of Athletics, 1033 Springfield Ave., Cranford, NJ 07016, (201) 276-2600 ext. 419. NJCAA, Garden State Athletic Conference. 1 BB: partial. 2 BB, 2 SOC: full. CC, G, TEN: non-scholarship.

NEW MEXICO

COLLEGE OF SANTA FE, Robert Sweeney, Athletic Director, St. Michaels Dr., Santa Fe, NM 87501, (505) 473-6501. NAIA. 8 TEN, 12 VB: partial.

EASTERN NEW MEXICO UNIVERSITY, B.B. Lees, Athletic Director, Greyhound Arena, Portales, NM 88130, (505) 562-2153. NCAA, NAIA. 6 BB, 1 T&F, 4 VB: partial. 6 BB, 1 T&F, 4 VB: full.

NEW MEXICO HIGHLANDS UNIVERSITY, Orlando Brown, Athletic Director, Baca Ave., Las Vegas, NM 87701, (505) 425-7511 ext. 351. NAIA. 15 BB, 6 CC, 15 SB, 10 VB: partial.

NEW MEXICO STATE UNIVERSITY, Karen Fey, Assistant Athletic Director, Box 3145, Pan American Center, Las Cruces, NM 88003, (505) 646-1028/4048. NCAA, High Country Athletic Conference, IA. 13 G, T&F/CC: partial. 17 SB, 18 S&D, 8 TEN: partial to full. 15 BB, 12 T&F: full.

UNIVERSITY OF NEW MEXICO, Judy Ray, Assistant Women's Athletic Director, Carlisle Gym, Albuquerque, NM 87131, (505) 277-6479. NCAA, High Country Athletic Conference, I. 7 SKI, 10 S&D,

HOUGHTON COLLEGE, E. Douglas Barke, Athletic Director, Houghton, NY 14744, (716) 567-2211. NAIA, Dist. 18. 6 BB, 6 FH, 6 SOC, 6 VB: partial.

HOFSTRA UNIVERSITY, Cindy Lewis, Women's Athletic Director, Hempstead, NY 11550, (516) 560-6750. NCAA. 8 BB, 10 FH, 5 GYM, 8 LAX, 2 SB, 6 VB: partial. 4 BB, 3 VB: full.

IONA COLLEGE, Rick Mazzuto, Athletic Director, 715 North Ave., New Rochelle, NY 10801, (914) 636-2100. NCAA. 4 BB: partial. 8 BB: full. CREW, SOC, SB, S&D, TEN, VB: non-scholarship.

THE KINGS COLLEGE, Tome Hughes, Athletic Director, Lodge Rd., Briarcliff Manor, NY 10510, (914) 941-7200 ext. 293. NAIA, NCAA. 7 BB, 9 FH, 7 SB, 4 TEN, 3 T&F, 6 VB: partial.

LONG ISLAND UNIVERSITY, James G. Thompson, Associate Athletic Director, University Plaza, Brooklyn, NY 11201, (212) 403-1031. NCAA, Cosmopolitan, ECAC, I. 12 BB, 4 CC, 8 GYM, 8 SB, 4 TEN, 8 T&F: full.

MANHATTAN COLLEGE, Kathy Solano, Women's Basketball Coach, Manhattan College Pkwy., Riverdale, NY 10471, (212) 920-0228. NCAA, MAAC, I. 11 BB, 2 T&F: full. SB, TEN, VB: non-scholarship.

MARIST COLLEGE, Patricia Torza, Basketball Coach, McCann Recreation Center, Poughkeepsie, NY 12601, (914) 471-3240. NCAA, Cosmopolitan, I. 12 BB: full. CREW, CC, S&D, TEN, T&F, VB: non-scholarship.

MERCY COLLEGE, Neil Judge, Athletic Director, 555 Broadway, Dobbs Ferry, NY 10522, (914) 693-4500 ext. 220. NCAA. 3 BB, 3 SB, 1 T&F, 3 VB: full.

MOLLOY COLLEGE, Denise Cohen, Director of Athletics, 1000 Hempstead Ave., Rockville Centre, NY 11570, (516) 678-5000 ext. 308. NCAA, ECAC, II. 2 RIDING: partial. 6 BB, 2 TEN, 2 VB: full. SB: non-scholarship.

Rochester, NY 14618, (716) 586-4140 ext. 286. NCAA. 9 SOC, 6 VB: partial. 6 BB: full.

ST. JOHN'S UNIVERSITY, Kathleen Meehan, Associate Athletic Director, Grand Central and Utopia Pkwy., Jamaica, NY 11439, (212) 990-6161 ext. 6173. NCAA, Big East, I. 4 FENC, 9 SB, 12 S&D, 6 TEN, 20 T&F: partial. 15 BB: full.

ST. THOMAS AQUINAS COLLEGE, Barbara Vano, Assistant Professor, Rte. 340, Sparkill, NY 10976, (914) 359-9500. NAIA, CACC. BB, SB, VB: partial.

SIENA COLLEGE, Joyce A. Legere, Women's Athletic Director, Rte. 9, Loudonville, NY 12211, (518) 783-2532. NCAA. 11 BB: full. CC, FH, SOC, SB, TEN, T&F, VB: non-scholarship.

SOUTHAMPTON COLLEGE, Mary Topping, Athletic Director, Montauk Hwy., Southampton, NY 11968, (516) 283-4000. NCAA. 1 VB: partial.

SYRACUSE UNIVERSITY, Jake Crouthamel, Manley Field House, Syracuse, NY 13210, (315) 423-2384. NCAA, Big East, I. 8 CREW, 8 FH, 5 S&D, 4 TEN, 8 T&F, 8 VB: partial. 15 BB, 3 S&D, 4 TEN: full.

THE COLLEGE OF SAINT ROSE, Cathy Cummings Haker, Athletic Director, Albany, NY 12203. NAIA, Central Atlantic College Conf. CC, SOC, SB, S&D, TEN, VB: partial. BB: non-scholarship.

UTICA COLLEGE, Jim Spartano, Athletic Director, Utica, NY 13502, (315) 792-3050. NCAA. 6 SOC, 8 S&D, 3 TEN, 2 T&F: partial. 6 BB: full.

VILLA MARIA COLLEGE, Ron Griffin, Athletic Director, 240 Pine Ridge Rd., Buffalo, NY 14225, (716) 896-0700. NJCAA, PennYork, Junior College. 4 VB: partial. 2 VB: full.

WAGNER COLLEGE, Gela Mikalauskas, Associate Athletic Director/Basketball Coach, 631 Howard Ave., Staten Island,

Coordinator of Women's Athletics, 467 Franklin St., Bloomfield, NJ 07003. (201) 748-9000 ext. 363. NAIA, CACC. 1 **BB**, 1 **SB**: full. **VB**: non-scholarship.

CALDWELL COLLEGE, Kathy Morgan, Athletic Director, Ryerson Ave., Caldwell, NJ 07006. (201) 228-4424 ext. 264. NAIA, III. 3 **BB**, 2 **VB**: partial. **FENC**, **SB**: non-scholarship.

FAIRLEIGH DICKINSON UNIVERSITY, Barbara Leshinsky, Acting Director of Athletics, 1144 River Rd., Teaneck, NJ 07666. (201) 692-2242/43. NCAA, Cosmopolitan, I. 12 **BB**, 4 **FENC**, 3 **T&F**, 7.5 **VB**: partial to full.

GEORGIAN COURT COLLEGE, Kathy Perri, Director of Athletics & Recreation, Lakewood Ave., Lakewood, NJ 08701. (201) 363-2374. NAIA, NJAIAW, Central Atlantic Coastal Conference, District 31. **BB**, **CC**, **SB**, **VB**, **KARATE**: partial.

MIDDLESEX COUNTY COLLEGE, Robert Zichak, Athletic Director, Woodbridge Ave., Edison, NJ 08818. (201) 548-6000. NJCAA, GSAC. 1 **BB**, 1 **CC**, 1 **SKI**: partial. **SOC**, **SB**, **TEN**: non-scholarship.

MONMOUTH COLLEGE, Joan Martin, Assistant Athletic Director, Cedar Ave., W. Long Branch, NJ 07764. (201) 222-6600 ext. 363. NCAA, COSMO-ECAC METRO, I. 2 **BB**, 1 **CC**, 4 **SOC**, 5 **S&D**: partial. 10 **BB**: full.

RIDER COLLEGE, John B. Carpenter, Athletic Director, Box 6400, Lawrenceville, NJ 08648. (609) 896-5054. NCAA. 12 **BB**, 11 **FH**, 11 **SB**, 1 **TEN**, 4 **VB**: partial to full.

RUTGERS STATE UNIVERSITY OF NEW JERSEY, Rita Kay Thomas, Assistant Athletic Director, Rutgers Athletic Center, Rockefeller Rd., Piscataway, NJ 08854. (201) 932-4220. NLCAA, ECAC, Atlantic Ten, I. **CC**, **CREW**, **FH**, **G**, **GYM**, **LAX**, **SOC**, **SB**, **S&D**, **TEN**, **T&F**, **VB**: partial. 15 **BB**: full. **CREW**: non-scholarship.

ST. PETER'S COLLEGE, Barbara Church, Associate Athletic Director, 2641 Kennedy

16 **T&F**: partial. 13 **BB**, 6 **G**, 9 **GYM**, 11 **SB**, 6 **TEN**, 12 **VB**: full.

ADELPHI UNIVERSITY, Janet Ficke, Associate Athletic Director, South Ave., Garden City, NY 11530. (516) 663-1155. NCAA. 15 **SOC**, 12 **SB**: partial. 10 **BB**, 3 **SB**: full. **CC**, **G**, **S&D**, **TEN**, **T&F**: non-scholarship.

CONCORDIA COLLEGE, Eldan Kamla, Athletic Director, 171 White Plains Rd., Bronxville, NY 10708. (914) 337-7300. NCAA, NAIA, MCTC, Hudson Valley. 15 **BB**, 5 **CC**, 15 **SB**, 7 **TEN**, 12 **VB**: partial.

CANISIUS COLLEGE, Daniel Starr, Athletic Director, 2001 Main St., Buffalo, NY 14208. (716) 883-7000. NCAA. 1 **RIFLE**, 4 **SOC**, 6 **SB**, 2 **S&D**, 4 **TEN**, 6 **T&F**, 4 **VB**: partial. 10 **BB**: full.

DOMINICAN COLLEGE, Steve Kelly, Director of Athletics, 10 Western Highway, Orangeburg, NY 10962. (914) 359-6827. NAIA, HVWAC, CACC. **BB**, **VB**: partial. **SB**: non-scholarship.

DOWLING COLLEGE, Dick Jamison, Director of Athletics, Oakdale, NY 11769. (516) 589-6100. NCAA, II. 8 **TEN**, 10 **VB**: partial.

D'YOUVILLE COLLEGE, Ronald J. Bavmel, Director of Athletic Program, One D'Youville Square, 320 Porter Ave., Buffalo, NY 14201. (716) 881-7685. NLCAA. 3 **BB**, 3 **VB**: partial. **CREW**: non-scholarship.

FORDHAM UNIVERSITY, Chris Monasch, Acting Athletic Director, East Fordham Rd., Bronx, NY 10458. (212) 579-2448. NCAA, NYAIAW. 12 **BB**: full. 7 **S&D**, 4 **TEN**, 6 **T&F**: partial. **SB**, **VB**: non-scholarship.

HILBERT COLLEGE, Helen Lukasik, Financial Aid Director, 5200 S. Park Ave., Hamburg, NY 14075. (716) 649-7900 ext. 208. NJCAA. 8-9 **BB**, 6-8 **SB**, 6-8 **VB**: partial.

NEW YORK INSTITUTE OF TECHNOLOGY, Gail Wasmus, Women's Athletic Director, Wheatley Rd., Old Westbury, NY 11568. (516) 686-7626. NCAA. 8 **BB**, 8 **SB**, 10 **T&F**, 12 **VB**: partial.

NIAGARA UNIVERSITY, Nancy Riccio, Athletic Director, Niagara University, NY 14109. (716) 285-1212. NCAA, Upstate Women's Basketball Conference, I. 10 **BB**, 8 **SOC**, 8 **SB**, 8 **S&D**, 8 **VB**: partial. 4 **BB**: full.

NYACK COLLEGE, Jerry Sloaum, Athletic Director, Nyack, NY 10960. (914) 358-1710 ext. 217. NAIA, Hudson Valley WAC, III. 1 **BB**, 1 **SB**: partial. **CC**, **TEN**, **VB**: non-scholarship.

C.W. POST COLLEGE, Pat Lamb Kennedy, Women's Athletic Director, Northern Blvd., Greenvale, NY 11548. (516) 299-2287. NCAA, Empire State BB Conf., II. **FH**, **SB**, **T&F**, **VB**: partial. **BB**: partial to full.

QUEENS COLLEGE, Sharon R. Beverly, Assistant Director of Athletics, 65-30 Kissena Blvd., Flushing, NY 11367. (718) 520-7652/7215. NCAA, Cosmopolitan. 12 **BB**, 6 **CC**, 6 **SB**, 6 **S&D**, 6 **T&F**, 6 **VB**: full.

ROBERTS WESLEYAN COLLEGE, Dr. Kim Sisson, Athletic Director, 2301 Westside Dr., Rochester, NY 14624. (716) 594-9471. NAIA, NCCAA. 5 **BB**, 2 **CC**, 3 **SB**, 2 **T&F**, 3 **VB**: partial. **SOC**: non-scholarship.

ST. BONAVENTURE UNIVERSITY, Lawrence J. Weise, Athletic Director, Box G, St. Bonaventure, NY 14778. (716) 375-2211. NCAA. **BB**, **S&D**, **TEN**: partial.

ST. FRANCIS COLLEGE, Nate Salant, Assistant Athletic Director, 180 Remsen St., Brooklyn, NY 11201. (718) 522-2300. NCAA. 1 **BB**, 1 **TEN**, 1 **VB**: partial. 6 **BB**, 3 **S&D**: full.

ST. JOHN FISHER COLLEGE, Phillip I. Kahler, Athletic Director, 3690 East Ave.,

NY 10301. (718) 390-3470. NCAA, Cosmo/Metro, I. **BB**: partial. **CC**, **SB**, **TEN**, **T&F**: non-scholarship.

APPALACHIAN STATE UNIVERSITY, Judy Clarke, Assistant Athletic Director, Broome-Kirk Gym, Boone, NC 28608. (704) 262-3080. NCAA, Southern, I. 6 **CC**, 8-9 **FH**, 5 **G**, 5 **SB**, 5 **TEN**, 5 **T&F**, 6 **VB**: partial. 15 **BB**: full.

ATLANTIC CHRISTIAN COLLEGE, Bruce Curtis, Athletic Director, Box 5328, Wilson, NC 27893. (919) 237-3161. NAIA. 15 **BB**, 16 **SB**, 8 **TEN**, 14 **VB**: partial to full.

BELMONT ABBEY COLLEGE, Ken Davis, Assistant Athletic Director, Belmont Rd., Belmont, NC 28012. (704) 825-3711. NAIA. 6 **BB**: partial. 3 **BB**: full.

BREVARD COLLEGE, Jane Long, Women's Basketball/Tennis Coach, Brevard, NC 28712. (704) 883-8292. NJCAA, Western Carolina Junior College. 3.5 **BB**, 1 **SOC**, 1.25 **TEN**, 1 **T&F**: full.

CAMPBELL UNIVERSITY, Wendell L. Carr, Athletic Director, Box 10, Buies Creek, NC 27506. (919) 893-8591. NCAA, NAIA, Big South, I. 12 **BB**, 6 **CC**, 9 **SB**, 9 **TEN**, 9 **T&F**, 6 **VB**: partial.

CATAWBA COLLEGE, Head Coach, Salisbury, NC, 28144. (704) 637-4474. NAIA, Carolinas Conference, **BB**, **FH**, **SB**, **TEN**, **VB**: partial to full.

DUKE UNIVERSITY, Lorraine Woodyard, Assistant Athletic Director, Cameron Indoor Stadium, Durham, NC 27706. (919) 684-5881. NCAA. 10 **BB**, 4 **FH**, 5 **G**, 5 **TEN**, 4 **T&F**, 7 **VB**: full.

EAST CAROLINA UNIVERSITY, Pam Holt, Assistant Athletic Director, Minges Coliseum, Greenville, NC 27834. (919) 757-6417. NCAA. 8 **SB**, 11 **S&D**, 6 **TEN**, 11 **T&F**, 6 **VB**: partial. 12 **BB**: full.

ELON COLLEGE, Mary Jackson, BB/SB Coach/Karen Carden, VB/TEN Coach,

Box 2162, Elon College, NC 27244, (919) 584-2254. NAIA. .5 SB, .5 TEN, .5 VB: partial. 3 BB: full.

GUILFORD COLLEGE, Gayle Currie, Assistant Athletic Director, 5800 W. Friendly Ave., Greensboro, NC 27410. (919) 292-5511. NAIA. 12 BB, LAX, SOC, 10 SB, 8 TEN, 10 VB: partial.

HIGH POINT COLLEGE, Jerry M. Steele, Athletic Director, 933 Montlieu Ave., High Point, NC 27262. (919) 883-6218 or 885-5101. NAIA. 3 BB, 2 FH, 2 TEN, 2 VB: partial to full.

LENOIR-RHYNE COLLEGE, Athletic Director, Hickory, NC 28603. (704) 328-1741. NAIA. 3 BB, 1.5 SB, .75 TEN, 2 VB: partial to full.

LIVINGSTONE COLLEGE, Fred Ponder, Athletic Director, 701 W. Monroe St., Salisbury, NC 28144. (704) 633-7960/66. NCAA, NAIA. 5 BB, 4 SB, 4 T&F, 4 VB: partial to full.

MARS HILL COLLEGE, Pat Sams, Women's Athletic Director, Main St., Mars Hill, NC 28754. (704) 689-1229. NAIA. BB, TEN, VB: partial to full.

NORTH CAROLINA A & T STATE UNIVERSITY, Orby Moss, Director, Corbett Sports Center, Greensboro, NC 27411, (919) 379-7866. NCAA, Mid-Eastern Athletic Conference, IAA. BB, SB, TEN, T&F, VB: full.

NORTH CAROLINA STATE UNIVERSITY, Nora Lynn Finch, Assistant Athletic Director, Box 8501, Raleigh, NC 27650. (919) 737-2880. NCAA. 2 FENC: partial. 15 BB, 6 CC, 6 G, 6 GYM, 6 SOC, 12 S&D, 6 TEN, 12 T&F, 6 VB: full.

PEACE COLLEGE, Ruth Hopkins, Athletic Director, Raleigh, NC 27604. (919) 832-2881. NJCAA. 12 BB, 8 TEN: partial to full.

PEMBROKE STATE UNIVERSITY, Ann Webb, Assistant Athletic Director, Box 133, Pembroke, NC 28372. (919) 521-4214. NCAA, NAIA. 1 SB, 1 TEN, 1 VB: partial. 3 BB: partial to full.

WINSTON-SALEM STATE UNIVERSITY, C.E. Gaines, Athletic Director, Station A, Winston-Salem, NC 27102, (919) 761-2108. NCAA, NAIA. 10 BB, 12 SB, 4 T&F, 4 VB: partial. 3 BB, 1 SB: full.

MONTREAT-ANDERSON COLLEGE, Randy Unger, Athletic Director, Montreal, NC 28757. (704) 669-2696. NJCAA, Independent, I. SB, VB: partial.

MOUNT OLIVE COLLEGE, Larry Dean, Athletic Director, 403 E. College St., Mount Olive, NC 28365. (919) 658-5056. NAIA. 4 BB, 1 SB: full.

NORTH DAKOTA

MARY COLLEGE, Al Bortke, Athletic Director, Apple Creek Rd., Bismarck, ND 58501. (701) 255-4681 ext. 376. NAIA, WACND. 12 BB, 3 CC, 12 T&F, 8 VB: partial.

NORTH DAKOTA STATE UNIVERSITY, Lynn Dorn, New Field House, Fargo, ND 58105 (701) 237-7807. NCAA, North Central Conference, II. 3 SB: partial. 10 BB, 4 CC, 6 T&F, 8 VB: full. S&D, TEN: non-scholarship.

NORTH DAKOTA STATE SCHOOL OF SCIENCE, Don Engen, Athletic Director, Wahpeton, ND 58075, (701) 671-2283. NJCAA, I. 8 BB, 12 T&F, 8 VB: partial.

MAYVILLE STATE COLLEGE, Martin Johnson, Athletic Director, Mayville, ND 58257, (701) 786-2301 ext. 325. NAIA. BB, SB, T&F, VB: partial.

VALLEY CITY STATE COLLEGE, Darrell Anderson, Athletic Director, Valley City, ND 58072, (701) 845-7161. NAIA, Women's Athletic Conference of North Dakota. BB, GYM, SB, T&F, VB: partial. CC, G, TEN: non-scholarship.

UNIVERSITY OF NORTH DAKOTA, John Gasparini, Athletic Director, Box 8175 University Station, Grand Forks, ND 58202, (701) 777-2234. NCAA, NCIAC, WCHA, II. 7 BB, 5 S&D, 14 T&F, 1 VB:

Rd., Columbus, OH 43219, (614) 253-2741. NAIA. 12 BB, 12 SB, 12 VB: partial.

OHIO STATE UNIVERSITY, Phyllis J. Bailey, Associate Athletic Director, 410 Woody Hayes Dr., Columbus, OH 43210, (614) 422-0638. NCAA, Big Ten, I. 15 BB, 3 FENC, 9 FH, 5 G, 10 GYM, 11 SB, 14 S&D, 10 SYNC, 5 TEN, 15 T&F, 12 VB: full.

OHIO UNIVERSITY, Peggy J. Pruitt, Associate Athletic Director, Box 689, Athens, OH 45701, (614) 594-5013. NCAA, Mid-American, I. 15 BB, 8 FH, 10 SB, 10 S&D, 4 TEN, 10 T&F, 12 VB: full.

RIO GRANDE COLLEGE, John Lawhorn, Athletic Director, Athletic Dept., Rio Grande, OH 45674, (614) 245-5351. NAIA. 4 BB, 10 T&F, 8 VB: partial to full.

SHAWNEE STATE COLLEGE, Harry Weinbrecht, Athletic Director, Second St., Portsmouth, OH 45662, (614) 354-3205 ext. 219. NJCAA, OJCAA, Region XII. 10 BB: partial. TEN: non-scholarship.

UNIVERSITY OF AKRON, Mary Ann Tripodi, Assistant Athletic Director, Athletic Dept., 302 Buchtel Ave., Akron, OH 44325, (216) 375-7080. NCAA, OVC. TEN, T&F: partial. BB, SB, VB: partial to full.

UNIVERSITY OF CINCINNATI, Jean E. Tuerck, Associate Athletic Director, M.L. 21, Cincinnati, OH 45221, (513) 475-6763. NCAA. SOC: partial. S&D: partial to full. BB, VB: full.

UNIVERSITY OF DAYTON, R. Elaine Dreidame, Associate Director of Athletics, Athletic Dept., Dayton, OH 45469, (513) 229-4420. NCAA, North Star Conference, I. 6 SOC, 6 VB: partial. 12 BB: full. CC, SB, TEN: non-scholarship.

UNIVERSITY OF TOLEDO, Marnie W. Swift, Assistant Athletic Director, 2801 W. Bancroft St., Toledo, OH 43606, (419) 537-4334. NCAA. 15 BB, 9 FH, 11 SB, 6 TEN, 12 T&F, 12 VB: full.

URBANA COLLEGE, Bob Cawley, Athletic Director, College Way, Urbana, OH 43078,

RIDING, RIFLE, R, SKI, SOC, SB, S&D, SS, T&F, VB: non-scholarship.

EASTERN OKLAHOMA STATE COLLEGE, Joe Thomas, Athletic Director, College Addition, Wilburton, OK 74578. (918) 465-2361. NJCAA. 20 T&F: partial. 10 BB, 5 T&F: full.

LANGSTON UNIVERSITY, Anthony Lewis, Women's Basketball Coach, Box 175, Langston, OK 73050, (405) 466-2231 ext. 352. NAIA. 5 BB: full. T&F: non-scholarship.

NORTHEASTERN OKLAHOMA A&M COLLEGE, Boyd Converse, Athletic Director, Miami, OK 74354, (918) 542-8441. NJCAA. 3 BB, 5 RD, 15 SB, 6 TEN, 10 T&F: partial. 12 BB, 3 SB, 5 T&F: full.

NORTHEASTERN STATE UNIVERSITY, Jack Dobbins, Professor of Physical Education & Coordinator, Tahlequah, OK 74464, (918) 456-5511 ext. 3912. NAIA, OIC. 5 TEN: partial. 7 BB, 3 SB: full.

OKLAHOMA BAPTIST UNIVERSITY, Bobby Canty, Athletic Director, 500 W. University, Shawnee, OK 74801, (405) 275-2850 ext. 2143. NAIA. 8 BB, 4 SB, 4 VB: full.

OKLAHOMA CHRISTIAN COLLEGE, Max Dobson, Athletic Director, Rte. 1, Box 141, Oklahoma City, OK 73111, (405) 478-1661 ext. 340. NAIA. 6 BB: partial. 6 BB: full.

OKLAHOMA STATE UNIVERSITY, Myron Roderick, Athletic Director, Gallagher Hall, Stillwater, OK 74078, (405) 624-5855. NCAA. 15 BB, 6 G, 10 GYM, 11 SB, 8 TEN, 16 T&F: full.

ORAL ROBERTS UNIVERSITY, Cip Patterson, Women's Athletic Director, 7777 S. Lewis, Tulsa, OK 74171, (918) 495-7107. NCAA. 5 TEN, 2 T&F, 7 VB: partial. 15 BB: full.

PANHANDLE STATE UNIVERSITY, Jack Begley, Athletic Director, Box 430, Goodwell, OK 73939, (405) 349-2611. NAIA, Independent. 9 BB, 3 VB: full.

PFEIFFER COLLEGE, Tom Childress, Athletic Director, Misenheimer, NC 28109, (704) 463-5809. NCAA, NAIA. **BB, FH, SB, S&D, TEN, VB:** partial to full.

UNIVERSITY OF NORTH CAROLINA (ASHEVILLE), Ed G. Farrell, Director of Athletics, Dept. of Athletics, One University Heights, Asheville, NC 28804, (704) 258-6459. NAIA, Big South Conference, II. 12 **BB,** 5 **TEN,** 8 **VB:** partial.

UNIVERSITY OF NORTH CAROLINA (CHAPEL HILL), Dr. Beth Miller, Assistant Athletic Director, Box 3000, Chapel Hill, NC 27514, (919) 962-5411. NCAA, Atlantic Coast Conference, I. 15 **BB,** 10 **FH,** 6 **G,** 10 **GYM,** 11 **SOC,** 3 **SB,** 14 **S&D,** 7 **TEN,** 14 **T&F/CC,** 10 **VB:** full. **FENC:** non-scholarship.

UNIVERSITY OF NORTH CAROLINA (CHARLOTTE), Judy Wilkins, Associate Athletic Director, Athletic Dept., Charlotte, NC 28223, (704) 597-4955. NCAA, Sunbelt, I. 6 **BB,** 4 **CC,** 11 **SB,** 6 **TEN,** 7 **VB:** partial. 4 **BB,** 1 **VB:** full. **S&D:**

UNIVERSITY OF NORTH CAROLINA (WILMINGTON), Jackie Bartlett, Assistant Athletic Director, 601 S. College Rd., Wilmington, NC 28403, (919) 395-3824. **BB, G, SB, S&D, TEN, VB:** partial to full.

WAKE FOREST UNIVERSITY, Dorothy Casey, Director of Women's Athletics, Box 7265, Reynolds Sta., Winston-Salem, NC 27109, (919) 761-5858. NCAA, Atlantic Coast Conference, I. **VB:** partial. **CC, G, TEN, T&F:** partial to full. 10 **BB:** full.

WESTERN CAROLINA UNIVERSITY, Betty J. Peele, Assistant Athletic Director, Reid Gym, Cullowhee, NC 28723, (704) 227-7332. NCAA. 7 **BB,** 3.5 **SB,** 3.5 **VB:** partial to full.

WINGATE COLLEGE, Bill Connell, Athletic Director, Wingate, NC 28174, (704) 233-4061. NAIA, Carolinas Conference, I. 3 **BB,** 1.5 **SB,** 1.5 **TEN,** 1.5 **VB:** partial to full.

partial. 5 **BB,** 7 **VB:** full. **CC, FH, G, GYM, SB, TEN:** non-scholarship.

OHIO

ASHLAND COLLEGE, Sue Martensen, Associate Athletic Director, P.E. Center, Ashland, OH 44805, (419) 289-4142 ext. 5454. NCAA, Great Lakes Valley Conference, II. **BB, CC, FH, SB, T&F, VB:** partial.

BOWLING GREEN STATE UNIVERSITY, Carole J. Huston, Athletic Director, Athletic Dept.-Stadium, Bowling Green, OH 43403, (419) 372-2401. NCAA, MAC, I. 12 **BB,** 2 **G,** 7 **GYM,** 7 **SB,** 11 **S&D,** 4 **TEN,** 10 **T&F/CC,** 10 **VB:** full.

CLEVELAND STATE UNIVERSITY, Alice J. Kohl, Women's Athletic Coordinator, 2451 Euclid Ave., Cleveland, OH 44115, (216) 687-4756. NCAA. **BB, CC, FENC, S&D, TEN, T&F, VB:** full.

COLLEGE OF MOUNT ST. JOSEPH, Jean Dowell, Athletic Director, Mount St. Joseph, OH 45051, (513) 244-4311. NCAA. 2 **BB,** 6 **VB:** partial.

KENT STATE UNIVERSITY, Judy Devine, Associate Athletic Director, 150 Memorial Gym, Kent, OH 44242, (216) 672-5976. NCAA, Mid-American, I. 14 **BB,** 7 **FH,** 9 **GYM,** 10 **SB,** 7 **S&D,** 11 **T&F,** 10 **VB:** full.

MALONE COLLEGE, Joan K. Tomec, Women's Athletic Director, 515 25th St., Canton, OH 44709, (216) 489-0800 ext. 512. NAIA. 12 **BB,** 10 **TEN,** 15 **T&F,** partial.

MIAMI UNIVERSITY, Karen Womack, Associate Athletic Director, Millett Hall, Oxford, OH 45056, (513) 529-4902. NCAA, Mid-American Conference, I. 14 **BB,** 6 **FH,** 8 **SB,** 10 **S&D,** 5 **TEN,** 8 **T&F,** 11 **VB:** full.

OHIO DOMINICAN COLLEGE, Rickie Sue Grunden, Athletic Director, 1216 Sunbury

(513) 652-1301 ext. 324. NAIA. 3-4 **BB,** 2-3 **SB,** 3-4 **VB:** partial.

WALSH COLLEGE, Missy Long, Assistant Athletic Director, 2020 Easton Rd., Canton, OH 44720, (216) 499-7090 ext. 511. NAIA. 12 **BB,** 12 **SB,** 4 **TEN,** 12 **T&F,** 12 **VB:** partial.

WRIGHT STATE UNIVERSITY, Peggy Wynkoop, Assistant Athletic Director, Dayton, OH 45435, (513) 873-2771. NCAA, I. 1 **CC,** 1 **SB,** 1 **TEN:** partial. 6 **BB,** 5 **S&D,** 6 **VB:** full. **SOC:** non-scholarship.

XAVIER UNIVERSITY, Laurie Massa, Assistant Athletic Director, 3800 Victory Pkwy., Cincinnati, OH 45207, (513) 745-3043. NCAA. 5 **TEN,** 8 **VB:** partial. 8 **BB:** full. **CC, RIFLE, SOC, S&D:** non-scholarship.

YOUNGSTOWN STATE UNIVERSITY, Pauline Saternow, Assistant Athletic Director, 410 Wick Ave., Youngstown, OH 44555, (216) 742-3718. NCAA, Ohio Valley, IAA. 12 **BB,** 4 **SB,** 4 **S&D,** 2 **TEN,** 4 **VB:** full. **CC:** non-scholarship.

OKLAHOMA

BETHANY NAZARENE COLLEGE, Bobby Martin, Athletic Director, 6729 N.W. 39th Expwy., Bethany, OK 73008, (405) 789-6400 ext. 356. NAIA. 1 **TEN:** partial. 8 **BB,** 4 **VB:** partial to full.

CAMERON UNIVERSITY, Bill G. Shahan, Athletic Director, 2800 Gore Blvd., Lawton, OK 73505, (405) 248-2200 ext. 400. NAIA. 11 **BB,** 5 **SB,** 4 **TEN:** full.

CENTRAL STATE UNIVERSITY, John Keely, Assistant Athletic Director, 100 N. University Dr., Edmont, OK 73034, (405) 341-2980 ext. 501. NAIA. 9 **BB,** 8 **SB,** 2 **TEN,** 2 **T&F,** 2 **VB:** partial to full.

EAST CENTRAL OKLAHOMA STATE UNIVERSITY, Tim Green, Athletic Director, Ada, OK 74820, (405) 332-8000 ext. 364. NAIA. 9 **BB,** 2 **TEN:** full. **ARCH, BD, BOW, CREW, CC, FENC, FH, G, GYM, IH, LAX,**

PHILLIPS UNIVERSITY, Women's Basketball Coach, 2000 College Station, Enid, OK 73701, (405) 237-4433. NAIA, Sooner Conference. 10 **BB:** full.

ROSE STATE COLLEGE, Virgil Milliron, Athletic Director, 6420 S.E. 15th St., Midwest City, OK 73110, (405) 733-7350. NJCAA, Bi State, Western Division. 15 **BB:** partial.

SOUTHEASTERN OKLAHOMA STATE UNIVERSITY, Dr. Don Parham, Director of Athletics, Station 1, Box 4122, Durant, OK 74701, (405) 924-0121. NAIA, I. 6 **TEN:** partial. 8 **BB:** full.

UNIVERSITY OF OKLAHOMA, Donald D. Jimerson, Assistant Athletic Director, 180 W. Brooks, Rm. 201, Norman, OK 73019, (405) 325-6511. NCAA, Big Eight Conference. 15 **BB,** 6 **G,** 10 **GYM,** 11 **SB,** 8 **TEN,** 16 **T&F/,** 12 **VB:** full.

OREGON

CONCORDIA COLLEGE, Joel Schuldhaisz, Athletic Director, 2811 NE Holman, Portland, OR 97211, (503) 288-9371. NAIA, District 2. **BB, VB:** partial.

GEORGE FOX COLLEGE, Paul Berry, Athletic Director, Newberg, OR 97132, (503) 538-8383. NAIA, NCAA. **BB, CC, SB, T&F, VB:** partial.

OREGON STATE UNIVERSITY, Sylvia L. Moore, Deputy Director, 103 Gill Coliseum, Corvallis, OR 97331, (503) 754-2611. NCAA, NORPAC, I. 6 **G,** 11 **SB,** 14 **S&D,** 16 **T&F,** 12 **VB:** partial to full. 15 **BB,** 10 **GYM:** full.

PORTLAND STATE UNIVERSITY, Betty Rankin, Associate Athletic Director, Box 751, Portland, OR 97207, (503) 229-4400. NCAA. 4 **BB,** 3 **CC,** 6 **SB,** 3 **TEN,** 3 **T&F,** 4 **VB:** partial. 8 **BB,** 6 **VB:** full.

SOUTHERN OREGON STATE COLLEGE, Sally Jones Rushing, Associate Athletic Director, 1250 Siskiyou Blvd., Ashland, OR

97520. (503) 482-6236. NAIA, Cascade Collegiate Conference. **BB, CC, T&F, VB**: partial.

UNIVERSITY OF OREGON, Chris Voelz, Assistant Athletic Director, McArthur Ct., Eugene, OR 97403. (503) 686-4433. NCAA, NORPAC, I. 15 **BB**, 10 **GYM**, 11 **SB**, 14 **S&D**, 8 **TEN**, 16 **T&F**, 12 **VB**: full.

WARNER PACIFIC COLLEGE, Dave Bale, Athletic Director, 2219 S.E. 68th, Portland, OR 97215. (503) 775-4366 ext. 751. NAIA. 8 **BB**, 8 **VB**: partial. **SB**: non-scholarship.

PENNSYLVANIA

BLOOMSBURG UNIVERSITY, Joanne McComb, Associate Athletic Director, Nelson Field House, Bloomsburg, PA 17815. (717) 389-4363. NCAA. **BB, SB, S&D**: partial.

CALIFORNIA UNIVERSITY OF PENNSYLVANIA, Janice L. McConnell, Acting Athletic Director, Third St., California, PA 15419. (412) 938-4351. NCAA. **BB, SB, TEN, T&F, VB**: partial.

CLARION UNIVERSITY OF PENNSYLVANIA, Frances M. Shope, Associate Athletic Director, Tippin Gym, Clarion, PA 16214. (814) 226-2371. NCAA. **BB, GYM, S&D, VB**: partial to full.

DREXEL UNIVERSITY, Mary F. Semanik, Director of Women's Athletics, 32nd and Chestnut Sts., Philadelphia, PA 19104, (215) 895-2980. NCAA, PAIAW, ECC, I. **BB, FH, LAX, SB, S&D, TEN, VB**: partial to full.

DUQUESNE UNIVERSITY, Eileen B. Livingston, Athletic Director, 600 Union, Pittsburgh, PA 15282. (412) 434-6565. NCAA, Atlantic Ten Conference, I. **BB, SB, S&D, VB**: partial to full.

EAST STROUDSBURG UNIVERSITY, Robert G. Sutton, Interim Associate Athletic Director, East Stroudsburg, PA 18301. (717) 424-3310. NCAA, PA State Athletic Conference. **BB, SB**: partial. **CC,**

MILLERSVILLE UNIVERSITY, Marjorie A. Trout, Director of Women's Athletics, Brooks Hall, Millersville, PA 17551. (717) 872-3402. NCAA, Pennsylvania State Athletic Conference, II. **BB, LAX, SB, S&D, TEN, T&F**: partial.

PENNSYLVANIA STATE UNIVERSITY, Della Durant, Athletic Director, 206 Recreation Bldg., University Park, PA 16802. (814) 865-1104. NCAA. **BB, FH, GYM, LAX, S&D, T&F, VB**: partial to full.

PHILADELPHIA COLLEGE OF TEXTILES & SCIENCE, Julie Soriero, Women's Athletic Coordinator, Henry Ave., Philadelphia, PA 19144. (215) 951-2723. NCAA, ECAC, PAIAW, II. 12 **BB**, 1 **CC.**, 1 **SB**, 1 **T&F**, 1 **VB**: partial. **FH, LAX, TEN, VB**: non-scholarship.

POINT PARK COLLEGE, Jerry Conboy, Athletic Director, 201 Wood St., Pittsburgh, PA 15222. (412) 391-4100. NAIA, Penn Wood West. 10 **BB**, 8 **SB**: partial.

ROBERT MORRIS COLLEGE, C. Robert Miller, Acting Athletic Director, Narrows Run Rd., Coraopolis, PA 15108. (412) 262-8200. NCAA. 12 **BB, SOC**, 4 **TEN, T&F**, 3 **VB**: partial.

ST. FRANCIS COLLEGE, Deb Polca, Assistant Athletic Director, Stokes Building, Loretto, PA 15940. (814) 472-7000 ext. 244. NCAA, ECAC METRO, I. 8 **BB**: partial. **CC, RIFLE, SB, S&D, TEN, T&F, VB**: non-scholarship.

ST. JOSEPH'S UNIVERSITY, Ellen Ryan, Assistant Athletic Director, 5600 City Ave., Philadelphia, PA 19131. (215) 879-7614. NCAA, Atlantic Ten, I. 5 **FH**, 1 **SB**, 1 **TEN**, 5 **T&F**: partial. 12 **BB**: full.

ST. VINCENT COLLEGE, Kristen Zawacki, Associate Director of Athletics, St. Vincent College, Latrobe, PA 15650. (412) 539-9761. NAIA, District 18. **BB**: partial to full. **CC, SB, TEN, VB**: non-scholarship.

SHIPPENSBURG UNIVERSITY, Jane Goss, Director of Women's Athletics, Shippensburg, PA 17257. (717) 532-1541. NCAA, ECAC, PSAC. **BB, CC, LAX, SB,**

Department of PE & Athletics, Box M College Station, UPR, Rio Piedras, PR 00931. (809) 751-5590. NCAA, LAI of Puerto Rico. **BB, CC, SB, S&D, TEN, T&F, VB, JUDO**: partial.

UNIVERSITY OF PUERTO RICO (MAYAGUEZ), Manuel D. Ramierez, Athletic Director, Mayaguez, PR 00708. (809) 832-0400. **BB, SB, S&D, TEN, T&F, VB**: partial.

RHODE ISLAND

PROVIDENCE COLLEGE, Helen Bert, Associate Athletic Director, Alumni Hall, Providence, RI 02918. (401) 865-2588. NCAA, ECAC, BIG EAST, I. 12 **BB**, 12 **CC**, 6 **FH**, 6 **IH**, 6 **SOC**, 4 **SB**, 8 **S&D**, 6 **TEN**, 12 **T&F**, 10 **VB**: full.

UNIVERSITY OF RHODE ISLAND, Eleanor R. Lemaire, Associate Athletic Director, Keaney Gym, Kingston, RI 02881. (401) 792-2233. NCAA, ECAC, Atlantic Ten, I. **BB, CC, FH, GYM, SB, T&F, VB**: partial to full. **SOC, S&D, TEN**: non-scholarship.

SOUTH CAROLINA

ANDERSON COLLEGE, Individual Coaches, Anderson, SC 29621. (803) 231-2029. NJCAA, Western Carolinas. 5 **BB**, 2 **SB**, 2 **TEN**, 2 **VB**: full.

BAPTIST COLLEGE, Howard Bagwell, Athletic Director, Box 10087, Charleston, SC 29411. (803) 797-4116. NCAA, Big South, I. **BB, CC, SB, TEN, T&F, VB**: full.

CLAFLIN COLLEGE, P. Palmer Worthy, Athletic Director, College Ave. NE, Orangeburg, SC 29115. (803) 534-2710. NAIA. **BB, SB, T&F, VB**: partial.

CLEMSON UNIVERSITY, Kassie Kessinger, Assistant Sports Information Director, Box 31, Clemson, SC 29631. (803) 656-2114. NCAA, Atlantic Coast, I. 15 **BB**, 14 **S&D**, 8 **TEN**, 14 **T&F/CC**, 12 **VB**: full.

University Pkwy., Aiken, SC 29801. (803) 648-6851. NAIA. 4 **BB**, 2 **VB**: partial.

UNIVERSITY OF SOUTH CAROLINA (COLUMBIA), Bobby Foster, Assistant Athletic Director, Columbia, SC 29208. (803) 777-3829. NCAA. 12 **BB**, 6 **G**, 11 **SB**, 14 **S&D**, 8 **TEN**, 12 **VB**: partial to full. 3 **BB**, 3 **TEN**: full.

UNIVERSITY OF SOUTH CAROLINA (SPARTANBURG), Gene DeFilippo, Athletic Director, Spartanburg, SC 29303. (803) 578-1800. NAIA. 6 **BB**, 4 **VB**: partial to full.

USC-COASTAL CAROLINA COLLEGE, Bobby Richardson, Director of Athletics, Box 1954, Conway, SC 29526. (803) 347-3161 ext. 2813. NAIA, Big South. 5 **BB**, 1.5 **TEN**, 2 **VB**: full.

WINTHROP COLLEGE, Wanda Briley, Assistant Athletic Director, Athletic Dept., Winthrop Coliseum, Rock Hill, SC 29733. (803) 329-2140. NCAA, Big South, I. 6 **BB**, 1 **CC**, 2 **SB**, 1.5 **TEN**, 2 **VB**: full.

WOFFORD COLLEGE, Crystal Sharpe, Women's Athletic Coordinator, Church St., Spartanburg, SC 29301. (803) 585-4821. NAIA. 3 **BB**: full.

SOUTH DAKOTA

AUGUSTANA COLLEGE, Eileen Friest, Women's Athletic Coordinator, Sioux Falls, SD 57197. (605) 336-5527. NCAA. 2 **SB**: partial. 10 **BB**, 3 **SB**, 1 **TEN**, 3 **T&F**, 4 **VB**: full.

BLACK HILLS STATE COLLEGE, Coach of Specific Sport, Spearfish, SD 57783. (805) 642-6464. NAIA. **BB, RD, T&F, VB**: partial.

DAKOTA WESLEYAN UNIVERSITY, Connie Johnson, Women's Athletic Coordinator, 1200 W. University Ave., Mitchell, SD 57301. (605) 996-6511 ext. 246. NAIA. 4 **BB**, 2 **T&F**, 3 **VB**: partial.

MOUNT MARTY COLLEGE, Janet Stumps, Coach, 100 W. Fifth, Yankton, SD

FH, GYM, LAX, S&D, TEN, T&F, VB: non-scholarship.

EDINBORO UNIVERSITY OF PENNSYLVANIA, Kathleen Lipkovich, Associate Athletic Director, McComb Field House, Edinboro, PA 16444, (814) 732-2472. NCAA, PA State Athletic Conference, II. **BB, CC, VB:** partial to full. **SB, S&D, TEN, T&F:** non-scholarship.

GANNON UNIVERSITY, Women's Athletic Coordinator, University Square, Erie, PA 16541, (814) 871-7419. NCAA, II. 6 **BB**, 6 **S&D**, 6 **TEN**, 10 **VB:** partial. 6 **BB:** full.

GENEVA COLLEGE, Kim Gall, Women's Athletic Director, Beaver Falls, PA 15010, (412) 846-5100 ext. 278. NCCAA. **BB, SB, SOC, GYM, T&F, VB:** partial.

INDIANA UNIVERSITY OF PENNSYLVANIA, Ruth Podbielski, Associate Athletic Director, Field House, IUP, Indiana, PA 15705, (412) 357-2755. NCAA. 10 **BB**, 4 **GYM**, 1 **SB**, 8 **T&F:** partial. 2 **GYM:** full.

LAFAYETTE COLLEGE, Pat Fisher, Women's Athletic Coordinator, Kirby Field House, Easton, PA 18042, (215) 250-5474. NCAA, ECAC, ECC, I. **CC, LAX, SB, S&D, TEN, VB:** partial. **BB, FH, SB, T&F, VB:** full.

LASALLE UNIVERSITY, Kathleen Wear, Assistant Athletic Director, 20th and Olney Ave., Philadelphia, PA 19141, (215) 951-1523. NCAA. **FH, SB, S&D, T&F, VB:** partial. **BB:** partial to full.

LOCK HAVEN UNIVERSITY OF PENNSYLVANIA, Sharon E. Taylor, Associate Director of Athletics, 215 Thomas Field House, Lock Haven, PA 17745, (717) 893-2093. NCAA, PA State Athletic Conference. **BB, FH, SB:** partial. **CC, GYM, LAX, S&D, TEN, T&F:** non-scholarship.

MERCYHURST COLLEGE, Janet R. Price, Women's Athletic Director, 501 East 38th St., Erie, PA 16546, (814) 825-0225. NCAA. 12 **BB**, 15 **SB**, 8 **TEN**, 12 **VB:** partial.

S&D, TEN, T&F, VB: partial.

SLIPPERY ROCK UNIVERSITY, William C. Lennox, Athletic Director, Morrow Field House, Slippery Rock, PA 16057, (412) 794-7336. NCAA. 6 **BB**, 6 **GYM**, 2 **LAX**, 3 **SB**, 2 **TEN**, 8 **T&F**, 2 **VB:** partial.

TEMPLE UNIVERSITY, Head Coach of Sports, 104 McGonigle Hall, Philadelphia, PA 19122, (215) 787-1955. NCAA, Atlantic 10, ECAC, IA. 2 **BAD**, 15 **BB**, 2 **B**, 14 **CC**, 5 **FENC**, 11 **FH**, 10 **GYM**, 8 **LAX**, 8 **SB**, 8 **S&D**, 6 **TEN**, 14 **T&F**, 12 **VB:** full.

UNIVERSITY OF PITTSBURGH, Coach of Specific Sport, Box 7436, Pittsburgh, PA 15213, (412) 624-4623. NCAA, Big East, I-A. **BB, GYM, S&D, T&F, VB:** partial to full. **BB:** full.

UNIVERSITY OF PITTSBURGH (JOHNSTOWN), Ed Sherlock, Athletic Director, Johnstown, PA 15904, (814) 266-9661. NCAA, Mason Dixon, II. 5 **BB:** full. **CC, G, T&F, VB:** non-scholarship.

VILLANOVA UNIVERSITY, Coach of Specific Sport, Athletic Dept., Villanova, PA 19085, (215) 645-4130. NCAA, Big East, I. 12 **BB**, 13 **CC**, 5 **FH**, 6 **S&D**, 13 **T&F**, 8 **VB:** full. **BOW, CREW, G, LAX, SOC, SB, TEN:** non-scholarship.

WILSON COLLEGE, Rebecca Smith, Athletic Director, Philadelphia Ave., Chambersburg, PA 17201, (717) 264-4141 ext. 255. NAIA, District 19. 1 **BB**, 1 **FH**, 1 **GYM**, 1 **SB**, 1 **TEN**, 1 **VB:** partial.

WAYNESBURG COLLEGE, Rudy Marisa, Athletic Director, Waynesburg, PA 15370, (412) 627-8191. NAIA. 4 **VB:** partial to full.

WEST CHESTER UNIVERSITY, Sue Lubking, Associate Athletic Director, West Chester, PA 19383, (215) 436-2743. NCAA, PSAC, PAIAW, PSAC. **BB, FENC, FH, GYM, LAX, SB, S&D, T&F:** partial.

COLLEGE OF CHARLESTON, Scooter Barnette, Basketball Coach, 28 George St., Charleston, SC 29424, (803) 792-5556. NAIA. 6 **BB**, 3 **TEN**, 1 **VB:** partial to full.

COLUMBIA COLLEGE, Linda Warren, Athletic Coordinator, Columbia, SC 29203, (803) 786-3723. NAIA. **BB, TEN, VB:** partial.

FRANCIS MARION COLLEGE, Sylvia Rhyne Hatchell, Associate Athletic Director, Box 7500, Florence, SC 29501, (803) 669-4121. NAIA. 2 **BB**, 1 **SB**, 1 **TEN**, 1 **VB:** partial.

FURMAN UNIVERSITY, Ray Parlier, Assistant Athletic Director, Athletic Dept., Greenville, SC 29613, (803) 294-2150. NCAA, Southern Conference, I. 6 **BB**, 5.5 **G**, 3 **SB**, 4.5 **S&D**, 3 **TEN**, 2.5 **VB:** full.

LIMESTONE COLLEGE, Nancy Scoggins, Women's Athletic Coordinator, College Dr., Gaffney, SC 29340, (803) 489-7151 ext. 215. **BB, SB, TEN, VB:** partial.

NEWBERRY COLLEGE, Steve Watt, Athletic Director, College St., Newberry, SC 29108, (803) 276-5010. NAIA. 4 **BB**, 2 **SB**, 1 **VB:** full.

NORTH GREENVILLE COLLEGE, Jane Arledge, Coach, Tigerville, SC 29688, (803) 895-1410. NJCAA, WCJCC. 5 **BB**, 2 **SB**, 2 **TEN**, 2 **VB:** full.

PRESBYTERIAN COLLEGE, Judi Gillispie, Director of Admissions, Clinton, SC 29325, (803) 833-2820. NAIA, I. 4.5 **BB**, 3 **TEN**, 2 **VB:** full. **RIFLE:** non-scholarship.

SOUTH CAROLINA STATE COLLEGE, Willis Ham, Athletic Director, Box 1808, Orangeburg, SC 29117, (803) 536-7242. NCAA. 12 **BB**, 6 **TEN**, 14 **T&F**, 6 **VB:** partial to full.

SPARTANBURG METHODIST COLLEGE, Fred L. Branham, Athletic Director, Powell Mill Rd., Spartanburg, SC 29301, (803) 576-3911. NJCAA, WCJCC, Region X. .5 **SB:** partial. 3 **BB**, 1 **VB:** full.

UNIVERSITY OF SOUTH CAROLINA (AIKEN), Chris Faust, Coach, 171

PUERTO RICO

UNIVERSITY OF PUERTO RICO (RIO PIADRAS), Jose M. Portela, Director

57078, (605) 668-1529. NAIA, IOKOTA, District 12. **BB, G, SB, VB:** partial to full.

NORTHERN STATE COLLEGE, James Kretchman, Athletic Director, Aberdeen, SD 57401, (605) 622-2488. NAIA, Northern Sun Conference. **BB, CC, G, SB, TEN, T&F, VB:** partial.

SOUTH DAKOTA SCHOOL OF MINES AND TECHNOLOGY, Barbara Felderman, Coach, 500 E. St. Joe, Rapid City, SD 57701, (605) 394-2351. NAIA. **BB, VB:** partial.

SOUTH DAKOTA STATE UNIVERSITY, Harry Forsythe, Athletic Director, Box 282, Brookings, SD 57007, (605) 688-5625. NCAA. 10 **BB**, 1 **SB**, 6.5 **T&F**, 4 **VB:** partial to full.

UNIVERSITY OF SOUTH DAKOTA, Dr. Mary Mock, Assistant Athletic Director, Dakota Dome, Vermillion, SD 57069, (605) 677-5309. NCAA, North Central, II. 6 **CC**, 2 **SB**, .5 **TEN**, 6 **T&F**, 2 **VB:** partial. 10 **BB:** full. **S&D:** non-scholarship.

TENNESSEE

AUSTIN PEAY STATE UNIVERSITY, Bob Brooks, Athletic Director, Box 4515, Clarksville, TN 37044, (615) 648-7903. NCAA, Ohio Valley Conference, I. 2 **CC:** partial. 12 **BB**, 5 **TEN**, 8 **VB:** full. **G, SB:** non-scholarship.

BELMONT COLLEGE, Don Purdy, Coach, Athletic Dept., Belmont Blvd., Nashville, TN 37203, (615) 385-6420. NAIA. 4 **TEN:** partial. 9 **BB:** full.

BRYAN COLLEGE, Paul H. Ardelean, Athletic Director, Box 7000, Dayton, TN 37321-7000, (615) 775-2041. NCCAA, NAIA. 6 **BB**, 6 **SB**, 6 **VB:** partial. **CC:** non-scholarship.

CHRISTIAN BROTHERS COLLEGE, Lynda J. Simpson, Coach, 650 East Parkway S., Memphis, TN 38104, (901) 278-0100. NAIA. 12 **BB**, 3 **TEN**, 12 **VB:** partial to full.

COLUMBIA STATE COLLEGE, Elner Hamner, Columbia, TN 38401, (615) 388-0123. NJCAA. 5 **BB**: full.

COVENANT COLLEGE, Gene Fitzgerald, Athletic Director, Lookout Mountain, TN 37350, (404) 820-1560. NCCAA. 6 **BB**: partial.

EAST TENNESSEE STATE UNIVERSITY, Janice C. Shelton, Associate Athletic Director, Box 23710-A, Johnson City, TN 37614, (615) 929-4294. NCAA, Southern Conference, I. 12 **BB**, 2 **RIFLE**, 3 **TEN**, 7 **T&F**, 6 **VB**: full.

FREED-HARDEMAN COLLEGE, Charlie Smith, Athletic Director, Henderson, TN 38340, (901) 989-4611 ext. 280. NAIA, TCAA. 10 **BB**, 3 **TEN**: partial.

LAMBUTH COLLEGE, Sherry Walker, Women's Coach, Lambuth Blvd., Jackson, TN 38301, (901) 427-1500 ext. 232. NAIA, TCAC. 6 **TEN**, 6 **VB**: partial. 11 **BB**: full.

LEMOYNE-OWEN COLLEGE, Lula Skinner, Coach, 807 Walker Ave., Memphis, TN 38126, (901) 942-7328. NCAA. 14 **BB**: full.

LINCOLN MEMORIAL UNIVERSITY, Elaine Minton, Athletic Director, Harrogate, TN 37752, (615) 869-3611 ext. 242. NAIA. 10 **BB**, 10 **SB**, 3 **TEN**: partial. 3 **BB**, 1 **SB**: full.

MEMPHIS STATE UNIVERSITY, Lynn Parkes, Assistant Athletic Director, Athletics Office Bldg., Memphis, TN 38152, (901) 454-2315. NCAA. 6 **G**, 3 **TEN**, 3 **VB**: partial. 14 **BB**, 1 **G**, 2 **TEN**, 7 **VB**: full.

MIDDLE TENNESSEE STATE UNIVERSITY, Jimmy Earle, Athletic Director, Box 77, Murfreesboro, TN 37132, (615) 898-2300. NCAA. 12 **BB**, 5 **TEN**, 4 **T&F**, 4 **VB**: full.

MILLIGAN COLLEGE, D.B. Walker, Athletic Director, Box 26, Milligan College, TN 37682, (615) 929-0116. 7 **BB**, 4 **SB**, 7 **VB**: partial. **S&D, TEN**: non-scholarship.

SHELBY STATE COLLEGE, Bob Canada, Athletic Director, Box 40568, Memphis, TN

VANDERBILT UNIVERSITY, Emily H. Harsh, Women's Athletic Director, McGugin Athletic Center, 2601 Jess Neely Dr., Nashville, TN 37212, (615) 322-2888. NCAA, Southeastern, I. 2 **CC**, 8 **S&D**, 1 **TEN**: partial. 12 **BB**, 3 **S&D**, 7 **TEN**: full. **G, SOC**: non-scholarship.

VOLUNTEER STATE COMMUNITY COLLEGE, Richard Moore, Athletic Director, Nashville Pike, Gallatin, TN 37066, (615) 452-8600. NJCAA. 5 **BB**: partial to full.

TEXAS

AMARILLO COLLEGE, Kelly Chadwick, Athletic Director, Box 477, Amarillo, TX 79178, (806) 376-5111. NJCAA. 10 **BB**: partial to full.

ANGELINA COLLEGE, Guy Davis, Athletic Director, Box 1768, Lufkin, TX 75901, (409) 639-1301 ext. 284. NJCAA. 15 **BB**: partial to full.

BAYLOR UNIVERSITY, David Taylor, Associate Athletic Director, Box 6427, Waco, TX 76706, (817) 754-4648. NCAA. **BB, SB, TEN, T&F, VB**: partial to full.

BLINN COLLEGE, Leroy Dreyer, Athletic Director, 902 College Ave., Brenham, TX 77833, (409) 836-6603. NJCAA. 4 **TEN**: partial to full, 12 **BB**: full.

CLARENDON COLLEGE, Joe Mondragon, Athletic Director, Box 968, Clarendon, TX 79226, (806) 874-2293. NJCAA, WJCAC, I. **BB**: partial.

CONCORDIA LUTHERAN COLLEGE, Linda Lowery, Athletic Director, 3400 N. IH 35, Austin, TX 78705, (512) 452-7661. NAIA. **BB, TEN, VB**: partial.

COOKE COUNTY COLLEGE, Dr. Robert Chaloupecky, Athletic Director, Box 815, Gainesville, TX 76240, (817) 668-7805. NJCAA, USTA, Region V. 12 **VB**: partial. 9 **TEN**: full.

EAST TEXAS BAPTIST UNIVERSITY, Dr. Jim Webb, Athletic Director, 1209 N.

MIDWESTERN STATE UNIVERSITY, Kim Griffie, Coach, 3400 Taft St., Wichita Falls, TX 76308, (817) 692-6611. NCAA, NAIA. 4 **BB**, 4 **RIFLE**, 7 **TEN**: partial. 8 **BB**: full.

NORTH TEXAS STATE UNIVERSITY, Fred McCain, Athletic Director, Box 13917, TN Station, Denton, TX 76203, (817) 565-2662. NCAA. 8 **BB**, 6 **G**, 5 **TEN**, 8 **T&F**, 8 **VB**: partial to full.

ODESSA COLLEGE, Barry Rodenhaver, Athletic Director, 201 W. University, Odessa, TX 79764, (915) 335-6567. NJCAA. 12 **BB**, 6 **GYM**, 6 **TEN**: full.

PAN AMERICAN UNIVERSITY, John McDowell, Women's Basketball Coach, 1201 W. University, Edinburg, TX 78504, (512) 381-2221. NAIA, Independent. 13 **BB**, 6 **CC**, 10 **TEN**, 10 **T&F**, 10 **VB**: partial.

RICE UNIVERSITY, Martha E. Hawthorne, Assistant Athletic Director, Box 1892, Houston, TX 77251, (713) 527-4077. NCAA. 8 **S&D**: partial. 15 **BB**, 14 **T&F**, 12 **VB**: partial to full. 3 **TEN**: full.

SAM HOUSTON STATE UNIVERSITY, Kim Basinger, Coach, Box 2268, Huntsville, TX 77341, (409) 294-1745. NCAA. 10 **BB**, 8 **SB**, 3 **TEN**, 7 **VB**: full.

SAN JACINTO COLLEGE (CENTRAL), Dorothy L. Brown, Chairwoman, Women's Health/Physical Education, 8060 Spencer Hwy., Pasadena, TX 77505, (713) 476-1501 ext. 224. NJCAA. 6 **TEN**, 12 **T&F**, 12 **VB**: partial to full.

SAN JACINTO COLLEGE (NORTH), Jacalyn Junkman, Coach, 5800 Uvalde, Houston, TX 77049, (713) 458-4050. NJCAA. 12 **BB**: partial.

SCHREINER COLLEGE, B.R. Chambers, Athletic Director, Kerrville, TN 78028, (512) 876-5411. NAIA, I. 8 **BB**, 3 **TEN**, 3 **VB**: full. **CREW**: non-scholarship.

SOUTHERN METHODIST UNIVERSITY, Barbara Camp, Associate Athletic Director, SMU Athletic Dept., Moody Coliseum, Box 216, Dallas, TX 75275, (214) 692-2879. NCAA, Southwest Conference, I-A. **BB, G, S&D, TEN**: full. **CC, T&F**: non-scholarship.

15 **BB**, 6 **G**, 1 **RIFLE**, 11 **S&D**, 6 **TEN**, 9 **T&F**: full.

TEXAS LUTHERAN COLLEGE, Kathryn Yandell, Women's Athletic Coordinator, 1000 W. Court St., Seguin, TX 78155, (512) 379-4161 ext. 271. NAIA. 4 **BB**, 1 **TEN**, 3 **T&F**, 4 **VB**: partial to full.

TEXAS TECH UNIVERSITY, Jeannine McHaney, Athletic Director, Box 4079, Tech Station, Lubbock, TX 79409, (806) 742-3360. NCAA, Southwest, I. **CC, G, S&D, TEN, T&F**: partial. **BB, VB**: full.

TEXAS WESLEYAN COLLEGE, Richard Hoogendoorn, Athletic Director, Ft. Worth, TX 76105, (817) 534-0251. NAIA, NCAA. **BB, VB**: partial to full.

TEXAS WOMAN'S UNIVERSITY, Jo Kuhn, Athletic Director, Box 22133 TWU Station, Denton, TX 76204, (817) 387-7555. NCAA, I. 6 **BB**, 3 **GYM**, 3 **TEN**, 4 **VB**: full.

TRINITY UNIVERSITY, Emilie Foster, Coach, 715 Stadium Dr., San Antonio, TX 78284, (512) 736-8270. NCAA, Independent, I. 8 **TEN**: full. **BB, SOC, SB, VB**: non-scholarship.

TYLER JUNIOR COLLEGE, Billy J. Doggett, Intercollegiate Athletic Director, Box 9020, Tyler, TX 75701, (214) 531-2200. NJCAA. 3 **BB**: partial. 12 **BB**, 6 **TEN**: full.

UNIVERSITY OF HOUSTON, Mary Nyholm, Primary Women's Administrator, 3855 Holman St., Houston, TX 77004, (713) 749-7363. NCAA, Southwest Conference, I. 15 **BB**, 8 **TEN**: full.

UNIVERSITY OF MARY HARDIN-BAYLOR, Dennis Strube, Women's Basketball Coach, Box 358 UMHB, Belton, TX 76513, (817) 939-5811 ext. 239. NAIA. 6 **BB**, 6 **VB**: partial to full.

UNIVERSITY OF TEXAS (ARLINGTON), Bill Reeves, Athletic Director, UTA Box 19079, Arlington, TX 76019, (817) 273-2261. NCAA, Southland Conference, I. 12 **CC**, 12 **SB**, 4 **TEN**, 12 **T&F**: partial. 10 **BB**, 10 **VB**: full.

38174-0568, (901) 528-6754. NJCAA, Tenn. Jr. College Athletic Association, Western Division. **BB:** partial.

TENNESSEE STATE UNIVERSITY, Robert Lee, Athletic Director, 3500 John A. Merritt Blvd.,, Nashville, TN 37203, (615) 320-3598. NCAA. 16 **BB**, 5 **S&D**, 12 **T&F:** full.

TENNESSEE TECHNOLOGICAL UNIVERSITY, Marynell Meadors, Head Basketball Coach, Box 5057, Cookeville, TN 38501, (615) 528-3921. NCAA, Ohio Valley, I. 12 **BB**, 6 **VB:** full.

TENNESSEE TEMPLE UNIVERSITY, Ron Bishop, Athletic Director, Chattanooga, TN 37404, (615) 698-6021 ext. 220. NCAA. 4 **BB:** partial to full.

TENNESSEE WESLEYAN COLLEGE, Dwain Farmer, Athletic Director, Box 121, Athens, TN 37303, (615) 745-6712. NAIA. 6 **TEN:** partial to full.

TREVECCA NAZARENE COLLEGE, Carolyn Smith, Women's Athletics Coordinator, 333 Murfreesboro Rd., Nashville, TN 37203, (615) 248-1271. NAIA. **TEN, VB:** partial.

UNION UNIVERSITY, David Blackstock, Athletic Director, Hwy. 45 Bypass, Jackson, TN 38305, (901) 668-1818 ext. 285. NAIA. 10 **BB**, 3 **TEN:** partial to full.

UNIVERSITY OF TENNESSEE (CHATTANOOGA), Sharon Fanning, Women's Athletic Coordinator, Arena 410, Chattanooga, TN 37402, (615) 755-4376. NCAA. 6 **CC**, 6 **G**, 4 **RIFLE**, 4 **TEN**, 10 **VB:** partial to full. 12 **BB**, 4 **TEN:** full.

UNIVERSITY OF TENNESSEE (KNOXVILLE), Joan Cronan, Women's Athletic Director, 115 Stokely Athletic Center, Knoxville, TN 37996-3110, (615) 974-4275. NCAA. 15 **BB**, 12 **S&D**, 6 **TEN**, 16 **T&F**, 12 **VB:** partial to full.

UNIVERSITY OF TENNESSEE (MARTIN), Bettye Giles, Women's Athletic Director, P.E. Complex, Martin, TN 38238, (901) 587-7680. NCAA, Gulf South, II. 2 **SB**, 5 **TEN**, 8 **VB:** partial. 12 **BB:** full.

Grove, Marshall, TX 75670, (214) 935-7963. NAIA, Big State. 1 **TEN**, 3 **VB:** partial. 6 **BB:** full.

EAST TEXAS STATE UNIVERSITY, Dr. Margaret W. Harbison, Associate Director of Athletics, Department of Health/Physical Education, Commerce, TX 75428, (214) 886-5572. NCAA, Lone Star, II. 5 **BB**, 3 **TEN**, 5 **T&F**, 5 **VB:** full.

FRANK PHILLIPS COLLEGE, David Murphy, Coach, Box 5118, Borger, TX 79008, (806) 274-5311. NJCAA. 10 **BB:** full.

HARDIN-SIMMONS UNIVERSITY, Wayne Fletcher, Assistant Athletic Director, HSU Station, Abilene, TX 79698, (915) 677-7281. NCAA, NAIA. 9 **VB:** partial. 9 **BB**, 5 **TEN:** partial to full.

HOUSTON BAPTIST UNIVERSITY, Ed Billings, Athletic Director, 7502 Fondern Rd., Houston, TX 77074, (713) 995-3314. NCAA, TAAC, I. 6 **CC**, 6 **G**, 6 **GYM**, 6 **T&F:** full.

HOWARD PAYNE UNIVERSITY, Nancy Cobb, Women's Athletic Director, HPU Station, Box 175, Brownwood, TX 76801, (915) 643-3599. NCAA, Lone Star, II. 6 **BB**, 6 **VB:** full.

LAMAR UNIVERSITY, Patty Calvert, Assistant to Associate Women's Athletic Director, Box 10039, Beaumont, TX 77710, (409) 880-8705. NCAA, Southland, I. 8 **BB**, 6 **G**, 3 **SB**, 8 **TEN**, 7 **T&F**, 17 **VB:** full.

LEE COLLEGE, Ron Ummel, Athletic Director, Box 818, Baytown, TX 77520, (713) 427-5611 ext. 437. NJCAA. 6 **TEN**, 10 **VB:** partial to full.

LUBBOCK CHRISTIAN COLLEGE, David Carter, Coach, 5601 19th St., Lubbock, TX 79407, (806) 792-3221. NAIA, District 8. 12 **BB**, 5 **CC**, 10 **T&F**, 12 **VB:** partial.

MIDLAND COLLEGE, Del Poss, Athletic Director, 3600 N. Garfield, Midland, TX 79705, (915) 684-7851. NJCAA. 6 **TEN:** full.

SOUTH PLAINS COLLEGE, Lyndon Hardin, Coach, 1400 College Ave., Levelland, TX 79336, (806) 894-9611 ext. 224. NJCAA. 10 **BB**, 6 **TEN:** full.

SOUTHWEST TEXAS STATE UNIVERSITY, Dana Craft, Women's Athletic Coordinator, Strahan Coliseum, San Marcos, TX 78666, (512) 245-2139. NCAA. 5 **GYM**, 5 **SB**, 5 **TEN**, 10 **T&F**, 12 **VB:** partial to full. 15 **BB:** full.

SOUTHWESTERN CHRISTIAN COLLEGE, Bruce Johnson, Athletic Director, 200 Bowser Cir., Terrell, TX 75160, (214) 563-3341. NJCAA. 15 **BB**, 15 **T&F:** full.

SOUTHWESTERN UNIVERSITY, Dr. Carla Lowry, Athletic Director, SU-Station, Box 6271, Georgetown, TX 78626, (512) 863-1381. NAIA, Independent, I. 10 **BB**, 10 **VB:** partial. 2 **BB**, 2 **VB:** full. **TEN:** non-scholarship.

ST. PHILIP'S COLLEGE, Leonard Mittelman, Athletic Director, 2111 Nevada St., San Antonio, TX 78203, (512) 531-3243. NJCAA, Texas Junior College Athletic Conference. 12 **VB:** partial.

STEPHEN F. AUSTIN STATE UNIVERSITY, Sadie Allison, Athletic Director, Box 13041, Nacogdoches, TX 75962, (409) 569-3506. NCAA, Gulf Star Conference, I. 4 **CC**, 13 **SB**, 6 **TEN**, 12 **T&F**, 10 **VB:** partial. 15 **BB**, 1 **SB**, 1 **T&F:** full.

TEXAS A&I UNIVERSITY, Ron Harms, Athletic Director, Box 202, Kingsville, TX 78363, (512) 595-2411. NCAA. 2 **TEN:** partial. 8 **BB**, 7 **T&F**, 6 **VB:** partial to full.

TEXAS A&M UNIVERSITY, Lynn Hickey, Assistant Athletic Director, Athletic Dept., College Station, TX 77843-1228, (409) 845-1052. NCAA. 15 **BB**, 6 **G**, 11 **SB**, 14 **S&D**, 8 **TEN**, 16 **T&F**, 12 **VB:** full.

TEXAS CHRISTIAN UNIVERSITY, Carolyn Dixon, Associate Athletic Director, Box 32924, Fort Worth, TX 76129, (817) 921-7951. NCAA, Southwest Conference, I.

UNIVERSITY OF TEXAS (AUSTIN), Donna A. Lopiano, Director, BEL 606 IAW, Austin, TX 78712, (512) 471-7693. NCAA. 15 **BB**, 6 **G**, 14 **S&D**, 8 **TEN**, 16 **T&F**, 12 **VB:** full.

UNIVERSITY OF TEXAS (EL PASO), Maxine V. Neill, Director of Internal Operations, El Paso, TX 79968, (915) 747-5347. NCAA, Independent, I. 12 **BB:** partial. 5 **TEN**, 14 **T&F/CC**, 8 **VB:** full.

UNIVERSITY OF TEXAS (PERMIAN BASIN), Virginia Brown, Coach, 3743 Fern Circle, Odessa, TX 79762, (915) 362-1713. NAIA, Independent. 10 **TEN:** full.

UNIVERSITY OF TEXAS (SAN ANTONIO), Rudy Davalos, Athletic Director, Inter-collegiate Athletics, San Antonio, TX 78285, (512) 691-4444. NCAA. 5 **BB**, 7 **TEN**, 15 **T&F**, 3 **VB:** partial. 10 **BB:** full.

UNIVERSITY OF TEXAS (TYLER), Fred Kniffen, Tennis Coach, 3900 University Blvd., Tyler, TX 75701, (214) 566-1471. NAIA. 2 **TEN:** partial. 6 **TEN:** full.

WAYLAND BAPTIST COLLEGE, Sylvia Nadler, Athletic Director, 1900 W. 7th, Plainview, TX 79072, (806) 296-5521 ext. 454. NAIA, District 8. 13 **BB**, 13 **T&F:** full.

WEATHERFORD COLLEGE, B.J. Graber, Coach, 308 E. Park, Weatherford, TX 76086, (817) 594-5471 ext. 257. NJCAA. 8 **BB**, 4 **TEN:** partial to full.

WEST TEXAS STATE UNIVERSITY, Ken Sawin, Assistant Athletic Director, WT Station Box 49, Canyon, TX 79016, (806) 656-3701. NCAA. 1 **SB**, 1 **TEN**, 1 **VB:** partial. 8 **BB**, 1 **SB**, 2 **TEN**, 3 **T&F**, 4 **VB:** full.

WESTERN TEXAS COLLEGE, Dave Foster, Athletic Director, College Ave., Snyder, TX 79549, (915) 573-8511. NJCAA. 10 **BB:** partial.

UTAH

BRIGHAM YOUNG UNIVERSITY, Lu Wallace, Women's Athletic Administrator, 295 Richards Bldg., Provo, UT 84602,

(801) 378-4225. NCAA, High Country Athletic Conference, I. 1 **BB**: partial. 13 **S&D**, 14 **T&F**: partial to full. 12 **BB**, 6 **G**, 8 **GYM**, 8 **TEN**, 12 **VB**: full.

COLLEGE OF EASTERN UTAH, Chris Peterson, Athletic Director, Price, UT 84501, (801) 637-2120 ext. 248. NJCAA. 10 **BB**, 5 **SB**, 5 **VB**: partial to full.

DIXIE COLLEGE, Sherry Titus, Women's Athletic Director, 215 S. 700 E., St. George, UT 84770, (801) 673-4811. NJCAA. 2 **BB**, 2 **SB**, 2 **VB**: partial.

SNOW COLLEGE, Ann Bricker, Assistant Athletic Director, 150 College Ave., Ephraim, UT 84627, (801) 283-4021. NJCAA. 10 **BB**, 8 **SB**, 10 **VB**: partial.

SOUTHERN UTAH STATE COLLEGE, Kathryn Berg, Assistant Athletic Director, West Center, Cedar City, UT 84720, (801) 586-7821. NCAA, NAIA. 5 **BB**, 5 **GYM**, 5 **SB**, 5 **T&F**, 5 **VB**: partial.

UNIVERSITY OF UTAH, Fern Gardner, Women's Athletic Director, Special Events Center, Salt Lake City, UT 84112, (801) 581-8171. NCAA, High Country Athletic Conference, I. 12 **SKI**, 15 **SB**, 8 **TEN**, 16 **T&F/CC**, 12 **VB**: partial to full. 15 **BB**, 10 **GYM**: full.

UTAH STATE UNIVERSITY, Dr. Kaye Hart, Assistant Athletic Director-Women's Sports, Athletic Dept., Logan, UT 84322-7700, (801) 750-2060. NCAA, High Country Athletic Conference, IA. 3 **BB**, 1 **GYM**, 5 **SB**, 13 **T&F/CC**, 9 **VB**: partial. 9 **BB**, 9 **GYM**, 9 **SB**, 2 **T&F/CC**, 3 **VB**: full.

UTAH TECHNICAL COLLEGE, Mike Jacobsen, Athletic Director, Box 1609, Provo, UT 84601, (801) 226-5000. NJCAA, WICAC, II. 12 **BB**, 4 **RD**, 4 **SB**, 12 **VB**: full.

WEBER STATE COLLEGE, Richard Ordyna, Assistant Athletic Director, Box 2701, Athletic Dept., Box 2701, Ogden; UT 84408, (801) 626-6500. NCAA, Mountain West, I. 15 **BB**, 6 **G**, 8 **TEN**, 16 **T&F/CC**, 12 **VB**: full.

G, **GYM**, **LAX**, **S&D**, **TEN**, **T&F**, **VB**: partial to full. 12 **BB**: full. **ARCH**, **FENC**: non-scholarship.

LIBERTY BAPTIST COLLEGE, Brenda Bonheim, Women's Sports Coordinator, Lynchburg, VA 24502, (804) 237-5961 ext. 388. NCAA. 9.45 **BB**, 6 **SB**, 8 **T&F**, 5.3 **VB**: full.

LONGWOOD COLLEGE, Dr. Carolyn V. Hodges, Athletic Director, Farmville, VA 23901, (804) 392-9323. NCAA, MDAC, II. 9 **BB**, 11 **FH**, 7 **G**, 6 **GYM**: partial. 2 **BB**, 1 **G**, 2 **GYM**: full. **LAX**, **RIDING**, **SB**, **TEN**, **T&F**: non-scholarship.

OLD DOMINION UNIVERSITY, Mikki Flowers, Associate Athletic Director, Hampton Blvd., Norfolk, VA 23508, (804) 440-3358. NCAA, Sunbelt, South Atlantic, I. 6 **CC**, 9 **FH**, 8 **LAX**, 8 **S&D**, 5 **TEN**: partial. 15 **BB**, 5 **FH**: full.

RANDOLPH-MACON COLLEGE, Carroll LaHaye, Women's Athletic Coordinator, Athletic Dept., Ashland, VA 23005, (804) 798-8372. NCAA, II. 3 **BB**: partial. **FH**, **LAX**, **SOC**, **TEN**: non-scholarship.

UNIVERSITY OF RICHMOND, Ruth M. Goehring, Assistant Athletic Director, Robins Center, Richmond, VA 23173, (804) 285-6471. NCAA. **BB**, **FH**, **LAX**, **S&D**, **TEN**, **T&F**: partial to full.

UNIVERSITY OF VIRGINIA, James O. West, Box 3785, Charlottesville, VA 22903, (804) 924-3494. NCAA, Atlantic Coast, I. 15 **BB**, 5 **CC**, 5 **FH**, 5 **LAX**, 5 **SB**, 8 **S&D**, 4 **TEN**, 10 **T&F**, 6 **VB**: full. **SOC**: non-scholarship.

VIRGINIA COMMONWEALTH UNIVERSITY, Elizabeth Royster, Women's Athletic Coordinator, 819 W. Franklin St., Richmond, VA 23284-0001, (804) 257-1277. NCAA. 9 **BB**, 9 **FH**, 2 **SB**, 10 **S&D**, 3 **T&F**, 9 **VB**: partial.

VIRGINIA STATE UNIVERSITY, Leon Bey, Coach, Box 58, Petersburg, VA 23803, (804) 520-6232. NCAA. 8 **BB**: partial. 1 **BB**: full

281-2081. NCAA, NAIA, II. 6 **BB**, 3 **CC**, 8 **GYM**, 6 **T&F**: partial. 2 **CC**, 4 **T&F**: full. **CREW**, **TEN**: non-scholarship.

SHORELINE COMMUNITY COLLEGE, Mary Segle, Women's Sports Coordinator, 16101 Greenwood Ave. N, Seattle, WA 98133, (206) 546-4791. NWAACC, Region I. 8 **BB**, 3 **CC**, 9 **SB**, 3 **TEN**, 8 **VB**: full.

SKAGIT VALLEY COMMUNITY COLLEGE, Gary Knutzen, Athletic Director, 2405 College Way, Mt. Vernon, WA 98273, (206) 428-1240. Northwest Athletic Association of Community Colleges. 5 **BB**, 3 **CC**, 3 **TEN**, 3 **VB**: full.

EVERGREEN STATE COLLEGE, Sandy Butler, Acting Director of Athletics, CRC 302, Olympia, WA 98505, (206) 866-6000 ext. 6530. NAIA. 3 **SOC**, 2 **S&D**, 1 **TEN**: partial. **CC**, **T&F**: non-scholarship.

UNIVERSITY OF PUGET SOUND, Sally Leyse, Women's Athletic Director, 1500 N. Warner, Tacoma, WA 98407, (206) 756-3140. NCAA, NAIA. 12 **BB**, 10 **CREW**, 5 **SKI**, 5 **SOC**, 5 **SB**, 12 **S&D**, 10 **TEN**, 12 **T&F**, 10 **VB**: partial.

UNIVERSITY OF WASHINGTON, Catherine B. Green, Associate Athletic Director, Graves Bldg., GC-20, Seattle, WA 98105, (206) 543-2279. NCAA. 6 **G**, 14 **S&D**, 7 **TEN**: partial. 15 **BB**, 10 **GYM**, 14 **T&F**, 12 **VB**: full.

WALLA WALLA COMMUNITY COLLEGE, Gary Knecht, Athletic Director, 500 Tausick Way, Walla Walla, WA 99362, (509) 527-4306. NWAACC. **BB**, **TEN**, **VB**: partial.

WASHINGTON STATE UNIVERSITY, Marcia Saneholtz, Athletic Director, 107 Bohler Gym, Pullman, WA 99164, (509) 335-0311. NORPAC. 2 **RIFLE**: partial. 6 **G**, 14 **S&D**, 8 **TEN**, 16 **T&F/CC**, 12 **VB**: partial to full.

WHITWORTH COLLEGE, Bruce Grambo, Athletic Director, Spokane, WA 99251, (509) 466-3215. NAIA. 12 **BB**, 5 **S&D**, 5 **TEN**, 20 **T&F**, 12 **VB**: partial.

YAKIMA VALLEY COMMUNITY COLLEGE, Jerry Ward, Athletic Director, Box 1647,

WEST VIRGINIA STATE COLLEGE, Robert Maxwell, Athletic Director, Institute, WV 25112, (304) 766-3165. NAIA. 9 **BB**: partial.

WEST VIRGINIA UNIVERSITY, Ed Pastilong, Assistant Athletic Director, Box 877, Morgantown, WV 26505, (304) 293-3714. NCAA. 1 **BB**, 2 **GYM**, 12 **S&D**, 5 **TEN**, 11 **T&F**, 9 **VB**: partial. 12 **BB**, 7 **GYM**, 3 **S&D**, 4 **T&F**, 2 **VB**: full.

WEST VIRGINIA WESLEYAN COLLEGE, Kent Carpenter, Athletic Director, Buckhannon, WV 26201, (304) 473-8510. NAIA. **BB**, **TEN**: partial.

WHEELING COLLEGE, Janice Forsty, Athletic Director, 316 Washington Ave., Wheeling, WV 26003, (304) 243-2365. NAIA, WVIAC, I. **BB**, **SB**: partial to full.

WISCONSIN

MARQUETTE UNIVERSITY, Tat Shiely, Coordinator of Women's Athletics, 1532 W. Clybourn, Milwaukee, WI 53233, (414) 224-7707. NCAA, North Star, I. 6 **CC**, 6 **TEN**, 12 **T&F**, 12 **VB**: partial. 8 **BB**: full.

NORTHLAND COLLEGE, Steve Franklin, Instructor of Physical Education Women's Coach, 1411 Ellis Ave., Ashland, WI 54806, (715) 682-4531 ext. 243. NLCAA, Independent. 11 **BB**, 7 **VB**: partial.

UNIVERSITY OF WISCONSIN (GREEN BAY), Carol Hammerle, Assistant Athletic Director, Phoenix Sports Center, Green Bay, WI 54302, (414) 465-2145. NAIA. 12 **BB**, 12 **S&D**: partial to full.

UNIVERSITY OF WISCONSIN (MADISON), Paula Bonner, Assistant Athletic Director, 1440 Monroe St., Madison, WI 53711, (608) 263-5580. NCAA. 10 **GYM**, 14 **S&D**, 8 **TEN**, 16 **T&F**: partial to full. 15 **BB**, 2 **FENC**, 3 **G**, 12 **VB**: full.

UNIVERSITY OF WISCONSIN (MILWAUKEE), Daryl Leonard, Athletic Director, Box 413, Milwaukee, WI 53201,

VERMONT

COLLEGE OF ST. JOSEPH, Mark R. Cartmill, Athletic Director, Clement Rd., Rutland, VT 05701, (802) 773-5900. NAIA, Mayflower. 8 BB, 4 SOC, 2 SB, 3 VB: partial.

ST. MICHAEL'S COLLEGE, Sue L. Duprat, Women's Athletic Coordinator, Winooski Park, VT 05404, (802) 655-2000. NCAA. 8 BB: full. CC, FH, G, LAX, SKI, SOC, S&D, TEN, VB: non-scholarship.

UNIVERSITY OF VERMONT, Sally Guerette, Assistant Athletic Director, Patrick Gym, Burlington, VT 05405, (802) 656-4441. NCAA, Seaboard Conference. IAAA. BB, CC, SKI, T&F: partial to full. FH, GYM, LAX, SOC, SB, S&D, TEN, VB: non-scholarship.

VIRGINIA

BLUEFIELD COLLEGE, Gail Fisher, Women's Athletic Director, Box 28, Bluefield, VA 24605, (304) 327-7137. NCCAA, Independent. 6 BB, 6 VB: partial.

COLLEGE OF WILLIAM AND MARY, Mildred West, Women's Athletic Director, Adair Gym, Williamsburg, VA 23185, (804) 253-4360. NCAA. BB, CC, FH, G, GYM, LAX, SOC, S&D, TEN, T&F, VB: partial to full.

GEORGE MASON UNIVERSITY, Susan Collins, Assistant Athletic Director, 4400 University, Fairfax, VA 22030, (703) 323-2657. NCAA, Colonial Athletic Assoc., I. BB, SB, SOC, TEN, T&F, VB: partial to full.

JAMES MADISON UNIVERSITY, L. Leotus Morrison, Associate Athletic Director, Godwin Hall, Harrisonburg, VA 22807, (703) 568-6248. NCAA, Colonial Athletic Association, South Atlantic Field Hockey/Lacrosse Conference, I. CC, FH,

VIRGINIA TECH UNIVERSITY, Jo K. Kafer, Women's Athletic Director, Box 158, Blacksburg, VA 24060, (703) 961-6489. NCAA, Metro, IA. 5 CC, 6 S&D, 3 TEN, 5 T&F, 6 VB: partial. 11 BB, 3 CC, 1 TEN, 3 T&F, 2 VB: full.

VIRGINIA UNION UNIVERSITY, Wilbert Talley, Athletic Director, 1500 N. Lombardy St., Richmond, VA 23220, (804) 257-5655. NCAA. 6 BB, 2 T&F: full.

WASHINGTON

CLARK COLLEGE, Roger D. Daniels, Athletic Director, 1800 E. McLoughlin, Vancouver, WA 98663, (206) 699-0140. NWAACC. 24 BB, 9 TEN, 24 VB: partial.

COLUMBIA BASIN COLLEGE, Lynda Meyers, Athletic Director, 2600 N. 20th Ave., Pasco, WA 99301, (509) 547-0511 ext. 310. NWAACC, Washington-Oregon Community College. 8 BB, 3 TEN, 8 VB: partial.

EASTERN WASHINGTON UNIVERSITY, Mary Rubright, Athletic Director, HPEA Bldg., Cheney, WA 99004, (509) 359-2463. NCAA, Mountain West Athletic Conf., I. 12 BB, 1 TEN, 7 T&F, 8 VB: full. GYM: non-scholarship.

GONZAGA UNIVERSITY, Dan Fitzgerald, Athletic Director, E 502-Boone Ave., Spokane, WA 99258, (509) 328-4220. NCAA, West Coast Athletic, I. 10 VB: partial. 12 BB: full. CREW, CC, G, RIFLE, TEN, T&F: non-scholarship.

GRAY HARBOR COLLEGE, Diane Smith, Women's Athletic Commissioner, College Heights, Aberdeen, WA 98520, (206) 532-9020. NWAACC. 8 BB, 3 CC, 8 SB, 8 VB: partial.

HIGHLINE COLLEGE, Don McConnaughey, Athletic Director, Midway, WA 98031, (206) 878-3710. NWAACC. 8 BB, 5 S&D, 3 TEN, 10 T&F, 8 VB: partial.

SEATTLE PACIFIC UNIVERSITY, Keith R. Phillips, Athletic Director, School of P.E. & Athletics, Seattle, WA 98119, (206) Yakima, WA 98902, (509) 575-2393. NWAACC. 8 BB, 1 TEN, 10 T&F, 8 VB: partial.

WEST VIRGINIA

ALDERSON-BROADDUS COLLEGE, Joe Miller, Athletic Director, Philippi, WV 26416, (304) 457-1700 ext. 332. NAIA. BB, VB: partial to full.

CONCORD COLLEGE, Georgia Kelley, Coach, Athens, WV 24712, (304) 384-9817. NAIA. 4 BB, SB, 4 VB: partial.

DAVIS AND ELKINS COLLEGE, Edward McFarlane, Athletic Director, Elkins, WV 26241, (304) 636-1900 ext. 26241. NCAA, NAIA, WVIAC. 10 BB, 12 FH, 8 SB, 3 TEN: partial.

MARSHALL UNIVERSITY, Judy Southard, Assistant Athletic Director, Box 1360, Huntington, WV 25715, (304) 696-6782. NCAA. 4 TEN, 8 T&F, 10 VB: partial. 12 BB: full.

POTOMAC STATE COLLEGE OF WEST VIRGINIA, Sandra J. Elmore, Women's Basketball Coach, Keyser, WV (304) 788-3011 ext. 289. NJCAA. BB: partial.

SALEM COLLEGE, Harry Hartman, Athletic Director, Main St., Salem, WV 26426, (304) 782-5286. NAIA. 10 BB, 10 SB, 10 VB: partial.

UNIVERSITY OF CHARLESTON, R.A. Francis, Assistant Athletic Director, MacCorkle Ave., Charleston, WV 25304, (304) 357-4822. NCAA, NAIA. CREW: partial. 8 BB, 6 SB, 3 TEN: partial to full.

WEST LIBERTY STATE COLLEGE, Ed Martin, Athletic Director, W. Liberty, WV 26074, (304) 336-8082. NAIA. 6 BB, 1.5 SB, 1.5 TEN, 3 VB: partial.

WEST VIRGINIA INSTITUTE OF TECHNOLOGY, Neal Baisi, Athletic Director, Montgomery, WV 25136, (304) 442-3121. NAIA. 6 BB: partial. CC, SB, VB: non-scholarship.

(414) 963-5155. NAIA, II. BB, CC, SOC, S&D, TEN, T&F, VB: partial.

WYOMING

CASPER COLLEGE, Jean Wheatley, Athletic Director, 125 College Dr., Casper, WY 82602, (307) 268-2224. NJCAA. 13 BB, 13 VB: partial. 5 BB, 5 VB: full.

CENTRAL WYOMING COLLEGE, Bin Graefe, Athletic Director, 2660 Peck Ave., Riverton, WY 82501, (307) 856-9291 ext. 119. NJCAA. 7 BB, 3 RD, 5 VB:full.

EASTERN WYOMING COLLEGE, Verl Petsch, Athletic Director, 3200 West C St., Torrington, WY 82240, (307) 532-7111 ext. 244. NJCAA, WCCAC. 12 BB, 12 VB: full.

LARAMIE COUNTY COMMUNITY COLLEGE, H.W. Halverson, Athletic Director, 1400 College Dr., Cheyenne, WY 82007, (307) 634-5853 ext. 184. 7 BB, 7 VB: partial to full.

NORTHWEST COMMUNITY COLLEGE, Ken Rochitz, Athletic Director, Powell, WY 82435, (307) 754-6505. NJCAA. 12 BB, 12 VB: partial.

SHERIDAN COLLEGE, Lonnie Williams, Women's Athletic Director, Box 1500, Sheridan, WY 82801, (307) 674-6446. NJCAA, WY Conference. 12 BB, 12 VB: full.

WESTERN WYOMING COLLEGE, Dennis Thomas, Box 428, Rock Springs, WY 82901, (307) 382-2121 ext. 173. NJCAA. 4-7 BB, 4-7 VB: partial to full.

UNIVERSITY OF WYOMING, Mary Ellen Cloninger, Assistant Athletic Director, 3414 University Station, Laramie, WY 82071, (307) 766-2244/2292. NCAA, High Country Athletic Conference, I. CC, G, SKI, S&D, T&F: partial to full. 15 BB, 12 VB: full.

■ Organizations to Aid the Student–Athlete

Center for the Study of Sport in Society

The Center for the Study of Sport in Society at Northeastern University focuses on the needs of students and athletes from junior high school to the professional leagues. The center has become a major national force in the study of sports and education.

Dedicated to reform and to information for the student–athlete, the center works closely with professional athletes, teams, leagues, and the news media, as well as with scholars from across North America, on a number of programs: degree completion for professional, Olympic, and amateur athletes; counseling for younger athletes; minimum academic standards for high school athletes; curriculum development; research; and public awareness.

Middle- and High-School Age Outreach Program

The School Outreach Program helps well-known athletes share their experiences with students. This program arranges for personal visits from athletes, who bring several important messages to students, and especially to student–athletes. Two of the main messages are about:

1. **Education.** These athletes warn students about the importance of balancing sports dreams in the future with the reality of education now. Hearing your sports heroes talk about the value of

education will, we hope, help make you aware of your need to develop sports *and* educational skills.
2. **Drugs and alcohol.** The athletes also speak to students about the dangers of drug and alcohol abuse. Recent newspaper and television stories about "fallen heroes" have made everyone aware of the dangers to our nation's athletes. Making an all-out offensive against drug and alcohol abuse is more important now than ever before. The athletes give first-hand accounts of the terrible risks of drugs and alcohol.

The University Degree Completion Program

Another key part of the center's efforts is to prepare athletes for careers after sports through the University Degree Completion Program. This plan, developed with the help of professional sports leagues, teams, and players associations, gives current and former players a chance to finish the degrees they began before turning professional. These players can use Northeastern University as a central location for their education.

The Degree Completion Program provides academic and professional counseling to help ease the difficult move from playing careers to normal employment. A group of major universities throughout the United States and Canada has been established so the Degree Completion Program can reach athletes wherever professional sports are played. The program has formal support from the players associations of the National Basketball Association, the National Football League, the National Hockey League, the Major Indoor Soccer League and the United States Football League.

Well-known sports stars who support the program include:

Kareem Abdul-Jabbar	Doug Flutie	Magic Johnson
Evelyn Ashford	Dwight Gooden	Michael Jordan
Larry Bird	Nancy Hogshead	Bobby Orr
Mike Bossy	Brian Holloway	Mary Lou Retton
Ray Bourque		

You can write to the Center for the Study of Sport in Society at the following address:

Center for the Study of Sport in Society
Northeastern University
360 Huntington Avenue
Boston, MA 02115
(617) 437-5815
(617) 437-5816

Women's Sports Foundation*

Purpose

The Women's Sports Foundation has three primary objectives:

- Encourage and support the participation of women in sport and fitness activities for their health, enjoyment and personal development.
- Provide opportunities, facilities and training for girls and women in sport and fitness.
- Educate women and the general public on the value of participating in sport and fitness activities.

Background

The Women's Sports Foundation was founded by Billie Jean King and other elite female athletes in recognition of the need for one unified effort on behalf of women's sports and fitness. Other founding members included Olympic greats Donna de Varona, Micki King Hogue, Wyomia Tyus and Sheila Young Ochowicz.

Governed by a Board of Trustees, the Foundation acts as an umbrella organization for all those interested in the development of women's sports and fitness. Objectives and direction for the Foundation are provided by its over 60 Advisory Board members who represent female athletes, sport and youth organizations, sport and health related services and public supporters of women's sports.

---

*This material is reprinted courtesy of the Women's Sports Foundation.

What the Foundation Does

- Serves as a resource center and clearing house on all women's sports and fitness topics including: sports medicine, training, coaching, business, psychology, research, statistics, camps, scholarships, legal, agents, etc.
- Conducts Fitness and Sports Medicine programs around the country.
- Researches and publishes annual College Scholarship, Career, Sport Camp and Organization Guides.
- Sponsors Award Programs that recognize female athleticism: the High School All Star Awards, the Women's Sports Hall of Fame, the Sportswoman Awards, the Team of the Year Award, and the Up and Coming Awards.
- Maintains a speakers bureau referral service of experts on women's sports.
- Assists national youth organizations with girls' sports programming.
- Provides leadership and direction for the implementation of The New Agenda for Women's Sports & Fitness.
- Develops publicity materials for promoting sports and fitness for women.

For further information on any of the above activities, contact the Women's Sports Foundation.

342 Madison Avenue, Suite 728
New York, NY 10017
(212) 972-9170

Toll-free information:
(800) 227-3988 (except CA, HI, AK (415) 563-6266)

Index

Richard E. Lapchick is Director of the Center for the Study of Sport in Society at Northeastern University in Boston, Massachusetts. The Center has been hailed as a leading voice for reforming our sports system and for helping athletes at all levels. It has been featured in *Time, Newsweek, Business Week,* and most of the nation's leading newspapers. Dr. Lapchick, a well-known sports activist and researcher, has appeared on "The Today Show," "Face the Nation," "ABC World News," "ABC Sportsbeat," "Nightline," and other network programs. He is the author of a weekly advice column on the problems in high school athletics for United Press International outlets. The column is based on the information included in *On the Mark.* He is also the author of *Broken Promises: Racism in American Sport* (St. Martin's, 1984) and *Fractured Focus: Sport as a Reflection of Society* (Lexington Books, 1986).

Robert Malekoff is the Director of Research at the Center for the Study of Sport in Society at Northeastern University. He is also the coordinator of a National Consortium of university degree completion programs for professional, Olympic, and former college athletes. Prior to joining the Center staff, Mr. Malekoff served as the head coach of women's soccer (1979–1985) and the assistant coach of men's lacrosse (1978–1983) at Princeton University. He is a graduate of Bowling Green State University in Ohio, and holds a Master of Education degree from Harvard University.